YOU'RE HISTORY!

YOU'RE HISTORY!

HOW PEOPLE MAKE THE DIFFERENCE

Edited by Michelle P. Brown
and Richard J. Kelly

continuum

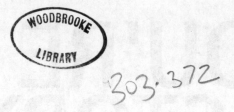

Continuum

The Tower Building
11 York Road
London SE1 7NX

15 East 26th Street
New York
NY 10010

www.continuumbooks.com

Action Aid, CAFOD, Christian Aid, Oxfam and Save the Children
are leading advocates for change, challenging the policies and
practices of rich countries and international institutions that
structurally impoverish half the world's people. Proceeds from
the royalties will be spent on promoting trade justice, more
effective aid, global corporate responsibility and children's rights.

First published 2005

British Library Cataloguing-in-Publication Data
A catalogue record for this book is available from the British Library.

ISBN 0 8264 8898 6

Designed and typeset by Benn Linfield
Printed and bound in Great Britain by MPG Books Ltd, Cornwall

Our deepest fear is not that we are inadequate.
Our deepest fear is that we are powerful beyond measure.
It is our light, not our darkness, that frightens us.

We ask ourselves, Who am I to be brilliant, gorgeous, talented and fabulous?
Actually, who are you not to be? You are a child of God.
Your playing small doesn't serve the world.
There's nothing enlightened about shrinking
so that other people won't feel insecure around you.

We are born to manifest in the Glory of God
that is within us. It is not just in some of us; it's in everyone.
And as we let our own light shine, we unconsciously give other people permission to do the same.
As we are liberated from our fears, our presence automatically liberates others.

Calligraphic artwork inspired by the vision of an integrated
Creation by leading British Sikh calligrapher, Satwinder Sehmi,
originally presented to Nelson Mandela

Contents

CONTENTS

viii

CONTENTS

ix

CONTENTS

Compiled by Rosemary Brown and Ciarán Quinn. *Giving some
information that may surprise and challenge you.*

A POET'S RESPONSE
De Rong Radio

BENJAMIN ZEPHANIAH

My ears are battered an burnt an I hav just learnt
Dat I've been listening to de rong radio station,
My mind has been brutalised now de pain can't be disguised
I've been listening to de rong radio station,
I waz beginning to believe I was a mindless drug freak
Dat couldn't control my sanity or my sexuality
I waz beginning to believe dat I couldn't believe in nothing,
Except nothing,
An all I ever wanted to do waz to get you, an do you,
I've been listening to de rong radio station.

My future has been blighted I'm so short sighted
I've been listening to de rong radio station,
I waz beginning to not trust me, in fact I wanted to arrest me
I've been listening to de rong radio station,
I've been dancing to music dat I can't stand
I've been reciting commercials to my girlfriends
I've been trying to convince myself dat what I really need is a
Sun bed
A mortgage
Sum hair spray, de kind of hair spray
Dat will wash my grey blues away,

DE RONG RADIO

I waz trying to convince myself dat I shouldn't care about
Anyone else
But myself,
I waz trying to convince myself dat I could ease my
  conscience
If I gave a few pence or a few cents to a starving baby
In Africa,
Because African babies needed my favours
Because Africa is full of dictators, an
Globalization will bring salvation,
I've been listening to de rong radio station.

I thought my neighbours formed an axis of evil
I wanna go kill people
I've been listening to de rong radio station,
I waz sure I didn't inhale
So why is my mind going stale?
I've been listening to de rong radio station.
I waz beginning to believe dat all Moslems were terrorist
An Christian terrorists didn't exist,
I really did believe dat terrorism couldn't be done by
Governments,
Not our governments, not white governments,
I just could not see what waz rong wid me
I gave hungry people hamburgers you see,
I waz beginning to believe dat our children wer better dan
Their children,
Their children were dying from terrorism
But I couldn't hear their children call
An a child from Palestine simply didn't count at all,

What despair? No children I waz not aware
I've been listening to de rong radio station.

For years I've been sedated
Now I think I'm educated
I've been listening to de rong radio station,
Every time I felt ill I took de same little white pill
I've been listening to de rong radio station,
When it started I waz curious but den it got so serious,
It waz cool when it began but now I really hate Iran
An look at me now I wanna make friends wid Pakistan
I wanna bomb Afghanistan
An I need someone to tell me where de hell is Kurdistan,
You can be my alli for a while
Until I come to bomb your child,
An I'm sure there's a continent called de Middle East
An I think I can bomb my way to Peace
I've been listening to de rong radio station.

I've been listening to de rong jams
De rong beats
De rong tones
From de rong zones,
De rong voices
I made mad choices
Listening to lies as spies
An de rong radio station.

I wanted to know what some pop star somewhere
Waz having for breakfast,

DE RONG RADIO

An dat I waz no longer working class,
I needed to know if de stock market rose one percent,
An dat I had a ruler to give me confidence,
I needed to know dat my life would improve loads
If I had an operation on my nose,
I needed to hear dat DJ say Good Morning Good Morning,
I felt dat he waz there just for me, I loved de way he would say
Dis show waz sponsored by
Oh my, he made me cry
I've been listening to de rong radio station.

Can you dig Dis?
I put myself on a hit list
I've been listening to de rong radio station,
I'm laughing an I'm crying
As I'm watching myself dying,
I've been listening to de rong radio station.
Listen to it
Can you hear?
Listen to me
Keep dis frequency clear.
Now tune in an drop out.

Contributors

Akbar Ahmed is one of the world's best known scholars on contemporary Islam. He is the former High Commissioner of Pakistan to Great Britain, and has advised Prince Charles and met with President George W. Bush on Islam. He is now Ibn Khaldun Chair of Islamic Studies and Professor of International Relations at the American University in Washington, DC. His books include *Islam Under Siege: Living Dangerously in a Post-Honour World* (Polity Press: 2003); *Discovering Islam: Making Sense of Muslim History and Society*, which was the basis of the BBC six-part TV series called Living Islam; his *Postmodernism and Islam: Predicament and Promise* was nominated for the Amalfi Award, and his 'Jinnah Quartet', a four-part project on Pakistan's founding father, M. A. Jinnah, has won numerous international awards.

Sabina Alkire is Research Associate at the Global Equity Initiative, Harvard University, Assistant Priest at St Stephen's Church, Boston MA, and an Associate Member of St Paul's Institute

Stephen Bates is religious affairs correspondent of *The Guardian*. An Oxford-trained historian, he has also been a journalist with the BBC, the *Daily Telegraph* and the *Daily Mail* and is a frequent broadcaster. He was named Religious Writer of the Year by the Churches Media Council in the 2005 Andrew Cross Awards and his book *A Church at War: Anglicans and Homosexuality* is published by Hodder and Stoughton.

Martin Bell was a correspondent for BBC News for more than 30 years. He was assigned to 80 countries and reported 11 wars, from Vietnam to Bosnia. He was wounded in Bosnia in 1992. In 1997, in controversial circumstances, he became the Member of Parliament for Tatton – the first elected Independent for nearly 50 years. He now travels on behalf of UNICEF-UK as its Ambassador for Humanitarian Emergencies.

Marie-Roger Biloa is a native of Cameroon who graduated from the universities of Abidjan (Côte d'Ivoire), Vienna and Paris, gaining a PhD for German Studies and Political Science, Diplomatic Academy, Vienna. She has been chief editor and publisher of *Africa International*, a leading monthly pan-African newsmagazine founded in 1958. She has received several media awards (including Unesco and French Press Club). 1n 1998, she received the Percy Qoboza – Journalist of the Year Award from the National Association of Black Journalists in Chicago. In 1999, the Cameroonian Government designated her as the 'Top Cameroonian Media Person'. Current projects include setting up a TV channel and launching a Top Executive Activity Center in Paris-Champs Elysées.

Michelle P. Brown obtained her PhD at the University of London, where she is a Senior Research Fellow (School of Advanced Studies and the Courtauld Institute). She is a Fellow of the Society of Antiquaries (London) and Visiting Professor at the University of Leeds (Medieval Studies). She has lectured widely, curated several exhibitions and authored and edited many books (*The Lindisfarne Gospels: Society, Spirituality and the Scribe*, was nominated for the British Academy Prize and The Times International Book of the Year, 2004, and the ACE/

Mercers Book Award). She was Curator of medieval and illuminated manuscripts, British Library (1986-2004). She remains at the British Library part-time, and freelances as an author/lecturer. She is a Lay Canon and member of Chapter at St Paul's Cathedral, London. Her work aims to help people to connect wires and consider the bigger picture, encouraging them to make the best use of their gifts and opportunities, whilst respecting others.

Rosemary Brown is a writer, journalist and editor who has worked for Save the Children, Co-op America and UNESCO and is now with the Rainforest Foundation. She has contributed to publications in the UK, US and France including *The Washington Post*, *New Society* and *New Internationalist*. She is a trustee and activist with organizations combating homelessness, inner-city deprivation and human rights abuses.

Bruce Clark writes on religion, and on European affairs, for *The Economist*. His book *An Empire's New Clothes* is a personal view of post-Soviet Russia, based on his time as Moscow correspondent for *The Times* in the early 1990s. He has also worked as diplomatic correspondent for the *Financial Times*, and as a reporter for Reuters in France and Greece.

Simon Counsell has been working to protect the world's rainforests for the last 20 years, first as a campaigner with Friends of the Earth, now as Director of The Rainforest Foundation. He has travelled widely in South America and Central Africa, learning from, and working with, indigenous forest communities. He is a leading advocate for a radical change in approaches to international wildlife conservation, which, he believes, should be much more in tune with the traditions, knowledge and livelihoods of local people.

xvii

CONTRIBUTORS

Richard Curtis is a well-known film director (his work including *Four Weddings and a Funeral* and *Notting Hill*), scriptwriter, author and a founder/co-ordinator of the fund-raising and awareness-raising initiatives 'Comic Relief' and 'Make Poverty History'.

Richard Dowden is Director of the Royal African Society and a journalist and commentator on African affairs. He was Africa Editor of *The Independent* and *The Economist* and also worked for *The Times*, visiting almost every African country.

Joyce d' Silva grew up on a farm in Ireland. After university (TCD) she lived and worked in India, married (the late) jazz guitarist Amancio D'Silva and later taught R. E. in a comprehensive school in Essex. Inspired by Gandhi's autobiography, she decided to become vegetarian and wrote Britain's second vegan cookbook. She has worked for Compassion In World Farming, the leading NGO campaigning against factory farming, since 1985 and was CEO for 14 years. She is now Ambassador for CIWF.

Scilla Elworthy is founder of Peace Direct, and founder and Chair of Oxford Research Group, established in 1982 to develop effective methods whereby people can bring about positive change on issues of global and local security by non-violent means. Previously she was a consultant at UNESCO on women's issues, a director of Minority Rights Group in France and has worked for ten years in southern Africa. In May 2003 she was awarded the Niwano Peace Prize and has three times been nominated for the Nobel Peace Prize.

William Frame is Curator of Modern Historical Papers at the British Library. He has researched widely on Britain in the 1930s and is currently preparing a book on the political history of the period. He grew up in North East England.

Sir Bob Geldof is a well-known musician and human rights campaigner. He is the founder/co-ordinator of 'Bandaid', 'Liveaid' and 'Live8'.

Carolyn Hayman OBE has been involved in the development of Peace Direct since 2002 and is now Chief Executive. After a career in DFID, the Cabinet Office and in venture capital, she joined the Foyer Federation as Chief Executive in 1997. Over the next seven years she grew its turnover eightfold. She served as a Board member of the Commonwealth Development Corporation from 1994 to 1999 and in 2003 was awarded an OBE for services to young people

Evan Heimlich has taught cultural theory and cultural history at Kobe University, Japan and at Haskell Indian Nations University, USA. He is writing books on Kerouac's experimentalism and on the movies of Cecil B. DeMille. He has campaigned against pollution, written for the Tibetan Refugee Documentary Project, facilitated intercultural understandings and lobbied for inclusion of minorities in education in the US and Japan.

Richard J. Kelly teaches and researches at the Faculty of Cross-Cultural Studies, Kobe University, Japan. He is also a visiting professor at the Faculty of Language and Culture, Osaka University, Japan. Professor Kelly, a graduate of the National University of Ireland, specializes in the study of medieval literatures, in particular the Christian prose and poetry of the Anglo-Saxon period (c. AD 449–1100). He is the author of a number of books as well as several articles and papers in academic books and journals, ranging in content from medieval literature, culture, art and manuscripts to linguistics and textual transmission. His most significant recent book is his edition and translation of *The Blickling Homilies*, which is one of the earliest extant examples of prose writing in English. He has a keen interest in issues of social justice and how they have been dealt with and articulated down through the ages to the present time.

Gerison Lansdown is an international children's rights consultant. She was the founder director, in 1992, of the Children's Rights Alliance for England, established to promote implementation of the UN Convention on the Rights of the Child. She has published and lectured widely on the subject of children's rights. She was involved in the establishment of the international working group, Rights for Disabled Children, and is currently a board member of UNICEF-UK, and project co-director for CRED-PRO, a new international initiative to develop child rights educational programmes for professionals working with children.

Kari Lydersen is a Chicago-based journalist working for *The Washington Post* (Midwest bureau) and freelancing for various publications including *Lip Magazine, In These Times, Punk Planet* and the *New Standard News.* She graduated from Northwestern University in journalism (1997). She is an instructor in the Urban Youth International Journalism Program, teaching journalism workshops to youth who live in public housing or attend alternative high schools in Chicago. She frequently reports on Latin America, and has written *Out of the Sea and Into the Fire: Latin American-US Immigration in the Global Age* (Common Courage Press).

Ricardo Navarro DSc is a prominent environmentalist. He is the founder and President of CESTA (Centro Salvadoreno de Tecnologia Apropiada), Friends of the Earth El Salvador. During El Salvador's 13-year civil war, Dr Navarro organized CESTA as a grass roots conservation group to promote community-based strategies to reverse past environmental destruction and prevent future degradation. He is also working with youth to plant a 'forest of reconciliation' on land damaged by the civil war. His awards include United Nations Environment Program's Global 500 award (1995); Goldman Foundation Environmental Award (1995). His publications include *El Pensamiento Ecologista (Centro Salvadoreno de Tecnologia Apropiada)* (co-author); *Necesidades Basicas y la Tecnologia (Basic Needs and Technology)*, International Symposium on Engineering (El Salvador: Universidad Centroamericana Jose Simeon Canas, 1980, 3d edn) (co-editor); and *Alternativas de Transporte en America Latina: La Bicicleta y los Triciclos* (St. Gallen, Switzerland: 1985).

Edmund Newell is Canon Chancellor of St Paul's Cathedral and Director of St Paul's Institute. He is a Fellow of the Royal Historical Society and was formerly a Research Fellow in Economic History at Nuffield College, Oxford.

Robin Philpot is a writer and researcher in Montréal, Québec. He lived in Africa in the 1970s and taught English and History in Burkina Faso from 1972 to 1974. The original French version of his book on the Rwandan genocide, *Ça ne s'est pas passé comme ça à Kigal,* has sold widely in Québec, in Europe and in Africa. *Rwanda 1994: Colonialism dies hard* is published on line by the The Taylor Report and Robin Philpot to ensure maximum readership, particularly in Africa.

CONTRIBUTORS

John Pilger was born and educated in Sydney. He has been a war correspondent, film-maker and playwright. Based in London, he has written from many countries and has twice won British 'Journalist of the Year', for his work in Vietnam and Cambodia. Other awards include 'International Reporter of the Year' and the 'United Nations Association Media Prize'. For his broadcasting, he has won an 'American Television Academy Award', an 'Emmy' and the 'Richard Dimbleby Award', given by the British Academy of Film and Television Arts. His books include: *The Last Day* (1975), *Aftermath: The Struggles of Cambodia and Vietnam* (1981), *The Outsiders* (1984), *Heroes* (1986), *A Secret Country* (1989), *Distant Voices* (1992 and 1994), *Hidden Agendas* (1998) and *The New Rulers of the World* (2002).

Dan Plesch is a writer, broadcaster and consultant on geo-political strategy. He is a Research Associate at the University of London's School of Oriental and African Studies and a Visiting Senior Research Fellow at Keele University. Previously he was Senior Research Fellow at the Royal United Services Institute and founding Director of the British American Security Information Council. He is a frequent contributor to the BBC and CNN and has written for a wide variety of print media including *The Times*, *Financial Times*, *Los Angeles Times*, *New York Times* and the *Washington Times*.

Ciarán L. Quinn teaches at Osaka University, Japan. He is a graduate in Celtic Studies from the National University of Ireland and in Medieval Art-History from Bangor, the National University of Wales. His recent research interests are in Anglo-Saxon translation, poetry and the iconography of the early Celtic Cross.

xxii

David, Lord Ramsbotham served in the Regular Army from 1957, when he came down from Cambridge, until 1993, retiring in the rank of General. From 1995 to 2001 he was Her Majesty's Chief Inspector of Prisons, during which time he visited or inspected – or both – every prison in England, Wales and Northern Ireland, as well as several in Scotland, America, Canada, Germany and the Caribbean. He published *Prisongate, the shocking state of Britain's Prisons and the need for visionary change* in 2003 and was appointed a crossbench member of the House of Lords in 2005.

Satwinder Sehmi is a Sikh writer, calligrapher and designer. He is African-born and is now based in London where he co-directs the graphic design company Alphabet Soup. His work draws upon a wide range of styles and cultural influences, reflecting the diverse character of his chosen home. His publications include *Calligraphy, the Rhythm of Writing* (Merehurst, London: 1993).

Salil Shetty joined the United Nations in 2003 as Director of the Millennium Campaign, which informs and encourages people's involvement and action in the realization of the Millennium Declaration and Development Goals. He was formerly Chief Executive of ActionAid – a leading NGO committed to poverty eradication. He is a Governor of the Institute of Development Studies in Sussex, Council Member of the Overseas Development Institute, London, a Member of the Advisory Council of the American-Indian Foundation, New York, and Trustee of the Board of Italy's largest secular international development NGO Azione Aiuto. An Indian National, he earned a distinction in a Masters of Science

in Social Policy and Planning from the London School of
Economics and a Masters in Business Administration from
the Indian Institute of Management in Ahmedabad. He
commenced his studies in Advanced Accountancy and Cost
Accounting at Bangalore University.

John Simspon CBE studied at Magdalene College, Cambridge.
In 1966 he joined the BBC as a trainee sub-editor in Radio
News, rising through the ranks to become the BBC's World
Affairs Editor in 1988. He has reported from more than 100
countries, including 30 war zones. Several of his awards are
related to his work in conflicts. In 2000, he was named RTS
(Royal Television Society) Journalist of the Year for his reporting
from Belgrade. Simpson received a CBE in the Gulf War Honours.
He won an International Emmy Award for reporting in
Afghanistan 2002, and two more RTS awards for reporting in
Afghanistan and Iraq in 2002. He holds an honorary doctorate
by St. Andrews University in Scotland. As well as writing
factual books, including his autobiography, *Strange Places,
Questionable People*, Simpson has authored the novels:
Moscow Requiem, and *A Fine and Private Place*.

Alan Titley is professor of Irish at St. Patrick's College (Dublin
City University) and the author of novels, stories, plays and
of literary scholarship. Awards for his writing including The
Butler Prize of the Irish-American Cultural Institute, The Pater
Prize for International Drama, The Stewart Parker Award
from the BBC, and the Éilís Dillon Award for Children's Literature.
He has scripted film documentaries on literature and has
presented radio and television book programmes. His
scholarly work concentrates on modern Irish and Scottish

Gaelic literature. He writes a weekly column on current and cultural affairs for *The Irish Times.*

Terry Waite CBE was Education Adviser to the Anglican Bishop and Provincial Training Adviser to the first African Anglican Archbishop of Uganda, Rwanda and Burundi, founding the Southern Sudan Project. In 1980 he became Advisor to the Archbishop of Canterbury, He negotiated release of hostages from Iran and Libya and in 1987 was himself taken captive in Lebanon – for 1,763 days. Elected Fellow Commoner at Trinity Hall Cambridge (1991), devoting himself to study, lecturing and humanitarian activities. Books include *Taken on Trust, Footfalls in Memory* and *Travels with a Primate.* Responsibilities include: Founder President of Y-Care. Trustee of the Butler Trust (UK prisons). President of Emmaus UK Trustee of the FreePlay Foundation, Member of the Advisory Council of Victim Support, and Founder Chairman of Hostage UK Ambassador for WWF-UK.

Kathi Zellweger is Director of International Cooperation for Caritas-Hong Kong. She has been working for Caritas for 27 years, and for the past ten years has had responsibility on behalf of the international Caritas network for the aid programme to North Korea. Caritas International is an international network of 162 Catholic relief, development and social service organizations present in 200 countries and territories.

Benjamin Zephaniah is a poet, novelist and playwright. He grew up in Jamaica and Birmingham, England, leaving school at 14 and moving to London in 1979. Awards include Writer in Residence, Africa Arts Collective, Liverpool; Creative Artist in Residence, Cambridge University; hon. doctorate in Arts and Humanities, University of North London; Doctor of

Letters, University of Central England; Doctor of the University, University of Staffordshire. Poetry includes *Pen Rhythm* (1980); *The Dread Affair: Collected Poems* (1985); *Rasta Time in Palestine* (1990); *Talking Turkeys* (1994); *Funky Chickens* (1996); *We Are Britain!* (2002); *Chambers Primary Rhyming Dictionary* (2004). His novels include *Face* (1999); and *Refugee Boy* (2001). His music recordings include *Us and Dem* (1990); *Belly of de Beast* (1996). His plays include *Dread Poets Society* (BBC, 1991); *Hurricane Dub* (BBC Young Playwrights Festival Award, 1998); *Listen to Your Parents* (BBC Radio 4, 2000).

The voices that you hear in this book are personal ones, as are the views expressed, rather than those of the editors or recipients of the royalties.

Foreword:
From Live Aid to Live 8

BOB GELDOF

This is a powerful book. The voices it contains will not whisper
softly to you or be discreet or polite. They will shout their
dismay with a loud intelligence, and though the end impression will be that of a coherent collective anxiety, each voice
is entirely singular.

In the middle of 2004, aware of the approaching twentieth
anniversary of Live Aid concert concomitant with Britain's
presidency of both the G8 and the European Union, I called
for a political and intellectual debate concerning extreme
poverty and its consequences, which I regard as the great
political problem of our age.

I wished for a discussion at the beginning of this young
century that would deal with the awful disparity between
an increasingly wealthy world and the appalling and abject
poverty that unnecessarily accompanies it.

For our prurient media the images we have been sated with
constitute nothing less than a pornography of poverty and yet
the parade of ill, dying, hungry, weak and powerless that mutes
our tea-time conversations seep from across our screens like a
great, weeping moral sore. It leaves us bewildered, sad and
impotent.

Nearly all now accept that our age and its terrors emanate
from this imbalanced moment. The hopeless and mute will

revert to a terrible barbarism. The impoverished will insist on their human dignity. The ideologically secure will discover that what they hold to be universal laws will turn out to be no more than parochial concerns. Those without a future will move to where they can acquire one.

Never before have we known so much about this disparity and done so little to rectify it. Or else we are simply bewildered that the world will not move smartly along to an accepted political or economic plan and that the forces which those plans put in train have severely unintended or misunderstood consequences.

It seemed that this year with its bizarre confluence of politics and populism within the UK might be the time to properly engage with this dilemma.

There are wholly new forces in play about us which we fail to perceive or understand. These phenomena are a consequence of a different modern world that has emerged since the Live Aid concert 20 years ago. And though part of Live Aid was the simultaneous suspicion and proof of media globalization, within a few years with the ubiquity of computerization and the consequent impact of 24/7 money, alongside the resulting demise of the power blocs of the cold war and their replacement by the trading blocs of financial and trade globalization, we had altered the hitherto known predictive post-war world.

This newer world is unknown to us. It appears haphazard and unpredictable. Much of it seems to make little economic sense and helps to break up social compacts we have grown accustomed to with little perceived benefit. In our lucky part of the world it creates anxieties and open revolt against institutions or individuals who try and coax us down its worryingly opaque road towards an unknown goal.

In the poorer part of the world its consequences, whether unintentional or not seems simply to kill people. They have no defence against this tide of dynamic worldwide financial novelty. By their very poverty, i.e. their lack of consequence either as consumers or producers to the global market they are excluded or unheard of in the very fora that shape most of their lives. They are too poor to be noticed. They are too poor to stay alive. Indeed it is only in the vast numbers of their dying that we begin to notice them, when the cameras descend vulture-like to record their whimpers amid the carnival of death.

On the other hand we are lucky and rich enough to not only make the rules that will further benefit our lives, but also, though we try and grope with the uncalled for social consequences of those rules, we are despite our anxieties and bewilderments, wealthy and therefore strong enough to simply surf the backwash of the global phenomena.

I believed that a second Live Aid was unnecessary. Given the immovability of the Cold War deadlock, 20 years ago Live Aid could only deal with the symptoms of poverty. Starvation, illness etc ... I fully understood that poverty was political and needed to be addressed thus and would not be remedied by Band Aid measures. In the meantime however one could not blithely stand by and watch the hungry while we through the economic imbalance of subsidy piled up our food stocks in vast Himalayas of surplus. It was truly sickening. Still is.

But that was then. The demise of the Cold War allowed for a newer political fluidity and I felt that a second Live Aid would not only be a mere and less-valued repetition but also ineffectual. If 20 years ago Live Aid dealt with the symptoms of poverty we could now finally begin to deal with the structures of poverty. We could begin to deal with issues of justice rather than charity. We could even maybe begin on the long road to making poverty history. I suggested that what was necessary was what I was calling an Intellectual Live Aid. A gathering of thinkers of our time in open, weeklong discussion. It would be televised and written about extensively in the press, provoking comment and debate within the general public and thus creating a groundswell of public opinion for political change prior to the arrival of the Group of 8 in Scotland.

Part of this would be the discussions within the Prime Minister's Commission for Africa which I had persuaded him was necessary using, partially, some of the arguments outlined above. It was a profoundly interesting experience for me, containing as it did several senior political figures from within and without the G8 and Africa. It also included academics, businessmen and intellectuals from many disciplines. Importantly the majority of the group were African. The resulting document provided the agenda for the African component of the Gleneagles summit, where 50 of its proposals were adopted and the significant debt/aid package was agreed upon and approved at the later IMF/World Bank meetings in Washington.

The Intellectual Live Aid idea never really happened, though there was significant press comment and public awareness of Africa as we now know through the Make Poverty History campaign and the Live8 concerts which I was finally persuaded were necessary in order to push the Commission's findings through the G8 by making each of the rich countries populations aware of the opportunity we faced.

xxx

This book however is the consequence of the earlier idea. It was part of the immediate response to my suggestion, taken up and extrapolated out in this great contribution to the debate.

It is often brilliant, sometimes shocking, usually frightening and always thoughtful. You feel within its pages a real attempt to understand our age and plot a way around its iniquities in order to move forward more appropriately in a just world. It will be a very interesting book to read in 2099.

Some of the writers you will know, others not. Some whose views you may be familiar with now take on a newer urgency. Others' voices, thoughtful and bothered, sneak into vacant cavities with all the vigour of fresh thought, new with their hitherto limited fame or relative obscurity. Either way there is a dreadful page-turning compulsion to the whole enterprise.

The left and the right are here, though for me these terms are becoming increasingly meaningless, if not actually unhelpful flags in this different age. There are those with an agenda and those who probably don't even recognize they have one. Here are the secular and the god-fearing. The idealistic and pragmatic. The sceptic, the cynic, the optimist and the fearful. But all of them are concerned, all impassioned and all firing wonderfully on all intellectual pistons. There should be more of this.

Preface:
The UN Millennium
Campaign

SALIL SHETTY, DIRECTOR, THE UN MILLENNIUM CAMPAIGN

When 189 governments from the North and South, as representatives of their citizens, signed up to the Millennium Declaration in the United Nations Millennium General Assembly of September 2000, there was a palpable sense of urgency. Urgency to 'free our fellow men, women and children from the abject and dehumanizing conditions of extreme poverty, to which more than a billion of them are currently subjected'.

The Declaration built on pledges made in the series of important UN conferences of the 1990s, and seeks to recognize the rising tide of discontent with the lopsided benefits of globalization. At the heart of the Declaration are human rights, peace, gender equity, the environment and the pressing priorities of the Least Developed Countries and Africa. The eight Millennium Development Goals (MDGs, which are printed in the Appendix to this book), a minimal set of interlinked outcomes that have to be met by 2015, are derived from the Declaration.

Given the proliferation of UN conferences and commitments, it's important for us to understand the uniqueness of the

Millennium Goals in many respects. They do represent, at the level of governments, a *compact* not only between rich and poor countries and the UN system based on shared responsibility, but also with the key institutions that determine the economic fate of the developing world: the World Bank, the IMF (International Monetary Fund), the regional development banks and increasingly the World Trade Organization. For the first time, the international financial institutions and rich-country governments have made explicit what they can be held accountable for: not just in process terms but in outcomes.

The world has never seen so much prosperity before. The hundreds of billions that are being spent in Iraq have put things in perspective. In 2004 alone, the world spent US $900 billion on arms. We might not need more than about US $100 billion of additional aid per year to meet the Goals. Financially, we are talking of small change.

Furthermore, performance against the goals will be monitored. These goals are not just lofty statements of intent; they are quite precise. Monitoring mechanisms have been put in place in terms of national MDG reports and the Secretary General's reports to the General Assembly. Many civil-society actors are starting independent tracking processes. Over 70 reports have already been produced at the national level.

The Goals are clearly achievable. Individual Goals have already been achieved in the space of 10–15 years by many countries, including China, Sri Lanka, Uganda and Ghana. Moreover, today we have not only the financial wherewithal but also the technical knowledge to realize the Goals.

Of course, it is equally true that at our current trajectory – if we carry on in a 'business as usual' mode – the goals will not be achieved by 2015. The reality is that progress at the ground level in poor countries across the world, particularly in Sub-Saharan Africa, is still unacceptably slow. The aggregates on performance on extreme poverty (Goal 1) at the global and indeed the national level are misleading. The Commission for Africa Report and the Millennium Project Report – the two major policy assessments – confirm this, as does the latest MDG progress report from the UN Secretary General. We still have 30,000 people a day dying from poverty, 120 million children (mostly girls) denied the right to even primary schooling, 3 million people succumbing to AIDS in 2004, and over half a million women dying annually during childbirth. The tragedy, of course, is that this is all preventable.

But to change this we need a major shift in the level of action by governments, the private sector and civil society. So far as governments are concerned, the issue of whether or not to take action boils down to political will. Where progress is evident, as for example in the European Union's recent commitment to increase aid levels by 2010, it is due in large part to the public placing sustained pressure on governments to take action towards the achievement of the MDGs. But there is still a very long way to go and the Millennium Campaign's explicit objective is to encourage and facilitate 'we, the people' to hold their governments and other key actors to account for the promises in the Millennium Declaration and the Millennium Goals.

National campaigns form the backbone of the international campaign. Non-governmental organizations, women's groups, faith groups among others are forming national coalitions in over thirty countries around the world to pressurize their governments to take concrete actions towards the achievement of the Goals. In poor countries, the focus is on the rights of poor people to realize the Goals: Are the appropriate policies in place? Is the government providing fundamental basic services such as education and health care free of charge to the poor? Are institutions responsive to the legitimate aspirations of poor and marginalized people? Is there adequate public accountability and transparency in budgeting processing? From the outset it has been clear that the credibility of the global campaign hinges on creating pressure for the achievement of Goal 8 in rich countries. Thus national coalitions in rich countries are focused on pressuring governments to increase the quantity and quality of aid, to make trade rules more equitable and to reduce the debt burden of the poor countries. Since its inception, the Millennium Campaign has been actively lobbying parliamentarians in rich countries on Goal 8 issues. In recent months the Campaign has also started engaging local authorities to raise awareness around the MDGs and to encourage citizens of rich countries to support the national campaigns.

The year 2005 offers an amazing range of possibilities for a real breakthrough towards achieving the Goals in the ten years remaining until 2015. The European Union announced some concrete and positive measures on improving aid quantity and quality in June 2005. The G8 announcements in July 2005 have built upon that, although most campaigners would have liked to have seen more, particularly from the non-EU countries, on aid and debt, and a stronger push for fairer terms of trade between North and South as a result of the Doha Round of trade negotiations. At the UN World Summit in New York in

September 2005, over 150 heads of state will review progress against the Millennium Declaration, including the Millennium Goals. There is an understandable concern amongst civil society that the development agenda and the MDGs will be overshadowed by other agendas at the Summit, in particular Security Council reform, a topic many rich (and indeed many poor) country governments will want to focus on. However, as outlined in Secretary General Kofi Annan's framing document for the UN World Summit – *In Larger Freedom: Towards Development, Security and Human Rights for All* – security, development and human rights are strongly interlinked and advances in any one of these areas are dependent on advances in the others.

> The world must advance the causes of security, development and human rights together. Humanity will not enjoy security without development, it will not enjoy development without security, and it will not enjoy either without respect for human rights ... Not only are development, security and human rights all imperative; they also reinforce each other. This relationship has only been strengthened in our era of rapid technological advances, increasing economic interdependence, globalization and dramatic geopolitical change. While poverty and denial of human rights may not be said to 'cause' civil war, terrorism, or organised crime, they all greatly increase the risk of instability and violence.

The Secretary General's Report itself draws heavily from the powerful recommendations of the UN High Level Panel on

xxxvii

Security – *A More Secure World: Our Shared Responsibility.*
This document reminds us: 'We live in a world of new and
evolving threats, threats that could not have been anticipated
when the UN was founded in 1945 – threats like nuclear
terrorism and State collapse from the witch's brew of poverty,
disease and civil war.' Of the six clusters of threats identified
by the Report that require urgent and sustained action at the
global level, the number one priority is assigned to economic
and social threats of poverty, infectious disease and
environmental degradation, i.e. the MDGs.

After the UN World Summit comes the World Trade
Organization (WTO) Ministerial Meeting in Hong Kong in
December 2005. As of now, trade discussions are in the
doldrums. There has been no movement on the dismantling of
agricultural subsidies and very little progress on increasing
market access for developing countries. The good news is that
as a result of growing public actions in recent years, the
general public in many rich countries today have a much
greater awareness and understanding around the Goal 8
issues of trade, aid and debt and are starting to demand that
their parliamentarians and governments take greater steps to
address them. A loose alliance of thousands of organizations
around the world that are campaigning for a breakthrough on
poverty, the Global Call to Action Against Poverty (GCAP) was
launched in January 2005. United by the symbol of a white
band, millions of citizens from Bangladesh to Bolivia, Chile to
Nepal, Italy to Indonesia are urging national governments and
international decision-makers to keep to the promises explicit in
the Millennium Declaration and make urgent and meaningful
policy change in trade, aid and debt. This gives hope and

encouragement to hundreds of thousands of people around the world who have been working tirelessly with the poor and marginalized for many years. Trade unions, faith groups, the media, celebrities, youth groups, local authorities and concerned citizens are standing shoulder to shoulder with those working in the development sector in their fight against poverty. All of these actors are gearing up for a massive global mobilization around the UN World Summit in September and the WTO in December. Ringing in their ears and inspiring them to continue with their struggle will be the words of Nelson Mandela, whose message to tens of thousands of campaigners gathered in Trafalgar Square earlier this year was clear: 'We won the struggle against slavery and then against apartheid, both of which seemed insurmountable at the time. The next big war is the one against poverty and we have to win this for the sake of humanity and our collective future.'

Websites

For information on the UN Millennium Campaign, the national MDG campaigns and on how to take action visit www.millenniumcampaign.org

For information on the Global Call to Action Against Poverty (GCAP) and on how to get involved in actions in your country visit www.whiteband.org

Introduction: History in the making

MICHELLE P. BROWN

The time of writing promises to be a momentous landmark in human history. Or at least, it offers the potential of being so. It is twenty years since a group of rock celebrities, led by Bob Geldof, started a campaign called Live Aid to raise public awareness and charitable giving to alleviate the plight of the world's poorest people. We have recently witnessed the greatest act of global spontaneous giving that has ever been seen, in response to the natural disaster and immense human tragedy of the Tsunami that devastated SE Asia, sweeping away some 300,000 lives and reminding us all of our transience and vulnerability. Britain holds the presidency of the G8 Summit of the wealthiest nations on the planet and its Labour government promises to use the opportunity to focus on global poverty and injustice. The Commission for Africa has been charged with exploring the causes and solutions of the problems facing the world's poorest continent. Charities, media, celebrities and public alike are joining forces in the 'Make Poverty History' campaign, recognizing that current generations are particularly well-placed to make a difference. And yet each generation's contribution can only really be effective in relation to those that have preceded them, and those that follow. All of this current popular activism stands

1

against the backdrop of the UN's Millennium Campaign that grew from attempts, such as Jubilee 2000, to mark the dawn of a new millennium by lifting the crippling burden of debt from the backs of the world's poor.

Such an epoch deserves to be chronicled and to be set in the context of past experience and future sustainability. The pieces by Bob Geldof and Richard Curtis give a personal insight into the motivation driving two of the leading co-ordinators of the Make Poverty History campaign and the Live 8 concerts. These are followed by a discussion of the longer-term aims of the UN Millennium Campaign by its director, Salil Shetty. In 2000, the largest gathering of world leaders ever assembled met in New York and agreed to the Millennium Development Goals (MDGs; these are printed, along with their objectives, in the Appendix). The schedule for their achievement may have slipped, but some major advances have already been made, saving millions upon millions of lives. The MDGs are the world's time-bound and quantified targets for addressing extreme poverty in its many dimensions - hunger, disease, lack of adequate shelter and exclusion - while promoting gender equality, education and environmental sustainability. They also recognize basic human rights - the rights of each person on the planet to health, education, shelter and security. They are designed to help halve poverty by 2015 - eight hundred years after the agreement known as Magna Carta (the 'Great Charter'), considered a foundation stone of civil liberties, was squeezed out of King John by his barons on a little island in the Thames, outside of London, known as Runnymede.

On July 6, 2005, a wave of optimism, of a magnitude not

experienced in decades, swept over London as the success of its bid to host the 2012 Olympics was announced. In the East End, one of the poorest parts of the capital, kids from across the 144 ethnic groups who live there were heard expressing their hopes that they might grow to represent their country. London's ability, like several other major British cities, to provide a home and opportunities for those from so many diverse cultures seemed supremely celebrated in this shared sense of belonging. That evening St Paul's Cathedral hosted an address by the UN Secretary General, Kofi Annan, with responses by a panel including the UK's Chancellor of the Exchequer Gordon Brown (a leading political advocate of the war on poverty). They were en route for Gleneagles and the G8 Summit. The cathedral was packed with an audience of 2,700 – all fired up with the campaign and keen to participate. The politicians could be seen to be touched themselves by the all-pervading energy and enthusiasm and spoke with a passion and commitment seldom displayed when addressing a political, business or media audience. All things were possible.

The next day, July 7, it was London's turn to fall victim to a series of terrorist attacks in which four young men (the youngest a mere boy of eighteen), some brought up in Leeds, thought that the best way they could raise public awareness for the injustices they perceived was to turn themselves into living bombs, blowing themselves and fifty-two innocent bystanders to eternity in three tube trains and a bus. So many others were maimed and scarred, in so many ways, by that tragic act. The next day the news coverage barely left room for mention of the lives lost in similar incidents in the hot-spots of the Middle East, the 'regular' atrocities that we have come to take for granted, without counting the cost of the lives lost or pausing to imagine them as real people with loved ones and precious lives to be lived. Recent estimates tell of some 23,000 civilian deaths during the conflicts in Iraq. And yet, the issue is not one of numbers – the loss of one innocent life, wherever it occurs, matters. For, to quote John Donne, the seventeenth-century poet-Dean of St Paul's,

> No man is an island, entire of itself; every man is a piece of the continent, a part of the main. If a clod be washed away by the sea, Europe is the less, as well as if a promontory were, as well as if a manor of thy friend's or of thine own were. Any man's death diminishes me, because I am involved in mankind; and therefore never send to know for whom the bell tolls; it tolls for thee ... (Meditation 17, *Devotions upon Emergent Occasions*, 1624.)

On July 8 the politicians emerged from the G8 Summit, which so many people had urged to increase aid, wipe out debts, adopt fairer trading practices and limit emissions endangering the environment. Their compromise package, in which increased aid and debt relief featured and trade and the environment did not (with the US leading opposition to meaningful measures in these areas), was announced and passed almost without comment. Nonetheless, some 10 million lives will be saved by 2010 as a result. The campaigners took heart, and returned to their plans to keep the pressure up in order to influence further significant meetings later in the year. What the ghastly contrast of those two days showed, however, was that, despite any attempts to perpetuate a political smokescreen, the issues surrounding poverty, aid and debt cannot and should not be approached in isolation from those of trade, defence and the situation of conflict in the Middle East - in which faith is but one ingredient in a volatile mixture of ethnic, territorial, economic and political alignments (as Akbar Ahmed's paper illustrates). Some three millennia ago the Psalmist said 'pray for the peace of Jerusalem'; he saw even then that peace in Jerusalem is a paradigm for peace in the whole world.

As the discussion of arms and warfare in the Appendix shows, there are issues that need to be addressed if we are serious about improving the lot of the poor:

- 85 per cent of global arms exports come from G8 countries.
- The top five countries profiting from the arms trade – USA, UK, France, Russia and China – are the five permanent members of the United Nations Security Council. This is because they have the most significant military capability. Therefore their pre-eminence in the arms trade is regrettable, but scarcely surprising.
- From 1998 to 2001, the USA, the UK and France earned more income from arms sales to developing countries than they gave in aid.
- Half the world's governments spend more on the military than on health care.
- Just 1 per cent of global annual military spending could educate every child on earth over the next decade.
- Global military expenditure and arms trade form the largest spending in the world at over US $950 billion in annual expenditure for 2003; the total budget of the UN – committed to preserving peace through international

co-operation and collective security – amounts to only
about a proportional 1.5 per cent of this sum.
- The developing world is often the destination for arms sales.

Time will judge whether we have lived up to the heightened
expectations of our time. Such challenges to apathy,
complacency, detrimental ambition and greed are timely
and necessary. But they cannot stand in isolation. Charitable
giving is a great thing, enshrined in many of the varying
codes of social behaviour and of faith that human beings
have constructed. However, charity does not consist solely of
the time-honoured practice of almsgiving. The word itself is
derived from the Latin *caritas* – which means 'love'. To love
our neighbours as ourselves is one of the oldest injunctions
to human rights, enshrined in the ancient law of Judaism,
which was bequeathed to Christianity and Islam alike. It is a
principle that the Buddhist, the Hindu, the Sikh, the New Age
Pagan and many others embrace in their creeds. Many secular
statements concerning human rights likewise stress the respect
and care due to others. If we are to show true 'charity', that
love demands justice, equity, mercy, compassion, tolerance,
mutual forgiveness and empathy. These are the qualities that
we are called to give of, as well as our material wealth, our
time and our pen and ink.

This book brings together papers on a range of issues relating
to social justice, dignity, equality and survival. The voices you
will hear belong to some of those who work ceaselessly to
address these issues: on the ground, through the media, through
political and public lobbying and awareness-raising, and to
some historians who are interested in the people of the present

and the future, as well as those of the past, and who seek to assess where we are and where we might be going through an understanding of where we have been already. Questions are turned round and viewed from different perspectives, the focus zooming in and out as the picture takes shape.

There have always been those stricken by poverty, illness, warfare and disasters, although not necessarily confined to the parts of the world with which we most frequently associate them today. They are not merely the victims of geography. The African continent, the Middle East, Asia, the Orient and South America have produced some of the world's greatest civilizations. But as history unfolds empires rise and fall, as empires always do. They become victims of their own over-extended ambitions, their own weight and obligations, internal corruption and conflict, dissent amongst those they rule or competition with rivals. The aftermath of empire and the challenges of post-colonialism take time to work through, especially if new super-powers are raising the game and seeking new client populations and markets to support their internal economies. The maelstrom that followed the collapse of the Roman Empire in the fifth century meant that new international relationships – political, economic, cultural and religious – had to be forged by the successor states that gradually crystallized in its wake to form Europe and the Middle East. Over the next 1500 years they remained haunted by the vision of empire, seeking to recreate it in their own likeness: the Byzantine Empire, the Carolingian and Ottonian Empires, the Mamluk, Seljuk and Ottoman Empires, the Mongolian Empire, the Angevin Empire, the Holy Roman Empire, the Portuguese and Spanish Empires, the Dutch Trade Empire, the

Austro-Hungarian Empire, the British Empire, the Third Reich ...

Does this pattern of big fish gobbling up little fish, and of little fish banding together to become big fish themselves, have to persist as a model of nationhood, governance and economics? Will we someday see the United States of Africa and the Democratic Republic of Colorado as one of a number of devolved states? If history is not necessarily linear and progressive, nor is it inevitably cyclical, condemning us to a perpetual 'groundhog day' in which we repeat the same experiments and errors. Neither need we subscribe solely to a Marxist theory of historical dialectic in which we lurch from one trauma to another. We can help to shape history, if only we take the trouble to understand it and to join up the dots in our thinking and behaviour.

Relationships between wealthy and poorer nations do not always have to take the form of clientage. It should be perfectly possible to mentor developing nations without imposing ideologies upon them or making them victims of the global labour market and 'free' trade. If their lot improves then so does ours. The world is too small a place for the problems of any one area to be contained. The solutions are complex, and faced with complexity we so often retreat into over-simplistic black and white, either/or, rather than working it through. We can do it though. We think of ourselves as sophisticated – let's be sophisticated in our thinking.

In the eighteenth and nineteenth centuries some of the poorest people in the world were the Celts of Ireland, Scotland and Cornwall. Forced from their ancestral homelands, their diaspora carried them around the world where their skills and imagination helped to shape the technology, economy, literature, drama and music of many younger nations. Africa is now the world's poorest continent, beset by famine, HIV/AIDS, warfare and genocide. It is not that way by chance, but because it is going through a similar process of reinvention following its imperial colonial experiences. The world powers of today, whilst paying lip service to the need for aid, debt relief and environmental controls, know that fast-tracking the process will impinge on the cushioned comfort zones of their own societies. Humanitarian impulses vie with the pragmatics of vested interest and the political web of inter-relationships that have been constructed between individuals, nations and multi-national corporations. Such webs can distort reality and tie you in knots. To the educated English and Irish readers of eighteenth-century tracts and political essays, the bitingly satirical 'Modest Proposal' advanced by Dean Swift (the author of *Gulliver's Travels*) seemed, at face value, a completely logical extension of policy in respect of the Irish Problem. Until they realised that it led, quite logically and expediently, to eating the children of the poor.

This is exactly what we are doing today. We may not be devouring the children of the poor, in cannibalistic fashion, but we are taking the food out of their mouths in order to support our own lifestyles. And we are not reading snippets of patchy information – we are watching them starve on our TV screens. They are, literally, dying in our living rooms. And yet we are not uncaring. If those people were in our homes, expiring beside our dining tables, many of us would feed and shelter them, try to give them a leg up in life. But they are not, and faced with the seeming frustration and futility of getting some of our plenty onto their plates, we turn away and render them invisible, just as we do the homeless on our pavements. The problems seem too big for us to tackle alone. That's what we elect governments for – if indeed we bother to vote and haven't decided that all politicians are the same and on the make. Democracy was hard-won and there are good, committed people within the ranks of governments and administrations, but they also need encouraging and reminding that they really can make a difference, if only they steadfastly allow conscience to guide compromise, rather than vice versa.

Most of the world's conflicts throughout history come down ultimately to competition for resources. If those starving children were really in our front rooms and grabbing the food from our own kids' plates, rather than expiring quietly in the corner, we may not feel so charitably inclined towards them. But hopefully, we would intervene with dialogue, not just with force, and ensure that everyone got a share – that nobody went hungry to bed or injured to hospital. Conflict resolution and valuing the rights of the individual as part of the social whole are crucial aspects of sustainable life.

The sustainability of human societies and of human history cannot be considered in isolation. It cries out to be considered in relation to the bigger picture of the relationship and natural contract between ourselves and other creatures, our shared habitats and the very fabric of the hospitable little planet we live on. Yet we persist in condemning sentient creatures to tortured, undignified existences in the cause of quick profit and careless consumerism. Cease to respect other life-forms and it becomes ever easier to devalue human life too. Likewise, our growing awareness of the implications of ravishing

10

non-renewable resources is in tension with our unquenchable thirst for energy and our unwillingness to significantly change or modify our lifestyles.

One of the reasons that prehistoric societies persisted in their way of life for so many millennia (some still helping to care for areas such as the Amazon to this day) was that smaller, simpler societies suited them. The rate of technological development quickened along with growing competition for resources. As agricultural and metallurgical capabilities developed so too did warfare, conquest, expansionism, tribal confederacies, trade, material culture and the arts. Civilization was born and its development has been speeding up ever since. But is this an open-ended scenario? Is development finite or infinite, and might it sometimes be advantageous to decelerate or un-develop somewhat in order to ensure sustainability and 'progress' in the best sense of the word?

We ignore the legacy of our environment at our peril. The wilderness landscapes on our doorsteps, such as Dartmoor, Exmoor and Bodmin Moor in Britain, are the very areas that were most over-exploited during Prehistory. They have still not recovered. Mexico City is now the most massive urban conglomeration on Earth, part of a South American tradition of city living that began in the ancient empires of the Mayans and Aztecs. It is becoming apparent that a significant factor in the disappearance of these 'civilizations' was their over-working and colonization of the land. They simply became too voracious, too populous and too big. Today immigrants from South America flock to the US, often to dwell in makeshift shanty-towns as underpaid migrant labourers, their women and children stranded back home. And yet it is also in Latin

11

YOU'RE HISTORY!

America that we can currently see some of the most promising signs of growing popular awareness and constructive political activism. We congratulate ourselves on civil rights victories, such as the abolition of slavery, and yet there are more people in what amounts to the condition of slavery in the world today (a staggering 27 million) than ever there were in the ancient world, or in the cotton fields and sugar plantations of the southern states of America and the West Indies. Today, however, those who exploit them bear no legal or moral responsibility towards them. The process of abolition began over 2000 years ago and was frequently achieved. Have we actually sustained the process, as well as congratulating ourselves upon it?

History is there for us to learn from. It is not purely progressive and we in the developed West are not on some sort of evolutionary fast-track in terms of historical or ethical development. There have always been people who care and who have sought to make a difference for the good – we have no moral monopoly on compassion today. Sometimes the circumstances are right or they can inspire enough others to produce a shift in public opinion and social practices which may subsequently be enshrined in policy and, more importantly, in law. The role of the press and of freedom of speech has frequently played a vital role in this; they have ensured that we can never again have peace of mind – unless we reflect and act upon such knowledge.

Once ordinary people become more socially and politically aware and active it can become harder for their governments to be wantonly exploitative and corrupt – unless society becomes so cynical and blasé about its politicians and their motives that it leaves them to get on with it without demanding better.

This applies not only to those living in corrupt third-world states, but also to citizens of developed democracies. Allowing our governments to capitalize on the PR benefits of championing aid and debt relief whilst they are also cutting back on the means of understanding the cultures and challenges of the beneficiaries, bolstering the arms trade and prioritizing the interests of their own business communities, is naïve and irresponsible. Cynics might justify inactivity by denying that any attempts to help the poor can succeed in the face of corrupt local regimes. This is no excuse for leaving the innocent to their suffering or failing to help set in motion the longer processes of change. The poor need access to education, as much as to food and water, in order to help shape their own destinies. Women, in particular, can make a little education go a long way when it comes to caring for the welfare and livelihood of their families and their neighbours, and improving their environments. The rights of women, children, the disabled and the elderly need to be advanced and safeguarded if we are to achieve our full social potential.

Ultimately some things matter more than property, position, or even the physical survival of you and yours – as so many people have found during wars and persecutions when they have risked everything to save a neighbour or a stranger, acting intuitively or knowing that they could not live with the personal sense of guilt if they did not. You have to be able not only to live, but to live with yourself. If, given all that we now know about what is going on in our world and what makes it tick, we choose to play the ostrich with its head stuck in the sand, if we fail to ask the questions, seek the answers and help to make the difference, how can we ever live with ourselves – and what will history make of us?

That people are prepared to exert themselves to help others, whom they will probably never meet, in so many ways, from creative performances and feats of physical endurance to phoning, texting, e-mailing or signing a standing order form for regular, planned giving, is in itself a source of affirmation and hope. That others place their own lives on the line and leave their comfort zones to meet others in their place of pain and need is even more remarkable. That people can be made to think, to connect wires, to ask questions and seek answers is an even more essential part of change for the better. Once mobilized, public opinion is a powerful force. Individual action or the force of circumstances may serve to wake it from its usual Sleeping Beauty slumber, but for real, lasting change to occur the reasons underlying it have to be explored and understood and provision made for future sustainability.

Our time is but one episode in the epic of human history – in evolutionary terms but the blink of a dinosaur's eyelid – if we are to make it really count we have to think of it in relation to the whole story. We have to truly value what we have in every respect, enough perhaps to really give some of it away and allow the whole world an equal share. The greatest gift we can have is peace of mind and the ability to live with ourselves as well as others. The only way we can do that, in this information-rich age, is not look at injustice, suffering and the threat of military and environmental annihilation, or to look them squarely in the face and challenge our own preconceptions and practices – and maybe even change them. You *are* history – so help make the difference.

Acknowledgements

At the beginning of the Make Poverty History campaign I was listening to a TV interview between Bob Geldof and Jonathan Ross. In the course of this, in his own inimitable and eloquent fashion, Geldof cast down a gauntlet to the intelligentsia – one of the most articulate sectors of society, theoretically at any rate – to become more involved. I may not belong to any such select club, but as a writer and teacher, interested in social and cultural history, I felt obliged to pick up that gauntlet. I had tried to do my bit, along with so many others, by giving, collecting, writing protest letters, marching and cheering others on in fun runs (I'm built for distance, not for speed), but here was an opportunity to contribute something that my skills equipped me for. Enthusing others and embroiling them in my madcap ideas is one of these, and so I set about approaching others who could make a valuable contribution to this book. One of the first to agree was my dear friend Richard Kelly, who lectures at the University of Kobe in Japan. His own energetic enthusiasm for the project and his network of contacts, which drew in other valued authors, soon made it apparent that we should co-edit the book. He has worked tirelessly on the project and has been an invaluable sounding board and source of encouragement.

Those who contributed pieces gave generously of their time and thought, responding at short notice amidst over-stuffed schedules. Their voices can be 'heard' here, eloquently expressing their views on areas in which they have experience – their own views, rather than those of the editors, publishers or charitable recipients of the royalties. Others helped to facilitate contacts or contributed information, including the following:

YOU'RE HISTORY!

Cecil Brown, Gina Cowne, Val Ferguson, Catriona Finlayson, Claire Foster and other members of the St Paul's Institute and members of the Royal African Society, Unicef and the UN, Ann Fox, Jim Fox, Emma Freud, Ciara Gaynor, Amanda Hon, Andrew Kelly, Joan Kelly, Mika Kinose, Kimiko Koi, Dee Kruger Simpson, Brigitte Lenon, Junko Matsunaga, Rie Matsuya, Elizabeth Moran, William O'Callaghan, Jerry O'Riordan, Tony O'Shea, David Stanton, Dermot White and Kate Worden.
Two other close friends, the teacher/poet Ciarán Quinn and the journalist/activist Rosemary Brown, also made an exceptional commitment to this work, including assembling the amazing array of information – much of it startling reading – in the Appendix.

Read it, and think. Then tell others, and act.

Making Poverty History

RICHARD CURTIS

It may seem strange that someone who does my job – trying
to convince people that tragedy consists of poor Hugh Grant
having a tiny tiff with Julia Roberts and then wandering
through Notting Hill to the tune of another great sixties
classic – should think he has any right to talk about
something as important as global poverty, and I would
agree. It's been a strange journey to here.

I think the seeds were initially sown because when I was
young I lived in the Philippines and was very aware, as we drove
from the airport in our air-conditioned car, that a million
people were living under corrugated iron roofs in slums by the
roadside. But my real interest was ignited by Live Aid. And by
a strange set of coincidences, I actually found myself in
Ethiopia in 1985 during the famine. I remember how struck
I was by the steely determination of the people working there.
They didn't shed many tears. They knew they were there to do
a job, to do practical things, to save lives. The time for crying
was over. I feel the same now.

Every day I watched the doctors, nurses and engineers
working to save lives in the camps, and every night over dinner
they'd turn to me and tease me and say – what the hell can you
do? I had no idea – but when I came home, I talked to friends
in the comedy industry about what I'd seen and we got together
and started Comic Relief – which has so far made £240 million

to help fight the root causes of extreme poverty in Africa.

The point is, it doesn't matter how unpromising your set-up seems to be – if you are determined to make a difference to the poor – you can. Of course Lenny Henry and I haven't made that £240 million – the British people have given it to us – because when faced with the fact that 30,000 children are dying every single day of extreme poverty and we know how to prevent it, people won't have it. I believe that passionate concern for the poor is very deep in most people – they just need it tapped and guided.

I've prayed for some terrible things in my time. I've prayed for Kate Moss to leave her boyfriend and bump into me. But this year I'm praying that everyone has this simple fact burnt into their consciousness – that in 2005 we could make poverty history – but we don't have a lot of time.

2005 has been a key year for the poor – the political stars have aligned, it's the twentieth anniversary of Live Aid, the UK have the presidency of the G8 and have put poverty and development at the top of the agenda, and it's the crucial five-year anniversary of the moment every single country in the world promised, in the magnificent Millennium Development Goals, to halve poverty by 2015.

So if we don't do something big this year, we'll all be liars. If we don't do it this year, extreme poverty will slip off the top of the political agenda and it'll be up to our children to deal with it. And some year – 30 years from now – they'll do what needs to be done and our kids will come up to us and say – you knew the solutions – you knew that 30,000 children were dying every day – and yet, on your watch, you let it happen. Shame on you.

This year there is a unique opportunity – eight men are going to be sitting in a room in Scotland on 7 July and there is a plan. A plan to deliver 'trade justice' so that world trade becomes part of the solution to poverty, not part of the problem. A plan that ends the third world debt crisis once and for all. And a plan that mobilizes more and better aid – at least US $50 billion (£26.7 billion) more each year. These eight men could start the ball rolling and finally change the face of extreme global poverty – so we must start mobilizing – write, talk, argue, march, investigate, raise our voices to the rooftops. It's not about giving cash – it's about getting your voice heard. We must create a sound so loud that every politician hears it – so that when they meet, they know they can't side-step it this time.

There's a phrase 'the tipping point' – the moment when suddenly something gets into the bloodstream of people and tips over into popular movement. We've got two tipping points here – if enough of us actually do something, suddenly the determination to make poverty history will tip over and become the theme of this year. And if it does – then at some moment, we will tip the politicians over – and they'll do something too. They know the answers – a mixture of debt, aid and trade justice – they just need to know that people care enough.

And you don't need to be Gordon Brown, the British Chancellor of the Exchequer, to make that difference. Let me just give you a few examples. I had lunch with a slightly scary Scottish shoe manufacturer – he owns Office – and at the end of the meal, he simply decided he'd give our campaign a million pounds. He's not a political man – he's not an expert on Trade and Aid, but he's doing his bit.

YOU'RE HISTORY!

At the totally different end of the scale, I received a letter from a woman telling me the astonishing true-life story of her husband's ten-year battle against AIDS and then cancer. She said 'we've never spoken about this in public before – but we've decided to now, because we're going to tell our tale and then say – don't feel sorry for us - we're the lucky ones – he's lived with AIDS for 10 years because we had access to drugs – in Africa they only have paracetamol – join the campaign – make poverty history.'

It doesn't matter what your job is, or how well off you are – you'll find a way to recruit people, to talk to people, to engage people, to motivate people. And it might be anyone who causes things to reach the tipping point – it might be you who gets justice for the poor at last.

We are fighting against something that is claiming many more lives than slavery or apartheid ever did. It can be solved. I'm praying that everyone this year will take a bit of time out from the way they normally look at things and try to look at life through the eyes of, say, a woman called Aberash whom Comic Relief filmed in Ethiopia last month.

She had AIDS. She had a five-day-old child. She didn't have money for drugs for her illness. She didn't have money to buy food for her child. But she didn't dare breastfeed for fear of passing on the virus. Two days after I'd seen the film I got an email from someone in the office: 'I have just spoken to our contact in Ethiopia and she has confirmed that Aberash's child died on December 4 – this is such an awful part to our job – oh dear.'

Whatever took the child's life medically, the real cause was poverty. Someone dies of poverty-related causes every three seconds – every day of our lives. Well, I think the time for letting this continue has gone. As Bob Geldof said: 'The tsunami was an act of God. African poverty is an act of man.'

So what can you do? Well, for a start go to our website and join our email army that is going to contact every world leader during the year to pay attention to this. Then get hold of a white band, and wear it. Then talk to your friends – get them to do the same. Write to your MP now. Write to the Prime Minister now. Look at your life and think 'is there anything I can do – I'm a lawyer, could I get all the lawyers to write to the Prime Minister and Michael Howard – both of whom started as lawyers? I'm in advertising – could I get some media space for adverts for Make Poverty History? I'm at school – can I get my school to join up to the huge international initiative, Send a Friend to School?' If you're a close personal friend of George Bush, take him out to dinner and tell him unless he joins the campaign, he's not getting any pudding.

I'd love you, as you read this, to ask yourself 'What can I do this year?' – and then do it. Everyone, young, old, rich, poor, trade unionist, businessperson, diplomat, Conservative, Labour, Liberal, Green, churchgoer, concertgoer, teacher, writer, actor, even – perhaps most important of all – politicians and journalists: please, I beg you, don't see this moment, this possibility for change, and then waste the opportunity to write about it by pretending that the important thing here, when so many people are dying, is a feud, real or imagined, between the politicians Gordon Brown and Tony Blair. For God's sake.

Every time we do Red Nose Day there's a whole bunch of people who give with astonishing generosity. We pray you will give again; but we also pray you'll take some kind of action as well to tell politicians that enough is enough. It's their turn.

Every time we do Red Nose Day there are those who don't care for it, who say: 'You can't solve the problems of the world by buying a red nose and spraying your hair red – this is politics.' Well, your moment has arrived too. Make Poverty History is not a fundraising campaign, so your time to do something has come.

I would even ask the real cynics about aid to use their cynicism to see better aid delivered, rather than just dismiss the whole thing.

I went to Johannesburg recently for a meeting of leaders of this campaign from forty countries. There was a lot of talk there of making sure that aid gets through to the right people. Interestingly, it was the representatives from Africa and the poorest countries who were most passionate about forcing their governments to clean up their act.

Everything must be done to create good governance so that aid works. That will be part of the solution. This is not the time to say: 'It's very tricky, so let's walk away.'

Make Poverty History is already a strange and broad coalition, from faith groups to charities, trade unions to the Mothers' Union. But we need everyone to ask politicians to really concentrate on this issue. The simplest thing you can do is go to our website, www.makepovertyhistory.org, and join our email army. Together we'll remorselessly email politicians and policy-makers throughout the world. Or you can contact any of the 157 members of the coalition. You may belong to one already and work with them.

When terrible things have happened, the poor have paid the

highest price. If there's a flood in Brighton, people get their carpets and belongings ruined; if there's a flood in Bangladesh, 10,000 people die. On Boxing Day 2004, when the tsunami struck, the world reacted with spectacular generosity and emotion. I was deeply chilled by one sentence about the tsunami that was published recently, a description of bodies on the beach. The writer was there, he'd seen death, and his last sentence was: 'And I thought heartbreak hurt.'

Let's take that passion – let's really face the fact that a silent tsunami is happening every day of our lives – that a holocaust is happening not far from here, more than 10 million people dying unnecessarily every year, in secret, away from the news.

Every day of the year we watch the news, and they forget to add that item. 'Chelsea won again – oh, and 30,000 people died who didn't have to.' '*The Incredibles* went back to number one at the box office – oh, and 30,000 real people died, totally avoidably.'

What we saw at the beginning of the year, in the astonishing generosity of the public around the world in response to the tsunami, is that, faced by the reality of unnecessary death people are massively generous and massively concerned. And countries can suddenly, quite rightly, find large reserves of money – just as they've always been able to when a Black Wednesday hits the economy or there's a war to be fought.

I'd ask people not to forget that passion and compassion. Hold on to it.

My friend Kevin says that it's as if we are all living with an elephant standing in our living rooms, but we just don't see it: this huge, simple truth that 15 million people will die preventable deaths this year – twice the population of London.

YOU'RE HISTORY!

We know how to stop it happening but we haven't yet convinced our politicians that we will not tolerate it any more.

In Britain one in 153 children die before their fifth birthday. In Sierra Leone, it's one child in four. I have four children ... You don't have to be Stephen Hawking to work out the maths on that one. Those children die from lack of food and clean water. They die in their thousands from curable diseases such as pneumonia, measles and malaria – and from a simple malady like diarrhoea that is just a joke to me and the kids. They die from AIDS, often contracted from their mother's milk. They die the day they are born for lack of basic natal care. But this year we finally have a chance to change that. I think it would be worth fighting all year to save one life, one life of equal value to mine or yours. How much more important to fight all year to save millions. And if we try, and if we succeed, we'll be able to look our kids in the eyes and say – we looked around – we saw what was happening – we saw that AIDS and malaria and diarrhoea and simple hunger were taking thousands of lives a day – and we would not let it stand.

POSTSCRIPT
This statement was released following the G8 Summit:

LIVE 8 STATEMENT – July 8, 2005
Kofi Annan, the Secretary General of the United Nations, called the Gleneagles G8 'the greatest summit for Africa ever'.

Only time will tell if this summit is historic or not. What is true is that never before have so many people forced a change of policy onto the global agenda.

And that policy today has been addressed.

20 years ago, Live Aid achieved a staggering $200m for those suffering death by starvation. We were addressing the symptoms of poverty.

Last Saturday Live 8 asked for $25bn per annum for Africa to attack the structures of poverty. And today Africa got it.

No longer will the lives of the African poor be framed by charity but rather defined by justice.

That long walk is now over. Brought to an end by the greatest act of mass advocacy in political history.

Live 8 was wonderful and devastatingly effective. The figures announced today are not simply cold numbers.

They mean 10m people alive because you danced for life.

They mean 20m children in school because we played our guitars.

5m orphans taken care of because we sang for joy.

600,000 people every year will not now die of malaria.

The list of excellence goes on. The list of lives stretches to the future.

You did this.

We invited you on a long walk and you went all the way. You are a great peaceful army of 3 billion who walked for those who could barely crawl. And you won.

Thank you so very much. Millions live because of you.

The Live 8 people

YOU'RE HISTORY!

AOL's Report of Events
That same day the following report appeared on the AOL website:

G8 Leaders in £30bn African Aid Deal
Lead role: Tony Blair speaks in front of other world leaders at the end of the G8 summit – Make Poverty History

A £30 billion (50 billion dollar) aid package for Africa agreed by the G8 will 'lift the shadow of terrorism', Tony Blair said. The Prime Minister contrasted the deal struck by leaders gathered at Gleneagles with the aims of those behind the London bombings. After uniting to condemn the attacks yesterday the heads of the eight richest nations had come together to help Africa, Mr Blair said.

The PM conceded the package did not meet the demands of all anti-poverty campaigners. But he insisted: 'We have made very substantial progress indeed. We do not, simply by this communique, make poverty history. But we do show it can be done and we do signify the political will to do it.'

Campaigner Bob Geldof said measures agreed at the summit would save 10 million lives. 'Today is a great day for those 10 million people', Geldof told a press conference at Gleneagles.

He added: 'Was this a success? On aid, 10 out of 10, on debt 8 out of 10. Time will tell, time only will tell if this has been historic or not.'

African development and climate change were the twin key issues placed on the agenda of the summit in Scotland by Mr Blair. Environmentalists savaged the conclusions on global warming which they say leaves the G8 'treading water' in the face of US intransigence. And agencies expressed varying degrees of disappointment over the development package, particularly the lack of moves to end subsidies in western countries.

Mr Blair insisted the agreements struck set a course to end global poverty and eventually bring the US on board to tackle greenhouse gas emissions.

In addition to the Africa deal leaders had agreed to £1.80bn (3 billion dollars) for the Palestinian Authority so 'two states Israel and Palestine, two peoples and two religions can live side-by-side in peace' he said. He admitted pushing for a deadline to end subsidies but predicted that would now happen at trade talks in December. US President George Bush had paved the way on agreement by suggesting American subsidies if the Common Agricultural Policy was scrapped. 'I believe it should be and will be 2010 when we can end subsidies; he said.

That move was among the demands of the Africa Commission, established by Mr Blair, which also set the target of increasing annual aid to Africa by £30bn (50 billion dollars) within 10 years. It has been described as a minimum by many aid experts, who argue the sum is relatively small by G8 standards and could be given immediately. However, Mr Blair said that taken with previously agreed debt cancellation and agreements on providing AIDS and Malaria treatment it would make a real difference. 'All of this does not change the world tomorrow. It is a beginning not an end; he said. 'None of it today will match the same ghastly impact as the cruelty of terror. But it has a pride and a hope and a humanity at its heart that can lift the shadow of terrorism and light the way to a better future.'

YOU'RE HISTORY!

Mr Blair compared the G8's attempts to save and improve lives with the terrorists who struck London. 'The purpose of terrorism is not only to kill and maim the innocent. It is to put despair and anger and hatred in people's hearts,' he said. 'It is by its savagery designed to cover all conventional politics in darkness, to overwhelm the dignity of democracy and proper process with the impact of bloodshed and of terror. There is no hope from terrorism nor any future in it worth living and it is hope that is the alternative to this hatred. So we offer today this contrast with the politics of terror.'

The UN Declaration of Human Rights

Printed with comments by
ELEANOR ROOSEVELT, MARY ROBINSON
AND IRENE KHAN

Eleanor Roosevelt regarded the Universal Declaration as her greatest accomplishment.

'Where, after all, do universal human rights begin? In small places, close to home – so close and so small that they cannot be seen on any maps of the world. Yet they are the world of the individual person; the neighborhood he lives in; the school or college he attends; the factory, farm, or office where he works. Such are the places where every man, woman, and child seeks equal justice, equal opportunity, equal dignity without discrimination. Unless these rights have meaning there, they have little meaning anywhere. Without concerted citizen action to uphold them close to home, we shall look in vain for progress in the larger world.'

Eleanor Roosevelt

'1. A world of true security is only possible when the full range of human rights – civil and political, as well as economic, social and cultural – are guaranteed for all people. What we need now is a new approach – which begins with a broader understanding of what defines human and global security.

29

Eleanor Roosevelt with the French-language version of the
Universal Declaration of Human Rights, 1949
© Franklin and Eleanor Roosevelt Institute

We must craft a policy that manages and balances our increasing interdependence with our increased vulnerability. Governments from both the North and the South must expand their thinking and policies to encompass a broader understanding of security beyond the security of states.
2. We must put into practice the values of freedom, equality, solidarity, tolerance, respect and shared responsibility which can unite North and South, rich and poor, left and right, religious and secular, us and them.'

Mary Robinson, Executive Director,
Realizing Rights: The Ethical Globalization Initiative,
UN High Commissioner for Human Rights 1997–2002,
President of Ireland 1992–1997

'Governments are betraying their promises on human rights. A new agenda is in the making with the language of freedom and justice being used to pursue policies of fear and insecurity. This includes cynical attempts to redefine and sanitize torture.

Violence by armed groups and increasing violations by governments have combined to produce the most sustained attack on human rights and international humanitarian law in 50 years. This was leading to a world of growing mistrust, fear and division.'

Irene Khan, Secretary General of Amnesty International

Universal Declaration of Human Rights

On 10 December 1948 the General Assembly of the United Nations adopted and proclaimed the Universal Declaration of Human Rights, the full text of which appears in the following pages. Following this historic act the Assembly called upon all Member countries to publicize the text of the Declaration and 'to cause it to be disseminated, displayed, read and expounded principally in schools and other educational institutions, without distinction based on the political status of countries or territories.'

PREAMBLE

Whereas recognition of the inherent dignity and of the equal and inalienable rights of all members of the human family is the foundation of freedom, justice and peace in the world,

Whereas disregard and contempt for human rights have resulted in barbarous acts which have outraged the conscience of mankind, and the advent of a world in which human beings shall enjoy freedom of speech and belief and freedom from fear and want has been proclaimed as the highest aspiration of the common people,

Whereas it is essential, if man is not to be compelled to have recourse, as a last resort, to rebellion against tyranny and oppression, that human rights should be protected by the rule of law,

Whereas it is essential to promote the development of friendly relations between nations,

33

Whereas the peoples of the United Nations have in the Charter reaffirmed their faith in fundamental human rights, in the dignity and worth of the human person and in the equal rights of men and women and have determined to promote social progress and better standards of life in larger freedom,

Whereas Member States have pledged themselves to achieve, in co-operation with the United Nations, the promotion of universal respect for and observance of human rights and fundamental freedoms,

Whereas a common understanding of these rights and freedoms is of the greatest importance for the full realization of this pledge,

Now, Therefore THE GENERAL ASSEMBLY proclaims THIS UNIVERSAL DECLARATION OF HUMAN RIGHTS as a common standard of achievement for all peoples and all nations, to the end that every individual and every organ of society, keeping this Declaration constantly in mind, shall strive by teaching and education to promote respect for these rights and freedoms and by progressive measures, national and international, to secure their universal and effective recognition and observance, both among the peoples of Member States themselves and among the peoples of territories under their jurisdiction.

Article 1.

All human beings are born free and equal in dignity and rights. They are endowed with reason and conscience and should act towards one another in a spirit of brotherhood.

Article 2.

Everyone is entitled to all the rights and freedoms set forth in this Declaration, without distinction of any kind, such as race, colour, sex, language, religion, political or other opinion, national or social origin, property, birth or other status. Furthermore, no distinction shall be made on the basis of the political, jurisdictional or international status of the country or territory to which a person belongs, whether it be independent, trust, non-self-governing or under any other limitation of sovereignty.

Article 3.
Everyone has the right to life, liberty and security of person.

Article 4.
No one shall be held in slavery or servitude; slavery and the slave trade shall be prohibited in all their forms.

Article 5.
No one shall be subjected to torture or to cruel, inhuman or degrading treatment or punishment.

Article 6.
Everyone has the right to recognition everywhere as a person before the law.

Article 7.
All are equal before the law and are entitled without any discrimination to equal protection of the law. All are entitled to equal protection against any discrimination in violation of this Declaration and against any incitement to such discrimination.

Article 8.
Everyone has the right to an effective remedy by the competent national tribunals for acts violating the fundamental rights granted him by the constitution or by law.

Article 9.
No one shall be subjected to arbitrary arrest, detention or exile.

Article 10.
Everyone is entitled in full equality to a fair and public hearing by an independent and impartial tribunal, in the determination of his rights and obligations and of any criminal charge against him.

Article 11.
1. Everyone charged with a penal offence has the right to be presumed innocent until proved guilty according to law in a public trial at which he has had all the guarantees necessary for his defence.
2. No one shall be held guilty of any penal offence on account of any act or omission which did not constitute a penal offence, under national or international law, at the time when it was committed. Nor shall a heavier penalty be imposed than the one that was applicable at the time the penal offence was committed.

Article 12.
No one shall be subjected to arbitrary interference with his privacy, family, home or correspondence, nor to attacks upon his honour and reputation. Everyone has the right to the

protection of the law against such interference or attacks.

Article 13.

1. Everyone has the right to freedom of movement and residence within the borders of each state.
2. Everyone has the right to leave any country, including his own, and to return to his country.

Article 14.

1. Everyone has the right to seek and to enjoy in other countries asylum from persecution.
2. This right may not be invoked in the case of prosecutions genuinely arising from non-political crimes or from acts contrary to the purposes and principles of the United Nations.

Article 15.

1. Everyone has the right to a nationality.
2. No one shall be arbitrarily deprived of his nationality nor denied the right to change his nationality.

Article 16.

1. Men and women of full age, without any limitation due to race, nationality or religion, have the right to marry and to found a family. They are entitled to equal rights as to marriage, during marriage and at its dissolution.
2. Marriage shall be entered into only with the free and full consent of the intending spouses.
3. The family is the natural and fundamental group unit of society and is entitled to protection by society and the State.

Article 17.

1. Everyone has the right to own property alone as well as in association with others.
2. No one shall be arbitrarily deprived of his property.

Article 18.

Everyone has the right to freedom of thought, conscience and religion; this right includes freedom to change his religion or belief, and freedom, either alone or in community with others and in public or private, to manifest his religion or belief in teaching, practice, worship and observance.

Article 19.

Everyone has the right to freedom of opinion and expression; this right includes freedom to hold opinions without interference and to seek, receive and impart information and ideas through any media and regardless of frontiers.

Article 20.

1. Everyone has the right to freedom of peaceful assembly and association.
2. No one may be compelled to belong to an association.

Article 21.

1. Everyone has the right to take part in the government of his country, directly or through freely chosen representatives.
2. Everyone has the right of equal access to public service in his country.
3. The will of the people shall be the basis of the authority of government; this will shall be expressed in periodic and

genuine elections which shall be by universal and equal suffrage and shall be held by secret vote or by equivalent free voting procedures.

Article 22.
Everyone, as a member of society, has the right to social security and is entitled to realization, through national effort and international co-operation and in accordance with the organization and resources of each State, of the economic, social and cultural rights indispensable for his dignity and the free development of his personality.

Article 23.
1. Everyone has the right to work, to free choice of employment, to just and favourable conditions of work and to protection against unemployment.
2. Everyone, without any discrimination, has the right to equal pay for equal work.
3. Everyone who works has the right to just and favourable remuneration ensuring for himself and his family an existence worthy of human dignity, and supplemented, if necessary, by other means of social protection.
4. Everyone has the right to form and to join trade unions for the protection of his interests.

Article 24.
Everyone has the right to rest and leisure, including reasonable limitation of working hours and periodic holidays with pay.

Article 25.

1. Everyone has the right to a standard of living adequate for the health and well-being of himself and of his family, including food, clothing, housing and medical care and necessary social services, and the right to security in the event of unemployment, sickness, disability, widowhood, old age or other lack of livelihood in circumstances beyond his control.
2. Motherhood and childhood are entitled to special care and assistance. All children, whether born in or out of wedlock, shall enjoy the same social protection.

Article 26.

1. Everyone has the right to education. Education shall be free, at least in the elementary and fundamental stages. Elementary education shall be compulsory. Technical and professional education shall be made generally available and higher education shall be equally accessible to all on the basis of merit.
2. Education shall be directed to the full development of the human personality and to the strengthening of respect for human rights and fundamental freedoms. It shall promote understanding, tolerance and friendship among all nations, racial or religious groups, and shall further the activities of the United Nations for the maintenance of peace.
3. Parents have a prior right to choose the kind of education that shall be given to their children.

Article 27.

1. Everyone has the right freely to participate in the cultural life of the community, to enjoy the arts and to share in

scientific advancement and its benefits.
2. Everyone has the right to the protection of the moral and material interests resulting from any scientific, literary or artistic production of which he is the author.

Article 28.

Everyone is entitled to a social and international order in which the rights and freedoms set forth in this Declaration can be fully realized.

Article 29.

1. Everyone has duties to the community in which alone the free and full development of his personality is possible.
2. In the exercise of his rights and freedoms, everyone shall be subject only to such limitations as are determined by law solely for the purpose of securing due recognition and respect for the rights and freedoms of others and of meeting the just requirements of morality, public order and the general welfare in a democratic society.
3. These rights and freedoms may in no case be exercised contrary to the purposes and principles of the United Nations.

Article 30.

Nothing in this Declaration may be interpreted as implying for any State, group or person any right to engage in any activity or to perform any act aimed at the destruction of any of the rights and freedoms set forth herein.

The Magna Carta
Courtesy of The British Library

'It's Positively Medieval': Challenging Some Preconceptions of History

MICHELLE P. BROWN

People in the developed world often seem to have a quaint misconception of their place in history – if they think about it at all, that is, other than tuning in to the occasional television offering of heritage entertainment. There seems to be a superstitious and naïve confidence that we are on some evolutionary fast track, biologically, scientifically, technologically, historically and morally. It is as if history and human behaviour are purely subject to Darwinian principles of natural selection and survival of the fittest. The humanist or neo-secularist may console her/himself with the belief that our existence derives meaning from our evolving place within the natural order and by claiming a growing humane responsibility in the absence of any higher creating force – 'enlightened' humanity having been freed from 'religion' whilst the 'unenlightened' remain in thrall. Yet this stance becomes hard to sustain in the face of our subversion of nature, our profligate over-consumption of resources at the expense of other species and members of our own, our philosophically/spiritually impoverished materialism and our childlike confidence that development must be good and that 'we can, therefore we should'.

43

In accordance with this view, those of us in the developed 'western' world are fortunate enough to have been historically 'fast-tracked'. The complexity and accelerated rate of change in our societies can lead us to assume a misplaced sense of superiority over other less developed peoples. And yet in this context 'western' or 'northern', and the implied distinctions from 'eastern' or 'southern' peoples is misleading. Japan, Hong Kong and many other oriental societies, for example, are every bit as 'advanced' as western nations. India is the world's largest democracy and home to the pernicious caste system with its 'untouchables'. A distinction between northern and southern hemispheres is likewise skewed by Australasia and its transplanted European and Asian population groups. Geography and climate may impose constraints of resource, but history can sometimes transcend such factors. Shortage of water may be hitting Australian farmers hard but it is difficult to imagine us watching their society, so like our own, sink into the morass of poverty, disease and indignity associated with the shortage of this precious life-giving resource in the third world.

For wealth is not the primary arbiter of a region's status. The greatest concentrations of wealth in the smallest number of grasping hands on the planet are vested not only amongst certain members of prosperous nations but in South America and the Middle East, often at the expense of the standards of living and liberty of the broad mass of their populations. We sometimes describe such societies as 'medieval'. The curious use of this term is revealing for it assumes that their problems stem from an arrested development, stuck at a stage from which we escaped some five hundred years ago. Anything we are forced to acknowledge as negative within our own past is often shunted into this remote age as a reassurance that it is something we have left behind long ago. Historical evolutionism wins again: 'we' are better than that; 'we' have progressed, 'we' have evolved. 'They' have not.

A better knowledge of our own past might help to deconstruct such misplaced perceptions of 'otherness', which we have carefully cultivated over the centuries in order to justify and maintain our own privileged positions at the expense of others and which have so often found expression in western art and literature in the caricaturing of the Jew, the Moslem and the Negro. What is it that we think we left behind so long ago? What are the forces over which we have triumphed and the advances we have made? They often seem to include civil liberties, freedom from tyrannical dictatorships or absolute monarchies, personal freedom of speech and of movement (often away from ties to the land), lessening of poverty and disease and recognition of the rights of 'minority' groups, such as women (seldom in fact a numerical minority), the disabled and incomers from other ethnic groups. Are these things that only 'we' know how to value and promote? Can only economically, industrially and technologically developed societies achieve them?

Let's look at the early history of 'undeveloped' Britain, as an example. As a woman, I'll start by considering women and their rights. The first local law-codes to be written down in England were those of the Anglo-Saxons, shortly after they arrived during the fifth and sixth centuries from Germany and southern Scandinavia. They came as mercenaries, raiders, settlers and economic migrants during the implosion of the super-power of the day – the late Roman Empire. This political and trading empire had stretched from the Atlantic seaboard to Syria and was seen as 'global' in its day. In the face of the rupture of its international economy new ways of running societies and of conducting international trade and diplomacy had to be found. As they converted to Christianity the leaders and people of the Germanic and Celtic successor states in Britain – the heirs of Rome – used the newly acquired authority of the written word, introduced along with Christianity's sacred texts, to safeguard and extend their laws. They thereby strengthened the fabric of their society and the effective functioning of the state, making them one of the success stories of the 'Dark Ages'. The first to be written down was the law code of King Ethelberht of Kent, allegedly by the Roman missionary St Augustine, shortly after 600. From this and others that followed – including the laws of Ine of Wessex and of Alfred the Great – we can tell a great deal about early English society. One thing that becomes clear is that in this period Englishwomen enjoyed the best legal status of any women in the world prior to the 1920s, when they finally achieved the right to vote after the hard-won campaigns of the Suffragettes. Some twelve hundred years earlier, however, women could enjoy the same social status and legal rights as men. Everyone's status was determined by a combination of birth and wealth. There were kings, nobles, freemen and freewomen and slaves. Social mobility from one category to another depended on which group you were born into initially but you could move from one to another if you acquired enough property. Even slaves could buy their freedom by working for wages on their days off. Baltildis, an Anglo-Saxon slave girl made good, even worked her way to the throne of Merovingian Gaul (although her personal charms may have played a significant part in this). Gender was not a restriction. If a wife brought more into a marriage than her husband she could 'wear the trousers'. Contemporary Celtic Irish law and society operated similarly in this respect.

Some male historians found this hard to accept during the nineteenth and early twentieth centuries, and distorted the information by their own prejudices. One law referred to heightened penalties to be exacted from any woman breaching the law who was 'lokborra' ('lock-bearing'). This, they assumed, must be because she had long flowing locks of hair, the sign of the pure, unsullied maiden. Her transgression must therefore have compromised her virginity. More recently a female historian, Christine Fell, demonstrated that the meaning was actually that such 'lock-bearing' women were the key holders, the estate managers whose probity was particularly highly valued and who incurred greater penalties if they abused their authority and positions of trust. Many early Anglo-Saxon female burials feature chatelains, metal hangers suspended from their belts, on which were suspended the keys. In ancient Celtic society women could be druids – the professional bards, jurists and priests who preserved the culture and memory of society and accordingly enjoyed special legal status as part of the *Aes dana* – the legal class of the intelligentsia and artists. Women could be rulers and they could be warriors. In the early English and Irish Churches if a monastery was a double house containing both men and women, it was governed by an abbess rather than an abbot. One such early Irish abbess, St Brigid, is even reported to have been a bishop! Yet some Christians are still struggling with the concepts of women's ministry and female bishops today.

This early period was one of looking outwards, of travel and cultural interaction. Early Britain was forged from successive waves of incoming population groups who were assimilated and made their own distinctive contributions, whilst retaining their own identities: indigenous prehistoric peoples, Celts, Romans, Germans, Scandinavian Vikings, Flemish and French. People travelled, on business and on pilgrimage. In the 730s St Boniface wrote from the Continent to the Archbishop of Canterbury complaining of the hordes of unaccompanied Englishwomen who journeyed around Europe, fearing for their safety and lamenting that there was not a brothel north of the Alps in which they were not exploited. In the 690s a Frankish bishop was blown off course during his voyage back from a visit to the holy sites of Jerusalem and Egypt and spent Christmas on the island of Iona off the western coast of Scotland, dictating his guidebook to Abbot Adomnán. In 667 the newly appointed Archbishop of Canterbury, Theodore of Tarsus, was one of the most educated men of the Mediterranean world and had been born in Asia Minor; he was ably assisted by Abbot Hadrian, a North African. Together they founded a school at Canterbury that was one of the finest in Europe. In the eighth century Christians in England used prayer-mats during their veneration of the Cross on Good Friday (echoed in the painted carpet-pages of the Lindisfarne Gospels which adorned the shrine of St Cuthbert on Holy Island), recalling the shared rituals inherited by Judaism, Christianity and Islam within the Middle East; and in 773 King Offa, based at Tamworth in the kingdom of Mercia, was minting coins modelled on dinars of the Abbasid Caliph al-Mansur, bearing the name of Allah as well as his own. This was an age of diversity and enquiry, in which a new culture was born from the interaction of many peoples, and yet the term 'Anglo-Saxon' is now in danger of being equated with right wing fascism in Britain; hijacked, like the English flag, which bears the cross of a Middle Eastern saint, George.

The Celts and Anglo-Saxons were also deeply conscious of nature and the environment, and their place within them. Aldhelm, bishop of Sherborne during the early eighth century, wrote in one of his riddles, designed for teaching purposes in the schoolroom, of Nature as a mother whose breasts were lacerated by her ungrateful, careless offspring. Saint Columbanus, who in his old age journeyed across Europe around the year 600 to revive spirituality and learning, wrote of how Nature was a second revelation, to be 'read' alongside Scripture to deepen our knowledge of God. He was proposing what today might be considered a more creative Christian environmentalism than the conventional theology of stewardship and the assumption that we have been set above the rest of Creation to do with it as we will. Other Irish and Anglo-Saxon authors used their own language to convey, to great effect, their love of Creation, blending an ancient affinity for Nature with Christian teaching. They sought to ask the big questions of both how and why, exploring dimensions of being through theology, meditation and prayer, just as we are now beginning to glimpse the possibility of doing through the medium of quantum physics. They studied the natural world and the heavens; in the eighth century Bede (who had entered the twin monasteries of Monkwearmouth and Jarrow as a boy of seven and who rarely left their walls) knew that the Earth was round and how it related to the Sun, the Moon and certain

other stars and planets, drawing upon the remnants of classi-
cal learning. They applied rules of sacred geometry to their art
and verse which they thought reflected the master-plan
underlying Creation and which featured measurements and
numbers that we now associate scientifically with the basic
building-blocks of life and matter.

There have always been those who recognised the
connection between care for the environment and the fight
against disease and poverty. As early as the 1220s Eufemia,
Abess of Wherwell, as part of her reform of the nunnery
under her care, instilled rules of hygiene and overhauled
the plumbing, recognizing that clean water was an essential
prerequisite of health. In the late fifteenth century Leonardo
da Vinci tidied up forty years of working notes to form what
is now known as the Leonardo or Arundel Codex in the British
Library (its companion volume is now owned by Bill Gates of
Microsoft fame). It includes designs for the use of mirrors
and light refraction to power kilns for industry – a clean,
environmentally friendly solar source of energy that warrants
greater exploration today. Perhaps more radical still is the note
he wrote beneath his designs for an ideal city for François I,
King of France, in which he suggested that when the monarch
and his courtiers were not in residence the ordinary workers in
the field might be allowed to enjoy it. Needless to say, it was
never built. Nineteenth-century philanthropists and the more
responsible of employers toyed with pioneering workers' estates
and twentieth-century modernist architects and planners
returned to the quest for a life-enhancing, democratic
high-rise built environment, but without perhaps a full enough
grasp of the implications of social engineering and the more

organic needs of community. Nonetheless today, in even the wealthiest nations, the poor still often dwell in sub-standard housing that is conducive to health problems and used as a dumping ground for those with 'social problems', where violence and drug abuse can flourish. The fight against tuberculosis was a hard-fought one, only won in Britain and Ireland after World War II. It is now back on our streets again amongst the homeless and the poorer economic migrants.

At the time of writing, the fabric of US society is unravelling in the New Orleans area, with the poor abandoned to death, disease and lawlessness in the wake of Hurricane Katrina. How thin indeed is the fabric of 'civilization'! No society can bury its head in the sand and insulate itself against the ills that flow from the toleration of poverty in its midst – neither can the world. We live on a small planet: the problems and challenges besetting one social group, one nation or one continent are increasingly likely to affect us all.

The tyranny of poverty has constrained the lives of so many that it is every bit as pernicious as the deprivation of personal liberty that we connect with slavery, the notion of which we find intolerable, even though 27 million people still live in a de facto state of slavery today. Both have been used to ensure the comfortable lifestyle and economic security of one part of the populace at the expense of another. This is still the case. Underpaid workforces in some of the poorest parts of the world still slave to support the consumer demands and business interests of others. The biggest difference is that those exploiting them no longer bear even the vestiges of any legal or moral responsibilities towards them. We associate the legal abolition of slavery with nineteenth-century figures such as William

Wilberforce and Abraham Lincoln, but the fight against it was much older; it took shape, but fortunately did not die with the rebel slave-leader Spartacus, who was crucified in the first century BC. The British Parliament finally passed the Abolition of the Slave Trade Act in 1807, which had to be reinforced by the Slavery Abolition Act of 1833 as sea-captains caught in breach of the former Act resorted to the simple expedient of tossing their human cargo overboard when caught. The Abolition of Slavery was eventually added as the 13th Amendment to the US Constitution in 1865. And yet the first documents to grant liberty to slaves on moral grounds were inscribed in the margins of Gospelbooks, on which oaths were also sworn and legal transactions solemnified, in Wales, Cornwall and Anglo-Saxon England during the mid-ninth and early tenth centuries. Members of the early Christian Church spoke out energetically against slavery, which had already underpinned the fabric of society for over two and a half millennia. The teachings of Jesus Christ were radical and transforming and at this period many people were trying actively to live them out. They could and did lead seasoned warriors, used to the slaughter of hand to hand combat on the battlefield and reared on heroic epics such as *Beowulf* in the mead hall (the equivalents of the super-hero action movie and the pub) to embrace pacifism. They inspired kings to free slaves, overturning the establishment that they were meant to represent, laying their lives on the line and becoming victims of assassination, as in the case of King Sebbi of Essex during the seventh century, just as Abraham Lincoln would later be. Another seventh-century ruler of Essex, Sigebert, was forced to leave the monastery he had entered as a monk to go before his people in battle as he was the only leader left alive – he chose to do so armed only with a wooden staff and was among the first to fall.

Figures of the magnitude of Martin Luther King, with similar levels of commitment, compassion and courage, were around then too. People called them saints – a tribute to their service to society and a recognition of their value as role models which was accorded by popular public acclaim, rather than bestowed by senior churchmen, rulers or governments. Today we too have our secular saints, such as the remarkable Nelson Mandela, champion of the anti-apartheid movement and ambassador for reconciliation and human rights.

Saint Cuthbert of Holy Island in north-east England, who died in 687, was likewise renowned as an eloquent speaker, an astute politician, a spiritual ascetic and a tireless worker for social justice. He, like so many other men and women inspired by their faith, would travel to the most remote poverty-stricken, war-torn areas bringing humanitarian aid and an eternal message of hope. Even during his times of retreat as a hermit he did battle with his own demons on the harsh rock of the Inner Farne islands on behalf of everybody and everything, not relinquishing the world but renewing the energy to recommit. He is reported as saying 'If I could build a cell for prayer with walls so high that all I could see was the sky, I would still be afraid that the love of money and the cares of the world would steal me away'.

This is exactly what he did build, on a small islet just offshore from the formidable royal citadel of Bamburgh, seat of a local king, Ecgfrith, who was nominally an enlightened, civilized modern ruler but who was not averse to a little genocide and ethnic cleansing if the ends justified the means (sound familiar?).

Every time that he and his courtiers looked out from their seat
of government and prosperity they saw the bleak little island
and knew that on it sat Cuthbert – an emaciated, vulnerable,
indomitable, Gandhi-like reminder of the responsibilities that
accompany wealth and power. Cuthbert had been trained in
the Irish monastic tradition, and in Irish law the ultimate
means of obtaining redress for an injustice was to sit outside
the perpetrator's gate and shame them into proper action by
fasting (the origins of the hunger strike). Just as Gandhi's
passive resistance movement shifted the British Empire, so
Cuthbert's lifestyle, his values and his passive activism for social
justice brought about significant change in public and political
opinion and behaviour. We know all about the cult of celebrity
today, but do we really understand the value of such earlier
figures and their influence as role models in society? They should
certainly give us pause for thought in our innate assumptions of
modern moral superiority and cause us to question what values
we enshrine in our modern 'heroes' – such as the ability to look
good in front of a camera, to be decorative clothes-hangers
and to over-consume material goods and sexual partners?

The Anglo-Saxons were ruled by a number of regional kings,
whose power increased as big fish ate little ones and national
identity coalesced into 'England' in the face of threats of
invasion. But from its earliest stages the free members of early
English society contributed to their own government through
the folk assembly – the Thingemoot – at which issues were
discussed and decisions taken. Rulers were advised by a council,
the Witan, which had real powers. Saint Paul's Cross, at the
east end of St Paul's Cathedral's churchyard, was something of
a proto-parliament at which the medieval citizens of London

met to discuss the way in which their city was run. It was an early focus for freedom of speech. Announcements and opinions proclaimed there were the forerunners of the newspaper and free press and it stood at the core of what came to be the radical hub of the printing industry in Britain, in and around nearby Paternoster Square. Yet it also witnessed a backlash and attempts to control and limit access to knowledge, for it was here that Tyndale's edition of the New Testament in the more commonly accessible English language was burned in the early sixteenth century as heretical, at the dawn of the 'modern' age. The Anglo-Saxons and the Irish had experienced no such qualms when, from as early as the eighth century, they translated the Gospels into their own languages, using whatever tools they had at their disposal to share the 'Good News' (Old English 'Godspell'). In the process they developed the earliest written vernacular languages in Europe. Yet many local languages are in danger of being lost today in the face of the imperialism of the international languages of commerce, and even after World War II Charles de Gaulle decreed that Breton children heard speaking their own Celtic language at school should have their heads shaved, to ensure the homogeneity and purity of French culture. Minority languages are still dying out or being suppressed today. Such freedoms come and go. They need to be actively promoted, valued and defended in order to endure.

The freedom of expression and enquiry enjoyed by Bede and others during the early Middle Ages was not accorded to Tyndale and Galileo some eight hundred years later. But their persecution was the result of the baser human urge to control and of the surveillance of the over-powerful State (which electronic biometrics and tracking and monitoring devices are doing so much to extend in the present), and of the man-made aspects of religiosity, not of faith itself. Attempting to abolish faith does not suppress such urges.

Some of these early democratic trends in English society were lost as a result of the Norman Conquest of England in 1066, after which a more feudal structure prevailed. Serfs were tied to the land and the lords they served. Women and children lost most of their earlier rights. Government was vested in the hands of an absolute monarchy whose senior representatives at a local level were members of a military aristocracy which held its land from the Crown, derived from the spoils doled out to the mercenaries who had helped William the Conqueror to seize the throne and the land at the Battle of Hastings in 1066. Something of the pre-Conquest spirit of participative government must have survived, however, for in 1215 the barons cornered King John on the island of Runnymede in the Thames and would not let him off until he appended his seal to the Articles of the Barons, in which they set out a manifesto that became the basis of the resulting document known as Magna Carta – the 'Great Charter' – which was proclaimed throughout the cities of the realm. This contained many clauses, key amongst which were that the king could not arbitrarily raise taxes without consulting his leading subjects and that nobody could be executed without a trial. This is acknowledged worldwide as a foundation stone of civil liberty. The assembly of the barons gradually grew and was transformed into Parliament, the 'talking place' at the Palace of Westminster from which laws issued. Magna Carta was an important milestone in the establishment of social contract; there have been many others, before and since. The Millennium Development Goals seek to set in place further provisions and agreements that aim to significantly reduce world poverty and inequality by 2015 – eight hundred years later.

The fourteenth century has been branded 'the worst century ever'. Virulent pneumonic plague swept westwards from Asia and was accompanied by devastating famine. They wiped out a third of the population of Europe. It was even more terrifying than HIV and AIDS. In England it was preceded, accompanied and followed by repressive government and civil strife. Nonetheless, it also marked an important stage in the assertion of workers' rights and property ownership. It was widely acknowledged in the early decades of the century that the over-exploitation of land and the concentration of profit within too few hands needed to be limited. The landed and wealthy sought to ever enlarge their holdings, enclosing traditional common land and taking it as their own, appropriating common liberties – even claiming the right to 'airspace' and the honey from any bees that settled on the land, regardless of who gathered it. Before plague struck in 1348 ordinary folk were challenging these claims and asserting their customary rights, with recourse to law. Some even won. In the aftermath of the cataclysm the population had shrunk and labour was at a premium. Emboldened by this and frustrated by failures of central government, unpopular methods of taxation (the notorious poll tax in which everyone was taxed at the same rate, per head/poll, regardless of their income) and abuses of power and the law – even by members of the legal profession – the rural populace rebelled and marched on London to meet with their King. This was the Peasants' Revolt of 1381. When in recent times Prime Minister Margaret Thatcher attempted to revive this unjust poll tax, Blackheath in southeast London was once again the rallying place for protesters, as it had been six hundred years earlier for the rebel leader Wat Tyler, the preacher John Ball and their followers. Their quest was for justice and equality, epitomized in the verse they sang: 'When Adam delved and Eve span, Who was then the gentleman?' – espousing the ideal that all are created equal. Tyler may have been cut down (by the mayor) as a threat to authority, but the memory of his stand endures.

Today British citizens may not necessarily risk death when they take to the streets, but how many really register the fact that under the Criminal Justice Act two or more of them can be arrested as a public assembly simply for talking together: a curious basis of mistrust, however it is justified on grounds of national security, for a much vaunted 'democracy'. Even the most authoritarian of medieval despots did not possess such a legal tool for the potential repression of the populace.

Don't get me wrong. I'm not advocating a return to the 'Dark Ages', however misnamed I consider them to be. I know too much about medicine and surgery in the Middle Ages to want to live in them – although such barbarities had more to do with lack of knowledge than with today's gross inhumanity of inflexible government targets and inefficient hospital administrations which apply false economies that imperil patients, undo the good work of medical and surgical staff and betray the trust of all concerned. These were violent times with a perpetual undertow of warfare, just as there has been throughout the twentieth and twenty-first centuries, the difference being that more of it was conducted on actual

British and neighbouring soil, in the pursuit of British claims to ownership of parts of France, Scotland, Wales and Ireland. The public were coerced or tricked into funding and condoning military invasions and occupations and the losers were often tortured, humiliated and economically exploited – just as they are today, as aspects of recent Allied involvement in Iraq show all too well. Our medieval forebears also exported war, but they did not trade as widely in the instruments of warfare, using the arms trade to promote instability and create an uneven playing field on foreign ground in order to advance their ambitions of territorial and economic aggrandizement – as we do today. Capital punishment was favoured as a cheap alternative to imprisonment and as a palliative to uninformed mass opinion, as it was in Britain until the 1950s and still is in many North American states. Hunting was a favourite occupation of the landed classes, but at least they ate their quarry and were not merely engaged in ritualized blood-letting; and if we think that the barbarisms of the Roman arena and the dog-fighting pit are gone, we need look only to the bullrings of Spain and the backroom dives of our own inner cities to find them still. Nature could be 'red in tooth and claw', but at least human beings acknowledged that they were part of it and that they needed to respect and care for their livestock and their environment if they were to survive well within it. Parents watched their children die of disease, thirst and starvation, just as 30,000 of them still do every day around our world.

No, there were many things about medieval life that would not have recommended themselves to me. But are we really so very far away from them? If the things that horrify us about that life are not still apparent in our own backyards, they are still part of our world. Medieval thinkers and ordinary, motivated people sought to change them throughout history, without the advantages of mass communication, advanced scientific, medical and technological skills, developed international economies and surpluses. What excuse do we have?

What I have challenged is the assumption that the West is somehow socially more advanced simply because it has developed or evolved, that it holds some sort of moral high-ground, and that the social injustices it has itself experienced were confined to the remoter, earlier phases of its historical development which might be characterized as 'medieval' primitivism. Individuals have always had their own moral codes, aspirations and inspirations, which they have had to reconcile with those of society, or with which they have challenged it. In certain respects some medieval people were as advanced in their thinking on matters of social justice and personal morality as we like to think we are today. But many hard-won advantages were subsequently relinquished, as they are always in danger of being if they are not valued and nurtured by the individual and by society – even now. There are many theories of history. What it is not is a self-fulfilling prophecy. We need not be constrained by it, but we can learn from it – if we so choose – and find more creative responses. The West has not been on some evolutionary fast track of historical development. 'Progress' is not a relentless, unquestionable force and centralization, scientific, economic and cultural imperialism and the right to unbridled consumption of resources are not inevitable social and economic imperatives. History is dominated by the rise and fall of successive civilizations and their enduring influences. Ours will undoubtedly pass away. Let's ensure that we leave a sustainable, valuable legacy of our own to whatever may follow.

Further Reading

C. Breay, *Magna Carta* (London: British Library Publications, 2002).

M. P. Brown, *The Lindisfarne Gospels: Society, Spirituality and the Scribe* (London and Toronto: British Library Publications and Toronto University Press, 2003)

—*The World of the Lindisfarne Gospels* (London: British Library Publications, 2003).

—*How Christianity Came to Britain and Ireland* (Oxford: Lion Hudson, 2006, forthcoming).

C. Fell, *Women in Anglo-Saxon England* (London: Colonnade, British Museum, 1984).

Websites

British Library: www.bl.uk

National Archives: www.nationalarchives.gov.uk/

Labyrinth, a resource for medieval studies, hosted by Georgetown University: http://labyrinth.georgetown.edu/

Jonathan Swift (1677–1745)
© National Portrait Gallery, London

Inequality:
A Modest Proposal?

RICHARD J. KELLY

Although historians have cast doubt that Marie Antoinette ever uttered the now famous phrase, *Qu'ils mangent de la brioche*, 'Let them eat cake', it was her callous indifference to the plight of the poor and underprivileged in late-eighteenth-century France that culminated in her being brought to the guillotine along with her husband, Louis XVI. While we in the developed world of the early twenty-first century have little chance of being brought to the guillotine, we are for the most part indifferent to and unaware of the plight of our fellow humanity in the developing and industrializing world. Hunger, disease, illiteracy, unemployment, homelessness, corruption and ever-burgeoning debt are not generally abating there; in fact, a number of such nations are spiralling to ever-greater levels of crisis. One may ask the question: Is it a waste of time and effort to strive to help the deprived to help themselves? Jonathan Swift (1667–1745) must have asked a similar question of himself before he sat down to write 'A Modest Proposal' (1729), and the answer that can be gleaned from his essay is neither an emphatic 'no' nor an unconditional 'yes'. In the critical appraisal of 'A Modest Proposal' that follows, we will come to realize that Swift's greatest achievement in composing this piece of caustic satire was to heighten consciousness on all sides and at all levels.

63

Swift vents his increasing annoyance at the ineptness of the ruling class – epitomized by the double standards of the Anglo-Irish gentry – and at the squalor and degradation in which he sees so many Irish people living. While the essay documents the bleak social and economic situation of eighteenth-century Ireland under English rule (Ireland did not achieve independence from Britain until 1922), it also expresses Swift's revulsion at the seeming inability of the Irish peasantry to do anything except to subsist. Without excusing any group, the essay shows that not only the English but also the Irish are responsible for the nation's ominous mess. His concern for the wretchedness of the Irish is a merciless one, and he includes a critique of their incompetence in dealing with their own tribulations.

Political pamphleteering was a popular pursuit in Swift's day, which saw vast numbers of dissertations and treatises advocating political ponderings and proposing solutions for economic and social injustices. Swift's essay impersonates the style and method of these, and the grim sarcasm of his own solution reveals his personal despair at the failure of this writing to achieve any tangible results. His piece protests the utter inefficacy of Irish political authority and it also attacks the orientation of so many reformers at the time toward utilitarianism. While Swift himself was an observant fiscal and social thinker, he often expressed contempt for the application of supposedly scientific management ideas to humanitarian concerns.

The main rhetorical challenge of this intensely satirical piece is to gain the attention of an audience whose indifference was notorious. Swift makes his point negatively by juxtaposing a shocking plethora of morally untenable ideas in order to cast blame and vituperation far and wide. The essay progresses through a series of surprises that first astounds the reader and then causes him/her to think critically about social depravity and the policies that may underlie it. The inequality and depravity of Swift's Ireland, though almost three hundred years previous, is not completely alien to that which exists in our contemporary world, especially (but by no means exclusively) in several under-industrialized and industrializing nations.

The full and original title of Swift's essay is 'A Modest Proposal for preventing the children of poor people in Ireland from being a burden on their parents or country, and for making them beneficial to the publick'. The tract is an ironically conceived attempt to 'find out a fair, cheap and easy method' for converting the starving children of Ireland into 'sound and useful members of the common-wealth'. The one who could devise such a solution deserves according to the author to have 'his statue set up for a preserver of the nation' because all previous suggestions and attempts at an amelioration have miserably failed. Across the country in Swift's era, poor children (Catholics mainly) were living in squalor because their families were too poor to sustain them with basic food and clothing. Swift argues by hard-edged pecuniary analysis and by assuming a self-righteous moral stance for a way to turn this problem into a solution. His proposal is to fatten up these undernourished children and feed them to Ireland's Anglo-Irish gentry. Children of the poor could be sold to a meat market at the age of one, he argues, thus combating overpopulation and unemployment, sparing families the expense of child-rearing while providing them with a little extra income, improving the culinary experience of the wealthy and contributing to the overall economic well-being of the nation.

The author presents statistical support for his hypothesis and gives specific data about the number of children to be sold, their weight and price and the projected consumption patterns. He suggests some recipes for preparing this delicious new meat, and he feels sure that innovative cooks will be quick to create more. He also anticipates that the practice of selling and eating children will have positive effects on family morality: husbands will treat their wives with more respect and parents will value their children in ways hitherto unknown. His conclusion is that the implementation of this novel scheme will do more to solve Ireland's complex social, political and economic problems than any other measure that has been hereto proposed.

Swift's opening section offers a starkly realistic, although compassionate, portrait of the destitute families in Ireland. It presents a straightforward and matter-of-fact description yet goes on to propose judgements and explanations about such rampant depravity: for example, he states that mothers not being able to work for a wage is a contributing factor to their current poverty and humiliation. Swift's language here reverses the prevailing sentiment of his day, which held that if paupers were deprived, it was largely due to their own incompetence. The reader is unsure at this point whether to take Swift's professed compassion for the underclass as sincere or ironic. In fact, the issue never becomes completely clear because in this passage, and in the tract as a whole, he tends not to choose sides; his stance is one of general exasperation with all parties in this complex quagmire. Swift is generous with his disdain, and his irony works both to censure the poor and to excoriate the society that enables their demise. The remark about Irish Catholics who go to Spain to fight for the Pretender (the son of James II, who lost the throne of England in the Revolution of 1688) offers a good instance of the complexity of Swift's judgements: he is commenting on a woeful lack of national loyalty among the Irish, while at the same time denouncing a nation that drives its own citizens to mercenary activities. He makes a similar stab at national policies and priorities with the quip that takes for granted that poor Irish children will always be unemployed because 'we neither build houses (I mean in the country), nor cultivate land'.

One is initially inclined, as is the rhetorical intention, to identify in part with Swift's proposal. His compassion in the first paragraph, the matter-of-fact tone of the second, his apparent objectivity in evaluating other proposals and his moral outrage at the frequency of abortion and infanticide – all indicate a genuine desire for reform. Yet he habitually describes, using equine imagery, a newborn child as 'just drooped from its dam' and identifies women as mere 'breeders'. The use of such equine wordage is an effective stylistic way for the author's proposal to reduce human beings to mere statistical numbers and tradeable commodities.

It soon becomes clear that this is to be a fiscal argument despite the fact the proposal has moral, religious, political and nationalistic implications. Notwithstanding his own moral indignation, when the author suggests that most abortions are initiated by financial rather than moral considerations, he assumes that people's motivations are basically materialistic. This is not, of course, Swift's own assumption; he presents a shockingly extreme case of cold-blooded 'rationality' in order to make his readers reconsider their own priorities. Swift parodies the style of the pseudo-scientific proposals for social engineering that were so popular at his time. His piece is partly an attack on the economic utilitarianism that instigated so many of these proposals. Although Swift was himself an astute rational thinker, he here draws attention to the incongruity between a ruthless (though impeccably systematic) logic and a complexly human social and political reality. Part of the effect will be to make the reader feel that the argument is bad, without knowing quite where to intervene – to pit moral judgement against more purely logical pragmatism.

The irony of Swift's piece functions on the assumption that his audience, regardless of their national or religious affiliations or their socio-economic status, will all agree to the fact that eating children is morally reprehensible. The reader registers a shock at this point in the proposal and recognizes that a literal reading of Swift's pamphlet will not be sufficient. Swift is not literarily suggesting that the children of the poor are to be eaten at the tables of the rich, and so the task becomes one of identifying where his actual argument lies. This involves distinguishing the persona of the intended author from the person of Swift himself. The former is clearly a caricature; his values are shocking, but despite his cold rationality and his self-righteousness, he is not morally indifferent. Rather, he seems to have a single, glaring blind spot regarding the reprehensible act of eating children, but he is perfectly ready to make judgements about the incidental moral benefits and consequences of his proposal. The relater of the essay per se is not a recipient of Swift's mordant satire; rather he is the means of conveying some stinging parodies on prominent ways of social thinking.

'A Modest Proposal' draws attention to the self-degradation of the nation as a whole by illustrating it in shockingly literal ways. The idea of fattening up a starving population in order to feed the rich casts a grim appraisal on the nature of social relations in Ireland. The language that likens people to livestock becomes even more prevalent in this part of the propositional argument. The breeding metaphor underscores the fiscal pragmatism that underlies the idea. It also works to frame a critique of the domestic values in Irish Catholic families, who regard marriage and family with so little sanctity that they are effectively not unlike breeding animals. Swift draws on the long-standing perception among the English and the Anglo-Irish ruling classes of the native Irish as an uncouth people. Swift neither totally confirms nor negates this assumption. He admonishes the Irish Catholics for the extent to which they dehumanize themselves through their baseness and lack of self-respect. He also, however, berates those who would accuse the poor for their inhumane lack of compassion and excoriates the barbarism of a mode of social thought that takes economic profitability as its sole standard.

With the introduction of the idea of cannibalism, a number of associated implications come into play. Swift cultivates an analogy between literal and metaphorical cannibalism – humans consuming humans through injustice and cruelty. Yet Ireland's complicity in its own oppression translates the guilt of cannibalism to a narrower national scale; this is not just a case of humans being cruel to other humans, but a nation consuming itself and its own resources. Swift's aside about the fact that wealthy Anglo-Irish landlords have already 'devoured' most of the poverty-stricken parents caustically voices a protest against their exploitation of such peasants.

One of Swift's techniques is to let abstract ideas resonate in multiple ways. The word 'profit', for example, refers at various points to fiscal issues, morality and personal indulgence. When Swift looks at who stands to profit from the sale of infant flesh, he includes not only the family that earns the eight shillings, but also the landowner who will earn a certain social status by serving such a delicacy and the nation that will obtain relief from some of its most pressing problems. In this way, Swift keeps reminding his audience of the different value systems that bear on Ireland's social and political problems.

The author identifies himself as a member of the Anglo-Irish ruling class, who were predominantly Protestant. His reference to embattled Protestants forced to leave the country is mainly ironic. Swift is denouncing the practice of absenteeism among Irish landlords, who often governed their estates from abroad, thus funnelling much of the fruits of Irish peasant labour abroad and out of Ireland. His cultural allegiance is to that of the Anglo-Irish gentry, yet it is at these that he directs some of his fiercest derision. Swift's disdain for the irresponsibility, greed and moral indifference of the elite is matched only by his disgust at the total incompetence of Ireland's political leaders. Swift begins moving away from the fiscal economics of child breeding in order to home in on the realities of Ireland's real economic dilemma. Many of the arguments the essay advances have to do with the very real problem of building a viable Irish national economy. Swift reveals that his objection is not so much with the basic mercantilist idea that the people are the most valuable resources of a nation, but rather with Ireland's failure to value that resource in any meaningful and nationally constructive way.

Swift elaborates with a certain relish on his critique of domestic mores among the Irish poor. His citing them as needing a monetary incentive to wed, to love their children and spouses and to refrain from domestic violence is an obvious strike against them. Yet there is a certain inherent ambiguity in the excursus as it hints of prejudice. Swift is a complex thinker who acknowledges multiple sides to an issue.

The account of the long and exhausting years of wrestling with Ireland's problems can be interpreted as Swift's own. His catalogue of supposedly unrealistic alternative solutions marks a turning point in the pamphlet and a break in the satire. The ideas the proposal rejects represent measures that Swift himself had spent a great deal of energy advocating, to exasperatingly little effect. They are a set of steps by which the Irish might hope to break out of their cycle of victimization without the need for England's specific co-operation. Swift's modus operandi is a programme of civic-minded, patriotic and principled behaviour designed to effect change from the inside. The audience is confronted with the startling proposition that there are real and practicable solutions to ameliorate Ireland's demise; a demise that has been created for the greater part by the greed, self-indulgence and indifference of those with the responsibility of ruling.

In emphasizing that his remedy has been tailored mainly for Ireland, Swift is calling attention to the degree of how bad things have gotten. The author's statement that much of the population would have been better off dead is an embellishment, yet the irony is cutting; it is intended as a proof of the dire

71

national consequences of such rampant civic neglect. Only in Ireland, he seems to say, could a policy of cannibalism possibly be considered a social improvement.

The author's closing statement offers a last scathing indictment of the ethic of convenience and personal gain. We are urged to believe in his impartiality not because of his moral standards or his high-mindedness, but because he happens not to be susceptible to the particular fiscal temptation that might compromise his position. The manner of his assertion here reminds us that the author's unquestioned assumption throughout the entire proposal is that anyone with children would in fact be perfectly willing to sell them. This declaration also undercuts, once again, the separation between the privileged Protestant author and the Catholic masses. What unites them is their priority: improvement in the economic, social and moral standards of the population.

Even though Swift's essay was composed at another time and in another era, its relevance still resonates in our present age. No society in the industrialized and developed world may today overtly resemble what Swift portrays in 'A Modest Proposal', but one does not have to look too earnestly throughout the industrializing and developing world for parallels to the plight of the poor in eighteenth-century Ireland. The horrors of hunger and famine, the ever-mounting plethora of diseases and viruses, the failure to provide basic literacy, the scourge of poverty, unemployment and homelessness as well as spiralling national debt and corruption are ever prevalent in our time. The most important achievement of Swift's essay is not its poignant portrayal of the plight of the poor and the shocking proposed solution, but in the public highlighting of their plight; in other words, Swift, through this essay, instigated much public awareness and discussion with the aim that such might eventually instigate real and not cosmetic change.

In tone, Swift is sometimes not far from Mandeville, over 350 years before him. Mandeville spoke of an island he visited where children were eaten, describing their flesh as 'the best and sweetest flesh in the world'. Swift offers as a solution to the Irish Problem the marketing of the Irish children of the poor to the elite for consumption at their tables. The reading public (especially the English reading public) would have been understandably shocked and horrified, unable to garner the humour or his serious concern. But this, according to Swift, is the nature of satire because 'Satire is a sort of glass, wherein beholders do generally discover everybody's face but their own' (*The Battle of the Books*, 1704). Today, a quarter of a millennium after Swift, the plight of the majority of humanity is not that different: deprived and powerless. Ideologies of greater freedom and greater democracy as preached by leaders in industrialized countries sound fine and noble, but more often than not what is absent is the practising and/or the bringing to fruition of what is promulgated. The first step must be an all-pervasive awareness and the next step is to act: from this will slowly grow eventually the seeds of meaningful amelioration where people regardless of race or colour or nationality will be afforded a fairer opportunity to help themselves and enjoy a better quality of life.

Further Reading

C. Fox, ed., *The Cambridge Companion to Jonathan Swift* (Cambridge: Cambridge University Press, 2003).

J. McMinn, *Jonathan's travels: Swift and Ireland* (Belfast: Appletree Press, 1994).

C. J. Rawson, *God, Gulliver and Genocide: Barbarism and the European Imagination 1492 –1945* (Oxford: Oxford University Press, 2001).

C. Van Doren, ed., *The Portable Swift* (Harmondsworth, Middlesex: Penguin Books, 1987).

Websites
The History of Economic Thought Website: Jonathan Swift, 1667–1745: http://cepa.newschool.edu/het/profiles/swift.htm

The Victorian Web: Jonathan Swift: www.victorianweb.org/previctorian/swift/swiftov.html

The Other, Man-made Tsunami

JOHN PILGER

The West's crusaders, the United States and Britain, are giving
less to help the victims of the 2004 tsunami than the cost of
a Stealth bomber or a week's bloody occupation of Iraq. The
bill for George Bush's inauguration party would rebuild much
of the coastline of Sri Lanka.

Bush and Blair increased their first driblets of 'aid' only
when it became clear that people all over the world were
spontaneously giving millions and a public relations problem
beckoned. The Blair government's current 'generous' contribution
is one sixteenth of the £800 million it spent bombing Iraq before
the invasion and barely one twentieth of a billion pound gift,
known as a 'soft loan', to the Indonesian military so that it
could acquire Hawk fighter-bombers.

On 24 November 2004, one month before the tsunami struck,
the Blair government gave its backing to an arms fair in Jakarta,
'designed to meet an urgent need for the [Indonesian] armed
forces to review its defense capabilities', reported the *Jakarta
Post*. The Indonesian military, responsible for genocide in East
Timor, has killed more than 20,000 civilians and 'insurgents' in
Aceh. Among the exhibitors at the arms fair was Rolls-Royce,
manufacturer of engines for the Hawks, which, along with
British-supplied Scorpion armoured vehicles, machine guns

and ammunition, were terrorizing and killing people in Aceh up to the day the tsunami devastated the province.

The Australian government, currently covering itself in glory for its modest response to the historic disaster befallen its Asian neighbours, has secretly trained Indonesia's Kopassus special forces, whose atrocities in Aceh are well documented. This is in keeping with Australia's forty-year support for oppression in Indonesia, notably its devotion to the dictator Suharto while his troops slaughtered a third of the population of East Timor.

The government of John Howard – notorious for its imprisonment of child asylum seekers – is presently defying international maritime law by denying East Timor its due of oil and gas royalties worth some US $8 billion. Without this revenue East Timor, the world's poorest country, cannot build schools, hospitals and roads or provide work for its young people, 90 per cent of whom are unemployed.

The hypocrisy, narcissism and dissembling propaganda of the rulers of the world and their sidekicks are in full cry. Superlatives abound as to their humanitarian intent while the division of humanity into worthy and unworthy victims dominates the news. The victims of a great natural disaster are worthy (though for how long is uncertain) while the victims of man-made imperial disasters are unworthy and very often unmentionable. Somehow, reporters cannot bring themselves to report what has been going on in Aceh, supported by 'our' government. This one-way moral mirror allows us to ignore a trail of destruction and carnage that is another tsunami.

Consider the plight of Afghanistan, where clean water is unknown and death in childbirth common. At the Labour Party conference in 2001, Tony Blair announced his famous crusade to 're-order the world' with the pledge: 'To the Afghan people, we make this commitment, we will not walk away ... we will work with you to make sure [a way is found] out of the poverty that is your miserable existence.'

The Blair government had just taken part in the conquest of Afghanistan, in which as many as 20,000 civilians died. Of all the great humanitarian crises in living memory, no country suffered more and none has been helped less. Just 3 per cent of all international aid spent in Afghanistan has been for reconstruction, 84 per cent is for the US-led military 'coalition' and the rest crumbs for emergency aid. What is often presented as reconstruction revenue is private investment, such as the US $35 million that will finance a proposed five-star hotel, mostly for foreigners. An adviser to the minister of rural affairs in Kabul told me the government had received less than 20 per cent of the aid promised to Afghanistan. 'We don't even have enough money to pay wages, let alone plan reconstruction,' he said. The reason, unspoken of course, is that Afghans are the unworthiest of victims. When American helicopter gunships repeatedly machine-gunned a remote farming village, killing as many as 93 civilians, a Pentagon official was moved to say, 'The people there are dead because we wanted them dead.'

I became acutely aware of this other tsunami when I reported from Cambodia in 1979. Following a decade of American bombing and Pol Pot's barbarities, Cambodia lay as stricken as Aceh is today. Disease beckoned famine and people suffered a collective trauma few could explain. Yet, for nine months after the collapse of the Khmer Rouge regime, no effective aid arrived

77

from western governments. Instead, a western and Chinese
backed UN embargo was imposed on Cambodia, denying
virtually the entire machinery of recovery and assistance.
The problem for the Cambodians was that their liberators, the
Vietnamese, had come from the wrong side of the Cold War,
having recently expelled the Americans from their homeland.
That made them unworthy victims, and expendable.

A similar, largely unreported siege was forced on Iraq during
the 1990s and intensified during the Anglo-American 'liberation'.
In September 2004, UNICEF reported that malnutrition among
Iraqi children had doubled under the occupation. Infant
mortality is now at the level of Burundi, higher than in Haiti
and Uganda. There is crippling poverty and a chronic shortage
of medicines. Cancer cases are rising rapidly, especially breast
cancer; radioactive pollution is widespread. More than seven
hundred schools are bomb-damaged. Of the billions said to
have been allocated for reconstruction in Iraq, just US $29
million has been spent, most of it on mercenaries guarding
foreigners. Little of this is news in the West.

This other tsunami is worldwide, causing 24,000 deaths
every day from poverty and debt and division that are the
products of a super-cult called neo-liberalism. This was
acknowledged by the United Nations in 1991 when it called
a conference in Paris of the richest states with the aim of
implementing a 'programme of action' to rescue the world's
poorest nations. A decade later, virtually every commitment
made by western governments had been broken, making the
waffle of the British Chancellor (Treasurer) Gordon Brown
about the Group of Eight 'sharing Britain's dream' in ending
poverty just that: waffle.

Not one government has honoured the United Nations 'baseline' and allotted a miserable 0.7 per cent of its national income to overseas aid. Britain gives just 0.34 per cent, making its 'Department for International Development' a black joke. The US gives 0.15 per cent, the lowest of any industrial state.

Largely unseen and unimagined by westerners, millions of people know their lives have been declared expendable. When tariffs and food and fuel subsidies are eliminated under an International Monetary Fund (IMF) diktat, small farmers and the landless know they face disaster, which is why suicides among farmers are an epidemic. Only the rich, says the World Trade Organization (WTO), are allowed to protect their home industries and agriculture; only they have the right to subsidize exports of meat, grain and sugar and dump them in poor countries at artificially low prices, thereby destroying livelihoods and lives.

Indonesia, once described by the World Bank as 'a model pupil of the global economy', is a case in point. Many of those washed to their deaths in Sumatra on Boxing Day 2004 were dispossessed by IMF policies. Indonesia owes an un-repayable debt of US $110 billion. The World Resources Institute says the toll of this man-made tsunami reaches 13–18 million child deaths every year; or 12 million children under the age of five, according to a UN Development Report. 'If 100 million have been killed in the formal wars of the 20th century', wrote the Australian social scientist Michael McKinley, 'why are they to be privileged in comprehension over the annual [death] toll of children from structural adjustment programmes since 1982?' That the system causing this has democracy as its war cry is a mockery that people all over the world increasingly understand.

It is this rising awareness, consciousness even, that offers more than hope. Since the crusaders in Washington and London squandered world sympathy for the victims of September 11 2001 in order to accelerate their campaign of domination, a critical public intelligence has stirred and regards the likes of Blair and Bush as liars and their culpable actions as crimes.

The current outpouring of help for the tsunami victims among ordinary people in the West is a spectacular reclaiming of the politics of community, morality and internationalism denied them by governments and corporate propaganda. Listening to tourists returning from stricken countries, consumed with gratitude for the gracious, expansive way some of the poorest of the poor gave them shelter and cared for them, one hears the antithesis of 'policies' that care only for the avaricious.

'The most spectacular display of public morality the world has ever seen', was how the writer Arundhati Roy described the anti-war anger that swept across the world almost two years ago. A French study now estimates that 35 million people demonstrated on that February day and says there has never been anything like it; and it was just a beginning.

This is not rhetorical; human renewal is not a phenomenon, rather the continuation of a struggle that may appear at times to have frozen, but is a seed beneath the snow. Take Latin America, long declared invisible and expendable in the West. 'Latin Americans have been trained in impotence', wrote Eduardo Galeano the other day. 'A pedagogy passed down from colonial times, taught by violent soldiers, timorous teachers and frail fatalists, has rooted in our souls the belief that reality is untouchable and that all we can do is swallow in silence the woes each day brings.' Galeano was celebrating the rebirth of real democracy in his homeland, Uruguay, where people have voted 'against fear', against privatization and its attendant indecencies.

In Venezuela, municipal and state elections in October 2004 notched up the ninth democratic victory for the only government in the world sharing its oil wealth with its poorest people. In Chile, the last of the military fascists supported by western governments, notably that of Margaret Thatcher, are being pursued by revitalized democratic forces.

These forces are part of a movement against inequality and poverty and war that has arisen in the past six years and is more diverse, more enterprising, more internationalist and more tolerant of difference than anything in my lifetime. It is a movement unburdened by a western liberalism that believes it represents a superior form of life; the wisest know this is colonialism by another name. The wisest also know that just as the conquest of Iraq is unravelling, so a whole system of domination and impoverishment can unravel, too.

Website
Hidden Agendas: The Films and Writing of John Pilger:
http://pilger.carlton.com

Africa, the Crisis Continent?

RICHARD DOWDEN

Politicians don't often do things purely for altruistic, idealistic reasons. The nature of democracy is that they represent the interests of their supporters at home and abroad. People were puzzled when Tony Blair and Gordon Brown took up Africa's cause and put Africa at the top of the agenda for the G8 Summit and for Britain's six-month presidency of the European Union this year.

Britain has no particular interest in Africa any longer. Once an important source of raw materials, the continent has dwindled as a trading partner, more an object of charity than commerce. So, in his third term as Prime Minister, is Tony Blair looking for a legacy? Does he want to be remembered as the saviour of Africa? Or was he pushed by the charismatic Bob Geldof? The former rock star was instrumental in getting him to set up the Commission for Africa. Blair clearly enjoys being photographed with Geldof and Bono and it may have done him serious political harm if he spurned their passionately argued case for doing something about Africa. Perhaps too, Blair who once had a band called 'Ugly Rumours', felt a little of the adoration – envy even – that a failed rock star feels for a successful one. And perhaps there was an element of altruism too. Politicians are, after all, human.

So Blair set up the Commission for Africa, a global consultation about Africa with representatives from Africa, Britain, France, America, India and China. It oversaw the writing of the huge 461-page report on the state of Africa and what the rest of the world should do about it. The Year of Africa also produced an African season on the BBC that in turn sparked interest in aspects of Africa – art, culture, history – that had been neglected over the years. In the lead-up to G8 the Make Poverty History campaign was launched to focus the minds of politicians and people on achieving the Millennium Development Goals. Its aim was to focus on the targets to cut the death rate among babies in poor countries, get more children into school and launch a raft of other goals to make life better for the billions who live in permanent poverty. The whole campaign culminated in the Live 8 concerts across the world, which were seen by more people than any other television programme.

It was an amazing effort. What did it achieve? The answer lies somewhere in the gap between the reality of Africa and its image. How much do we engage with the reality of Africa and how much do we simply react to the image? Going back to the war for Biafran independence in Nigeria in the 1960s, the typical image of Africa has been one of a sick, starving child in a war zone, often affected by drought. In mid 1984 I was a reporter for *The Times* and I received a call from a contact at Oxfam. He told me that a terrible drought had hit northern Ethiopia; millions were facing starvation. I asked the editor of *The Times* if I could go. 'No,' he said, 'we saw quite enough of starving African babies during the Biafran war. I don't think our readers are interested in that sort of thing.'

I decided then that I would try to get to as many of these

ignored famines and wars as I could, and write about them. It was not easy. Africa rarely appeared in the top half of any news editor's schedule. There was little popular demand from readers and travel to Africa was expensive. But I managed to get to Angola, Mozambique, Uganda, Sudan and a host of other countries and write their stories.

Then a new movement started. Africans in Britain and others began to complain that I and other journalists working in Africa were giving the continent a bad name. Some even suggested a sort of racist conspiracy to always show Africa in a bad light. At first I was furious. These people seemed to be in denial. Then I began to see their point.

When, for example, we see floods in France on television we feel sorry for the victims but we don't think that France is permanently under water. We have in our minds other images of France, from holidays there or from friends, books and other more cheerful pictures of French life. But most people outside Africa have no other images of the continent than what they see on television, so they begin to believe that all African children are starving and the whole continent is engulfed by war. The accumulated stories of famine and war have become the narrative of the whole continent.

Journalism doesn't help. The further away the place, the more likely that the media will only report disaster and drama. It's what journalists do. They don't write about normality. Take the former Yugoslavia. Everyone has heard about Bosnia, Serbia, Kosovo. Who knows about the former province, Slovenia? That's because Slovenia left Yugoslavia without a fight and became a very successful small country. Slovenes may complain that their country is ignored. Perhaps they should be grateful.

The image of the sick, starving African child in a war zone is a real one but it is only a part of the story. Africa is a vast diverse continent. There is no single Africa, no common characteristic that covers the whole continent, nor any trait that is exclusive to Africa. North Africa, on the southern rim of the Mediterranean, has little in common with Africa south of the Sahara. Somalia in the northeastern tip is nothing like Ghana in the West. To the South, Botswana and South Africa are successful economies. But the states across the middle of Africa are not working well and it is these forty or so countries that cause most concern and which I am writing about here. Though potentially these countries could be rich, life in almost all of them is poorer and less secure than it was thirty years ago.

Not only is the media image of Africa giving the impression that everyone on the continent is starving but aid agencies use that image to imply that if you send money you can save Africa. Money can save lives, relieve suffering and help victims get back on their feet. That is what aid agencies do well. Most aid is not from aid agencies but from governments and international institutions like the United Nations and the World Bank. This aid is aimed at transforming lives but Africa has had hundreds of billions' worth of this sort of aid since the 1960s and there is little to show for it. The lesson is that you cannot draw whole societies out of poverty with aid, let alone a whole continent. Development – the transformation of societies from subsistence on the poverty line to dynamic wealth creation and a better standard of living for all – takes much more.

That is the flaw in the Make Poverty History campaign and in the British government's target of aid, trade and debt relief as the three thrust points for the G8 Summit. The Summit secured an agreement to double aid and write off debt for eighteen countries, fourteen of them African. On trade, where Blair hoped to get G8 leaders to agree a statement proposing a date for the abolition of export subsidies for agricultural produce, nothing happened. In theory rich countries' subsidies to their own farmers and exporters damage Africa because they lower the world price of food and cotton. Rich countries then dump the subsidized food on poor countries, undermining local agriculture.

But recent studies have shown that if all subsidies were dropped, Africa would not gain in the short or medium term. Countries such as Brazil or Indonesia are ready to feed the world with modern, well-organized agricultural sectors. In Africa only South Africa and Morocco could compete at global level. The cold fact is that at the moment Africa does not produce the right quality and quantity, in the right place and the right time. It is not blocked by tariffs in rich countries but by constraints in African countries, many of them created by the rulers of Africa.

Debt relief, an easy cause to fight for, is only a sideshow in terms of cash amounts. The deal only yields US $1.5 billion among the eighteen countries, a small proportion of the US $50 billion a year promised in aid by 2010. Many of those debts were not being serviced anyway and it is not clear where and how the debt relief money and the aid will be spent. What is clear is that only where governments are committed to change is there real national social transformation. Elsewhere aid boosts growth a little bit, for a while, but leaves nothing substantial. If the recipient government is not really committed, growth slips back when aid ends. It may even do harm by making those governments more corrupt and making them accountable to the aid donors, not to their own people.

Aid, trade and debt may have been the pillars on which the new approach to Africa is built but the foundations are African politics and these foundations are weak. The failure of many African countries is political failure. The political systems of these countries are based on 'winner-takes-all'. One man takes power, the army becomes his bodyguard, the law courts a political tool, the treasury his private bank account. The institutions of such African states are weak. In contrast to the enabling development state of the Asian Tigers in the 1970s and 1980s, African states have been dubbed anti-development states.

The reasons for this state of affairs are hotly debated but all agree that the careless creation of those states by imperial powers at the end of the nineteenth century has a lot to do with it. These states, which bore little relation to geographical or social realities on the ground, cutting across ethnic groups and natural boundaries, were then suddenly pitched into independence barely more than half a century later. Today these forty states contain some 10,000 political entities and different ethnic groups. Nigeria, for example, has more than four hundred languages. In many of these states people share no common history and have no shared sense of national identity. Hence they do not participate as true citizens in a nation state.

Their umbilical cords are still attached to their former colonial rulers. Until recently, links between colonies and their former British, French and Portuguese rulers were stronger than links between African neighbours. The roads and railways were designed to bring goods and raw materials from the interior to a port on the coast and from there to the rest of the world. Africa was a storehouse to be looted, not a place to be developed for the benefit of its own people.

So we, as British and part of the rich world, have had a huge part in the creation of modern Africa. That gives us a duty and a right to care, but not a right to intervene or dictate. Only Africans can develop Africa. That leaves us with a humbler support role.

Giving aid is one way of helping, but who should receive it and under what conditions? In the Cold War aid was given to 'allies'. As long as President X or Y was 'on our side' he was propped up with aid. Democracy, respect for human rights and the rule of law were secondary issues. As a western ally for three decades Mobutu Sese Seko of Zaire systematically looted his country, leaving it a broken wreck.

Since the end of the Cold War aid is still concentrated in countries where the donors have commercial interests, but it has been used more evenly. There is no agreement about conditions attached to aid. Some think it should just be given without any conditions. Others argue that aid should be given only to winners, those doing the 'right things'. This is the philosophy of the American Millennium Challenge Account (MCA), which has several conditions, many of them more to do with America's own interests than with those of the recipient countries. The heavy conditionality was designed as a lure to encourage better government in Africa but, after three years, the MCA had not dispensed a single dollar.

The first problem with giving only to the 'good guys' is that African leaders are like other human beings; sometimes good, sometimes not so good. President Yoweri Museveni for example has done much to strengthen Uganda's economy but does not believe in democracy. President Robert Mugabe on the other hand has destroyed Zimbabwe's economy but does hold elections, even if they are bad ones.

The second problem is that the vast majority of really poor people are in countries that have either bad rulers or no rule at all. There is no question of handing lots of aid to those governments, but how do you help the people? You can help them survive by sending aid through non-governmental aid agencies (NGOs) but they can't develop the country and they do not have the capacity to cover everyone. Great work is often suddenly wrecked by war or political disruption.

The Commission for Africa argues that now is the moment to double aid to Africa and forgive debt. Time for a 'Big Push'. It says there is no other possible source for the capital required to lift Africa out of poverty. It gives as examples of aid working countries such as Tanzania, Mali, Ethiopia, Mozambique and Ghana. But for every example of progress there are examples, such as Kenya, Cote d'Ivoire, Swaziland and now Ethiopia, of countries that have been doing well but have slipped back – always for political reasons. Elsewhere heavily aided countries are more dependent on foreign aid than they were in colonial times, with more than half their budgets coming from donors. Aid should not be seen as a fundamentally good thing. It creates a poisonous relationship. At best it should be a temporary measure to escape from difficult times. Even in countries doing well in Africa, there is no exit strategy and little sign that the demand for aid is diminishing.

Make Poverty History has been a wonderful motivator for

getting people out onto the streets and feeling they could make a difference but its danger was always that it is setting up everyone for disillusionment. It left the impression – though its creators and backers know the picture is a lot more complicated – that a new deal on aid, trade and debt would solve the problem. The campaign should have carried the sub-title: a fifty-year project.

Because that is how long it may take. It all depends on whether Africans can hold their governments accountable and force them to deliver services such as clinics and schools and roads, and spend less on presidential jets and international airports in the president's village. It is not just a question of corruption, though that is a serious problem in some countries. It is a matter of capacity, people with the skills, knowledge and experience to manage a government system that can get teachers, nurses and doctors paid, deliver drugs to far-flung clinics and build roads to the villages. In the badly managed attempts to force reform on African governments in the 1980s, the International Monetary Fund (IMF) and the World Bank forced huge cuts in civil services while at the same time forcing governments to float their currencies. Many civil servants ended up being paid the equivalent of US $10 a month. No wonder they left for the private sector or became deeply corrupt. The Commission for Africa report admits that much of the first dollop of new aid will have to be spent just rebuilding African civil services.

The demand for more aid and debt relief has overshadowed many other issues raised in the Commission for Africa report. Perhaps in the long run we will help Africa more by stopping policies and practices that hurt Africa, than trying to save

91

Africa by giving it too much aid. The damage we do Africa may cost it more than what we give in aid.

The trade tariffs and agricultural subsidies are one example, but more immediate is corruption. British based firms, particularly in the defence and energy industries, frequently bribe their way to big contracts. The Commission for Africa strongly supports the idea of forcing companies to publish what they pay, both formally and informally, to African governments. And then there is the issue of corruption money flowing back into western banks, many of them in the City of London. Some 40 per cent of African private wealth is held outside the continent and some of that is money stolen from aid or extracted in bribes. The Commission recommends that this money be traced, frozen and returned to Africa. There is also the issue of the recruitment by developed countries of Africa's professionals: teachers, nurses and doctors. This is a complicated issue but at present the individual worker wins by getting more opportunity and better pay, the country they come to wins by getting cheap expertise but the country they come from loses. We must find ways of turning win, win, lose into win, win, win.

It will be a long haul but also a complicated one. Making judgements about where and when to give aid or stop aid are crucial. That is why the most important thing is to understand Africa. Yet the British government, apparently so keen to help Africa, is diminishing Britain's capacity to understand and analyse it. The Foreign Office, the government's tool for gathering information, sifting it and making those judgements, is facing huge cuts. It has been forced to close three missions in Africa and cut back on desk officers in London – those people who watch particular countries day by day and act as a reference point for their citizens in Britain and for British businesses and NGOs working there. The reasons are not clear but the message it sends is that it is not important to understand Africa.

To prepare for the long haul of helping Africa, the government should be investing heavily in engaging with Africa, building Africa expertise and an institutional memory across its departments. Listening to Africa and gaining a better understanding of its history, cultures and societies might enable outsiders to respect Africa more and better engage with it.

How the Modern-day Missionaries Called 'Human Rights Activists' Help Wreak Havoc in Africa

ROBIN PHILPOT

Human rights are the unofficial religion and uncontested foreign policy of western countries and particularly the United States. Michael Ignatieff, a liberal turned hawk who heads Harvard's Carr Center for Human Rights, has said they are the 'semiofficial ideology' of the western world, the 'grace notes of a 21st century imperium' along with democracy and free markets. Like the environment, democracy and motherhood, who could ever think of being opposed to human rights? The problem is that the official proponents of human rights are also leaders of empires bent on expanding their imperial reach, and history has shown that countries and geographical regions targeted by empires have seldom reaped prosperity, economic development, peace and democracy. Instead, they have had poverty, economic dependence, war and dictatorships inflicted upon them. A careful look at events in Central Africa, specifically Rwanda and the Democratic Republic of Congo, shows how 'human rights' have become a terribly efficient form of imperial doublespeak and sloganeering and that anybody interested in making a difference in Africa or in making poverty history must know when and how to debunk them.

Ever since the first invasion of the Congo by Rwanda in November 1996, with backing by the United States, there has been a lot of hand-wringing about the extraordinarily high loss of human life in the Congo owing to the wars that followed. Estimates put losses at upwards of four million people. Added to these losses is the scramble by western corporations for control of the Congo's vast mineral resources. In fact, the massive loss of life has not prevented some of these corporations from walking away with millions. Thus, despite all the official hand-wringing, little has been done to help understand why this has happened, why it continues, and how it can be stopped. Some explanations tend to point to the Congo's complex demography – the old 'tribal wars' story – while others blame rapacious African warlords who hold power locally and who maintain the anarchy – the old 'African despot' story. Far too few dare investigate the imperial 'planned chaos' explanation, simply because it would mean revisiting the official, and blinding, story of the Rwandan tragedy, whence the chaos came, and that would mean taking on an enormous machine that operates in Hollywood and the Pentagon as well as in the offices of almost every human rights organization in the world.

A review of human rights doublespeak in Central Africa must begin at least in 1990 when the first international war was launched. On 28 September 1990, four thousand Ugandan soldiers and officers, including former army Commander and Ugandan Defence Minister Fred Rwigyema, left their barracks fully equipped with weapons and vehicles. They travelled hundreds of kilometres in Uganda to the Rwandan border and

attacked the few Rwandan border guards posted there on
1 October. They then advanced some 70 kilometres into Rwanda.
By 4 October, the invading troops were within 70 kilometres of
the Rwandan capital Kigali. These troops, though a mainstay
of the Ugandan army, became known as the Rwandan Patriotic
Front, the RPF. Victories loosen tongues, so we now know from
RPF leaders that the RPF also operated a fifth column
clandestinely in Rwanda. In fact, at the time of the invasion
it had 36 clandestine cells that were working mostly where?
In human rights organizations! These Rwandan organizations,
infiltrated by agents of the invading army, had strong ties with
the major European and North American human rights
organizations based in New York, London, Paris and Montreal.
So when the Ugandan troops invaded Rwanda in 1990 and the
Rwandan government took action to protect its sovereignty by
arresting people suspected of working with the invaders – every
country in the world would do the same – the human rights
activists in Rwanda with their powerful offices in western
countries roundly denounced the 'brutal' arrests, but kept
strangely silent about the invasion.

Was it normal in the search for justice to condemn one side
in a war for its human rights violations and not even question
the morality of the aggressors, those who violated the principles
of all the rights charters ever drafted? Is it right to shout about
how a government violates rights and then turn a blind eye to
the launching of an aggressive war? Unfortunately, the vast
majority of western human rights organizations and their
representatives must think it is right because they whitewashed
the invaders and denounced the invaded country, its leaders
and its people. It was like an armed break and entry against

which the homeowner defended himself. The Justice Department arrests the homeowner for arms possession and exonerates the break-and-entry artist. In 1990, it appears that human rights strategy was already marching together with imperial strategy? Their blatant contradiction and bias in favour of the Rwandan Patriotic Front, dominated by Tutsis, infected every human rights report thereafter.

The most egregious, and most devastating, was a report issued in March 1993 by an International Human Rights Commission sponsored by Human Rights Watch/Africa in New York (later to become Africa Watch), the Fédération internationale des droits de l'Homme in Paris, and the International Centre for Human Rights and Democratic Development in Montreal (now Rights and Democracy). The title of the report, based on a two-week visit to Rwanda in January 1993, betrays the bias: 'Report of the International Commission of Inquiry into human rights violations in Rwanda since October 1, 1990'. By definition, the scope of the report excludes examination of the worst crime in international law, namely the crime against peace and national sovereignty perpetrated by the invading RPF army. Judge Norman Birkett from the post-war Nuremberg Tribunal stated it clearly: 'The charges in the Indictment that the defendants planned and waged aggressive wars are the charges of utmost gravity. ... To initiate a war of aggression, therefore, is not only an international crime; it is the supreme international crime differing only from the other war crimes in that it contains within itself the accumulated evil of the whole.'

Why such selectivity? When criticized, the Commission replied that the dates were chosen by the host Rwandan human rights groups. However, we now know that the Rwandan human rights groups who received the Commission had been formed by clandestine RPF cells created either immediately before or right after the invasion. It should be noted that the RPF, which had 36 clandestine cells in October 1990, was operating 146 clandestine cells by August 1993 in Kigali alone. When the RPF took power in July 1994, leaders of Rwandan human rights groups became ministers in the first RPF government and it was revealed that at least one member of the supposedly neutral Commission of 1993 was an RPF operative and other members were soon on the direct payroll of the RPF government. They also became the unofficial spokespersons of the RPF government in Europe and North America.

The impact of that two-week tour of Rwanda made by ten human rights activists, none of whom spoke Kinyarwanda and six of whom had never visited Rwanda before, was overwhelming. First of all, immediately after these human rights tourists left Rwanda and before they had issued their report, the RPF army launched a murderous 'punitive' attack in reaction to the revelations of the Commission. This self-described 'punitive' attack broke a ceasefire, doubled the RPF-occupied territory, put the RPF within 30 kilometres of Kigali, and pushed the number of internal Rwandan refugees camped around Kigali from 300,000 to one million. In her book *Flight or Death in Zaire*, Marie-Beatrice Umutesi describes what that February 1993 punitive attack following the human rights Commission's visit to Rwanda really meant for people in the northern Rwandan city of Byumba: 'On Thursday morning the rebels [RPF] began rounding people up in the whole area. Everybody was brought together: men, women and children, supposedly for an informational meeting. People were confident. The rebels were courteous and the peasants had nothing to hide. Things apparently got worse when they reached the place where the meeting was to be held. The rebels had the people enter the surrounding houses and then locked them from outside. They then attacked the houses with grenades. Survivors were killed with knives. The man who told me the story miraculously survived the massacre because he ended up under the bodies of his dead friends.'

The 1993 International Commission Report is a sham because of the scope, it is a sham because of its pro-RPF bias, it is a sham because it was infiltrated by one of the parties to the war, and it is a sham for many other reasons that cannot be detailed in this short chapter. Nonetheless, because of the lobbying power of its sponsor organizations in the West, the report became the bible for all foreign embassies and foreign affairs departments, as well as for the large funding organizations like the World Bank and the International Monetary Fund (IMF). Belgium recalled its ambassador following publication of the report, Canada suspended $20 million in aid to Rwanda. The report became a pretext for an arms embargo on Rwanda, whereas the invading army had no trouble getting the weapons it needed. The report became the backdrop for all meetings with the Rwandan government until April 1994. To this day it is taken as the gospel about the so-called pre-genocide period in Rwanda. Yet any serious study of that Commission and its overall role shows that it was little more than a major public relations effort by an invading army that then took power and facilitated the remodelling of Central Africa in favour of American and British hegemony. After all, in mid-November, less than eighteen months after the RPF took power in Rwanda, its American- and British-backed troops invaded the Congo (then Zaire), supposedly to hunt down Rwandan 'génocidaires'.

In a November 2004 interview, Boutros Boutros-Ghali, who headed the United Nations during this key period for Central Africa, described these changes as follows: 'Central Africa has been the scene of a new Anglo-American conflict with France, and the Anglo-American block won through Uganda and Rwanda. Is this not a repetition of Fashoda?' he asked, referring to the fort on the Upper Nile (now in Sudan) where in 1898 French troops had to back down as the British tried to consolidate their 'possessions' from 'The Cape to Cairo'.

Ironically, almost on the very day Rwandan troops were invading the Congo in mid-November 1996 to bomb the camps where some two million Rwandans had taken refuge, assistant US Secretary of State John Kornblum told French journalist Jean Daniel that France should 'Watch out for Africa: France has it all wrong. The strong man is in Uganda, not in Kinshasa.' The 'strong man' in Uganda who would enjoy Washington's blessing refers to Yoweri Museveni who had backed the RPF invasion of Rwanda in 1990 and the power grab in 1994. Kinshasa referred to the late president Mobutu of Zaire (Democratic Republic of Congo).

In scope, the imperial remodelling of Central Africa equalled the American and British attempt to remodel the Middle East when they invaded Iraq. So what did the human rights activists have to say, particularly on the 1996 invasion of the Congo, the bombing of the refugee camps, and the pursuant murderous manhunt throughout Eastern Congo? Essentially, many simply provided moral backing for these illegal and devastating operations which continue to cause death and destruction.

Doctors Without Borders/Médecins sans frontières (MSF), for example, boasted in a 1997 statement that it provided intelligence to the United States on political and military organization of the two million Rwandan refugees, that it helped change US policy regarding the camps, and that it pulled out of the camps just before the invasion and the bombing of them. Intelligence provided to the US went straight to the Rwandan military brass that led the invasion of the former Zaire, bombed the camps and hunted down the refugees further west into that country. Moreover, MSF's absence meant that the refugees did not have the care and protection they needed. Adding to the destruction, as the invasion proceeded, the humanitarian activist Alain Destexhe, who had been MSF's Secretary General until 1995 before becoming a Belgian Senator, published a scathing attack on the UN's planned deployment of an international force to protect the refugee camps. In the article in the French daily *Le Monde*, he also made the blood-curdling comment that 'the refugees would not return to Rwanda unless they are forced or are starved into doing so'. And to support the illegal forced return of refugees, he added, 'sometimes a painful political solution is preferable to a policy of compassion'. It should be noted that among Rwandan refugees killed, Howard French of *The New York Times* reported that 80 per cent were women and children, and 50 per cent were believed to be under fourteen years old.

War has not stopped in the Congo since 1996. Officially, there have been four more invasions, yet very little has been done to stop the carnage. However, since 2004, all eyes have turned to Sudan where many of the human rights groups encountered in Rwanda and the Congo are now calling for 'decisive' military action in the Darfur region of Sudan including American and British intervention and/or a NATO-led invasion. The script is similar to that of Rwanda and the Congo. Self-described rebels attack a country, hold press conferences, and are spared being seriously scrutinized by the media and the human rights non-governmental organizations. Most human rights activists provide the simplistic picture of one very guilty party, the Sudanese government, and helpless innocent victims.

It is time to learn from what happened in Rwanda and the Congo. Having witnessed the destruction in the Congo and the dubious role played there by many human rights groups, people interested in making a difference in Africa must stop being blinded by the catchy names, vaguer virtuous intentions, and simplistic tales that are used to cover a new type of domination of Africa. Is it not possible that the Darfur human rights problems are being used to hide an attempt to dismantle, control and remodel Sudan, the largest and one of the richest countries in Africa?

In 2002, in a *cri du coeur*, Aminata Traore, the former Malian minister of culture, pointed out that one of every five Africans lives in a country at war. Moreover, there are more western troops in action in Africa now than there have been since most African countries became independent. It would appear that while the doctors, reporters and human rights workers who have generously granted themselves the noble 'without borders' title, are providing the moral high ground, large armies 'without borders' but with direct ties to European and North American capitals are doing what armies have always done – sowing death, destruction, and economic despair.

YOU'RE HISTORY!

Further Reading

R. Philpot, *Ça ne s'est pas passé comme ça à Kigali* (*Les Intouchables*) (2003), now available in English online: 'Rwanda 1994: Colonialism Dies Hard' at www.taylor-report.com. The book expands on points raised in this chapter and provides a selected bibliography.

Twenty Years with AIDS

MARIE-ROGER BILOA

AIDS. Short name, long story.

This is the issue that a European – or anyone from any other part of the world – is most likely to ask an African about. Sure, Africa has become the most spectacular casualty of that atrocious evil. But for me, this is the topic that I have been most reluctant to really confront.

As a journalist and a publisher, I have embraced the most sensitive, controversial and painful issues, in which Africa is particularly rich, ranging from the Rwandan massacres of 1994 to the Arusha war crime tribunal, always taking a strong and often highly controversial stand. While the trend was to court the man who took up arms against his country on an ethnic basis, and to call him a 'liberator' and a 'hero', I challenged Paul Kagame's role in and responsibility for the violence in Rwanda. I pointed to his role in the plane crash that triggered the Homeric killings and led to one of the most massive exoduses of recent history, into neighbouring Zaire where hundreds of thousands died. I challenged the unanimous western interpretation of these horrific slaughters in that Great Lake region, exceedingly biased in my view, by constant comparison to the Nazi-led genocide; this caused western journalists to promote a simplistic vision of the 'good' Tutsis and the 'bad' Hutus. Besides being untrue, this now standard

105

'political correctness' has prevented any sustainable peace between the now ruling Tutsis and the Hutu population, which happens to be the demographic majority.

This was a hard mouthful to chew ...

As a matter of fact, the Rwandan tragedy was a life-changing experience for virtually everyone who came in close contact with it. The orgy of hate and irrationality decimated hundreds of thousands and destroyed the lives of millions, in a way no living human had ever seen before. The conflict went on to involve many countries, including Uganda, former Zaire (now Democratic Republic of Congo), Congo, Angola, Kenya, Zimbabwe, Burundi, Gabon, Cameroon and South Africa, among others, when the refugees started to disperse across the continent.

There is another African tsunami *avant la lettre* spreading and involving not a dozen, but every single country of Africa: AIDS. This is an unprecedented disease that, we are warned, threatens to erase Africans from the world population. Looking back, however, I can't think of a significant upsurge of reporting commissioned by me for the magazine I have published since 1991, *Africa International*. As a matter of fact, not a single editorial of mine has focused specifically on the issue. I suppose this can be counted as a patent inhibition. For an activist promoting Africa's advancement, one renowned for her courage, this is a disturbing neglect: one that I am forced to come to terms with in this chapter. In other words, writing about AIDS here will take the form of explaining why I have not previously done so.

The first time I heard about AIDS was not especially frightening. It was sometime between 1984 and 1985 in Paris when I began my career as a journalist. According to reports at that time, the new sickness was developing among gay males in California, and nothing could have been more remote to a Cameroonian-born, Catholic-raised young woman. Moreover, estimates suggest that gays represent no more than 10 per cent of the population, which drops to less than 3 per cent in Sub-Saharan Africa. So AIDS seemed of little concern; until that is, reports started pointing fingers at Africa as the cradle of the new evil, an evil not linked to or conveyed by other humans, but by green monkeys! I remember the jokes this ignited in the editorial room. To my colleagues and me, white people just never missed an occasion to make Africa a scapegoat. The green monkey theory never accounted for the leap from the Central African rainforest to an epidemic within the gay urban community in Los Angeles. But this most bizarre introduction to what was to become a gigantic historical phenomenon, affecting for decades all continents and billions of people all over the world – and primarily Africans – definitely triggered in me an unconscious process of denial.

The second disturbing episode for me was the 1988 publication of a study by a French officer in a military journal. Based on the forecast that AIDS was going to decimate Africa's population in biblical proportions, the army general was complaining about the French inability to take advantage of the 'opportunity' as astutely as the Americans were by establishing for that purpose a secret mission centre in Nairobi, Kenya. According to him, some authoritative studies had established that the main reason for Africa's 'inability to develop' was the existence of Africans. With the Africans replaced by Indians, 'who have proven apt to adapt and prosper on the African soil', the continent would drastically change for the better and become a more efficient provider of raw materials and a sustainable market for western industries. This would also help solve overpopulation in Asia. That cynical construction was abundantly quoted and commented upon in *Africa International*, a then Senegal-based monthly news magazine which I knew at that time only as a reader. The reporter covering the story obviously did not take it seriously. 'What is the next absurdity which will be bred in a white brain?' asked the commentator. That was the universal reaction I encountered concerning that story: bemusement.

As for me, I did not find it funny, but revealing of the sort of plans that could be cooked up by weird extremists. The rise of the American right wing, the so-called 'neo-conservatives', who led their country into a disastrous war against Iraq, from the fringe to the core of the White House, only reminds us that every idea, good or bad, can grow big enough to become operative. The fear of appearing as a ridiculous and paranoid victim of some conspiracy theory made me dismiss without investigation rumours about experiments being conducted in South Africa by the apartheid regime. Years later, in 2002, after the racist scourge was officially abolished, Dr Wouter Basson was standing trial in Johannesburg for a wide range of frightening crimes. With government funding and foreign assistance, including money from France and Switzerland, Basson had led a secret biological and chemical research programme called Project Coast. The purpose was to produce lethal substances that were ethnically selective and destructive, in order to reduce the black population. The exact number of people who died in these experiments is unknown, though by some estimates it was several thousands. And is it significant that, after a bizarre trial, Basson was released on 12 April 2002 and is still actively engaged in research? The fact remains that South Africa is considered the most AIDS-infected country on the continent and probably in the world.

Last but not least, my attitude toward AIDS was shaped by an emerging awareness of how the disease originated. First there was the statement of Jonathan Mann, the first 'Mr AIDS' appointed by the UN in the early 1990s. Taking part in a CNN programme in which he had to answer viewers' questions about the incurable and deadly illness, I heard him say that little was known so far about the AIDS virus, but it was clearly 'man made'. This has since been reinforced by a number of studies, including *Emerging Viruses*, by Dr Leonard G. Horowitz (Tetrahedron, 1996–9), which demonstrate the probability that 'these bizarre germs are laboratory creations, accidentally or even intentionally via tainted hepatitis, polio, and smallpox vaccines in the US and Africa – as numerous authorities have alleged'.

Unaware of these studies, the urban crowds in African streets and bars actually made all kinds of jokes to dismiss the new disease as a hoax, at least to begin with. The most popular one among Francophones has long been changing the meaning of the AIDS acronym. SIDA: 'Syndrome Inventé pour Décourager les Amoureux' – syndrome invented to discourage lovers. That was the time when our coverage of the phenomenon tended to be anecdotal, avoiding a focus on its overwhelmingly sinister aspects. We disguised our perplexity by publishing funny pictures and cartoons from the anti-AIDS campaigns in the main capitals. It was incredibly difficult to write frequent editorials on a subject that appeared to us as binary: firstly, AIDS equals death, because there is no therapy and it is irreversible; secondly, if you have not caught it yet, the only protection is a condom. We also experienced the same saturation as our African colleagues, fed up with AIDS being almost the sole issue worth reporting in the western media. There was definitely a sort of escapism in the low level of AIDS coverage in African newspapers. AIDS has been such a biblical calamity coming from nowhere and suddenly labelled 'African' that most of us, consciously or not, refused to be locked into an imposed damnation, a hopeless despair. Why add to the continuous Africa-bashing? South African president Thabo Mbeki, a staunch African patriot, shocked many throughout the world by developing a strange theory alleging the uselessness of the much-praised tri-therapy. As a matter of fact, from the day it was known, AIDS has been a silent killer, hidden behind shame and denial, from Abidjan to Johannesburg. Putting the topic on the headlines was a certain scarecrow for readers. Who wants to buy newspapers that keep telling you that you are lost? Or that repeat the worst and inexorable news such as growing infection figures and skyrocketing prices for medicines that do not cure but are to be taken for life? Even hopeful announcements are hopeless; some 'treatments' dropped from several thousand dollars a month, to 'only' several hundreds, which just meant from 'unthinkable' to 'unsustainable' for most AIDS victims. I remember a woman from Burundi telling me that, as she would never be able to afford to pay 100 dollars a month for the treatment, she had better not even bother to start, but should instead dedicate the money to her children's tuition until her certain death.

110

Over the years, the selfishness of the wealthy has not decreased and some daring countries like South Africa and Brazil have had to challenge the billion-dollar pharmaceutical industries to provide medicines at more appropriate rates for the most affected countries. The battle was just another chapter in the larger, nameless war conducted by the world's happy few against three-quarters of the world's population that is living in sheer poverty. By all accounts, the funds allowed internationally to confront AIDS are far from adequate. No doubt about it. Still – I have been recently concerned with another aspect of the programmed inefficiency in tackling the epidemic: the intolerable discrepancy between the funds collected and the money actually spent to combat AIDS. While so many non-governmental organizations are voicing demands for more funding, few seem to care about the volume of the resources actually available for deployment. According to an estimate for Cameroon and Congo, only 10–40 per cent of the money collected is operative for AIDS patients. Red tape, surrealistic procedures, low expectations – and people continue to die in massive numbers.

Yes, AIDS is a depressing, but also an acute reality. Either 'accidentally or intentionally', the deadly thing is out there, and Africans are having a hard time facing it in a way that enables them to survive as a people. A sense of emergency is hard to detect on a large scale throughout a battered continent that has lived for centuries with another remorseless and permanent killer, malaria. As the monster continues to grow, the good news is neither medical, nor financial, but consists of the spirit of millions that remains unbroken across Africa. The other day, I phoned a good friend in Yaounde, Cameroon. He

had just attended the funeral of his maid, a thirty-year-old
mother of two, who was killed by AIDS, and he was driving to
his farm with the two orphans whom he had immediately
adopted. 'We will just grow more food for all of us,' he said
simply, alluding to his own five children. And he added: 'Gosh
– this thing is decimating our people, I'm telling you!' That
was the first time he ever mentioned so clearly what should
be a number one concern.

Yes, AIDS is no longer to be ignored. I have tried to explain
my reticence, but silence and denial are no longer tenable. It's
taken a long time for me to come to grips with AIDS, to
overcome my reluctance and to make combating AIDS one of
my priorities as an activist promoting African development. As
a result, the Club Millennium, a Paris-based high-level think
tank on the African future, established in January 2005, made
the fight against AIDS a top issue. The Club Millennium is about
appropriation, about Africans developing their own vision of
how to solve their problems, in order to sustain the enduring
spirit of hope embodied in the African people themselves.

As a valuable support, the tremendous energy and
commitment of some individuals helps to revive the focus on
Africa. Bob Geldof is one of them. This year I attended a
gathering with the rebellious Irish artist at the British Embassy
in Paris. Once again, he had managed to shake some bureaucracy
upside-down and put Africa again on the world agenda. I first
saw Bob Geldof in 1985 in Burkina Faso ('the land of men of
integrity') where he met with the unforgettable president
Thomas Sankara, a very selfless, proud and charismatic leader
who was overthrown and killed because he was promoting
self-based development, and perceived as a danger for French

local interests. I remember watching those two dedicated and enthusiastic figures walking almost hand-in-hand, surrounded by a cheerful crowd, keeping hope alive. I suddenly felt that every miracle was possible. It occurred to me then and now that too much scepticism, though justified by a history of broken promises and failures, could prevent us from seizing and supporting real opportunities to push a long-standing cause forward. Why should we not recall, amid disaster and cynicism, that generosity, action and freedom of mind are also 'man-made'?

Websites
Africa International: www.africainternational.info
Club Millenium: www.clubmillenium.org

Reviving Democracy

MARTIN BELL

What a fragile, fitful and sometime thing our vaunted democracy is! We recommend it to others as the holy grail of all possible systems of governance, rather than what it really is, which is the least worst yet devised for our own societies. We even presume occasionally to impose it on others by force of arms, an experiment mysteriously confined so far to countries with oilfields rather than countries without.

The glory of democracy lies in its simplicity: alone among political systems, it provides the means at regular intervals of peaceful and popular regime change. When I was a Member of Parliament (MP), I was asked by the electoral authorities whether, for a mere £150, I wished to register myself as a political party, and if so to choose a suitable symbol for it on the ballot paper. I declined, since it seemed a waste of money, and a party of Independents is a contradiction in terms, like a convocation of hermits. But I know what the symbol would have been: the removal van outside 10 Downing Street on the morning after an election. It denotes a constitutional *coup d'état.*

In modern times, in the matter of attracting voters to the polls, the new democracies have put the old ones to shame. The right to vote by universal franchise has been most enthusiastically embraced by those to whom in the past it was but a distant dream. In the elections in Portugal in 1976

115

and in South Africa in 1994 the turnout was as close to 100 per cent as is realistically and statistically possible in any democratic country. No less remarkable was the 59 per cent turnout in Iraq in January 2005, in conditions of lawlessness and intimidation, and the virtual boycott of the poll by the Sunni minority. You do not have to be a supporter of the war, on the spurious grounds advanced for it, to admire the courage of the millions of Iraqis who voted.

The turnout figure was almost exactly the same as in the British General Election of 2001. And in 2005 it was only 2 per cent better. But with us there were neither deterrents nor excuses – no suicide bombs, threats of reprisals or drive-by shootings to keep us from the polling stations. The New Labour government was elected for its second term by a huge majority of seats but a minority of votes. The Iraqis' 59 per cent was an expression of the people's determination to make a fresh start; ours was a victory for the Apathy Party. It was as if we had done with democracy, like an old suit fallen out of fashion, and had somehow lost interest in it.

This troubled and puzzled me, but perhaps not as much as it would have done but for my four years in the House of Commons. I arrived there, somewhat out of the blue in May 1997, after an implausible campaign that took me from being candidate to MP in the space of only 24 days. It was a democratic accident – something done to me rather than by me. I had hardly set foot in the place before, and never entertained any ambition of belonging there. I was astonished to find, in the Members' cloakroom, a coat hanger with my name on it and a pink ribbon attached on which to hang my sword. I regarded Parliament, initially, with more veneration than I now believe it deserved. I still revere the institution – it is the people within it who are, in many cases, rather harder to admire.

That is not to condemn the House of Commons and all who ply the profession of politics within it. I found many new friends there, among MPs of all parties who were models of diligence, integrity and applied idealism. I followed them into the voting lobbies and was grateful for their advice. They included Richard Shepherd (Conservative), Frank Field (Labour), Menzies Campbell (Liberal Democrat), Alex Salmond (Scottish National Party) and Elfyn Llwyd (Plaid Cymru). Yet I would warrant there is a lower proportion of such people in the House than in the country at large. That is because of the realities of electioneering – the daunting difficulties of securing and holding a seat. Electoral politics is not for the faint-hearted: it inevitably involves a determination to succeed at others' expense. The losers will outnumber the winners, in any constituency, by between three and ten to one. It takes someone of driving ambition to overcome the obstacles and disappointments, first of being selected and then elected; to suffer the intrusive scrutiny of the press and the ill-will of rivals; and, even if successful, to face the prospect of defeat and unemployment every four years, as the electoral train approaches the buffers of the dissolution of Parliament. And how employable is a former Member of Parliament? Not very, according to the melancholy experience of so many who had convinced themselves (such is human nature) that, whatever the fate of their party, their personal popularity would see them through. Alas, not so. My favourite (and probably apoc- ryphal) concession speech by one of these overconfident MPs was short and to the point: 'The people have spoken ... the

117

bastards!' I even know a man who traded his vote for a peerage. MPs represent us, but are not representative of us. The 2005 general election saw a rise of almost 100 per cent in the votes for parties and candidates outside the mainstream.

One of the causes of the present disaffection, I believe, is that politicians are regarded as a breed apart. That is because, in many cases, they are a breed apart. Such a state of affairs has never existed before, in any general and systematic way, over the three centuries in which we have enjoyed any form of democracy, however limited the franchise. Now, for the first time in our history, we have a class of professional politicians who neither have practised nor are qualified for any other form of employment. Only the fickle opinion of the voters stands between them and the queue for the Jobseeker's Allowance. They are young men and women who leave university – usually, alas, still the same two universities – with good degrees and even better connections. Oxbridge winnows them. Politics attracts them. They are intensely ambitious, bright, articulate and personable. They first find work in the foothills of the profession as researchers to MPs or parties, and in the private offices of ministers. If they are skilful, fortunate and unfailingly on message, they may scale the heights to a winnable seat by the time they are 30, and then hold on to it for as many as ten terms of Parliament. They will shape the future and make the laws for children yet unborn. But what do they know of the world for which they legislate? The answer, too often, is just about the square root of nothing.

The voters, peering into the Westminster village from outside, cannot relate to the scene refracted to them through press and television. They are unimpressed by the jeering, sneering

118

and ritualized mock combat of the House. They perceive it to be inhabited by careerists rather than idealists – an alien place where professional politicians, fearful of losing their seats, will vote shamelessly against measures they believe in (if indeed they believe in anything), and for measures that they don't. In the company of the compliant, a mere abstention is seen as an act of bravery. It doesn't appear like that in the world outside. The people shrug their shoulders, and turn away.

The sense of disconnection is felt most acutely on issues of war and peace. The most serious decision a government can take is to commit its armed forces to war. Such a decision should be taken collectively in cabinet. It should be in accordance with international law, and fully and explicitly authorized by the UN Security Council. For political and practical reasons – not least, the morale of the armed forces being put in harm's way – it should command the overwhelming support of the people. The decision to go to war in Iraq did none of these things. It was the decision of one man, and his alone. In a post-war speech to 7 Armoured Brigade near Basra, Tony Blair described it as 'The action that I ordered'.

It is clear to everyone now, as it was to many at the time, that a great and historic mistake was made by those who could have prevented it. As the war drums sounded in February and March 2003, the Parliament and cabinet failed to exercise their most basic functions of oversight and scrutiny. Lord Butler, the former cabinet secretary who served three Prime Ministers, observed: 'I think we are a country where we suffer very badly from Parliament not having sufficient control over the executive, and that is a very grave flaw.' And Peter Hennessy, the leading academic authority on the office of the Prime Minister, laid

119

the blame on a supine cabinet which allowed itself to be overridden on the critical issue of the legal justification for war: 'For me, this and other accumulations of failures to scrutinize and question in the privacy of the cabinet room amounts to a dereliction of cabinet government comparable only to 1956 ... Like the permanent stain on Eden's reputation, it will not be eradicated from the memory of the Blair premierships for many years to come.'

The values of a liberal democracy are strong and will prevail if only we care for them enough. I would like to be able to say the same for its processes, but those are not necessarily so. The failures in the analysis and presentation of the intelligence used to justify the war did not come to light as the result of some great, confessional act of glasnost by Whitehall and Downing Street. They were illuminated by two inquiries forced on the government – Lord Hutton's by the death of Dr David Kelly, and Lord Butler's by the parallel investigation established by the Bush Administration, after the much-publicized weapons of mass destruction turned out not to exist. In Lord Hutton's case the evidence went one way, and the verdict (that no one was to blame except the BBC) went the other. Lord Butler, however, identified serious structural and collective failures in the processes of government, especially in Downing Street. He didn't name names or call for resignations. Yet in another era it would have been – and even in ours I believe that it *should have been* – a resignation issue: with the resignations starting at the top.

But no one did resign, except chairman Gavyn Davies, director-general Greg Dyke and reporter Andrew Gilligan of the BBC. Yet the BBC was largely right on the central issue of the embellishment and falsification of intelligence, and the government was wrong. The people knew this. It strengthened the BBC's standing and weakened the government's. It eroded public trust in public life. It widened still further the ever-growing chasm between the government and the governed.

The government then urged us to move on. And we have moved on, but not forgotten the war that was fought on a falsehood and in our name. We have drawn from it, I believe, a new sense of ownership of the political process, an understanding that the democracy we practise is *ours* not *theirs*, and a belief that politics is too important to be left to the politicians. We have discovered from experience that, unchecked, they are not to be trusted with it. Where others have tended to despair, I am optimistic that the processes of democracy may be, after all, self-correcting. Things don't always go from bad to worse. In some ways, the most remarkable result of the 2005 general election was the 10 per cent polled in Tony Blair's Sedgefield constituency by the Independent Reg Keys, father of a soldier killed in Iraq; and the defining moment of the election night was the restrained, dignified and passionate speech in which he held the Prime Minister to account for an unnecessary and unlawful war. This was the democratic process at its best.

We cannot afford a future like our past, and are not condemned to one, either – certainly not without a strenuous attempt to resist it. Party politics isn't part of the answer, but part of the problem. The young especially find themselves politically homeless. The parties that should be attracting them seem irrelevant to their ideals and aspirations. As the parties' old soldiers fade away, new recruits are not taking their place in the ranks. As a result the parties are no longer mass movements, but ramshackle coalitions of the old and the ambitious. It is not uncommon for a constituency association, the basic political unit at grass roots level, to be composed of only five activists, three of whom are at daggers drawn with the other two. The war in Iraq both reflected and accelerated the parties' decline. It was a failure not only of intelligence and diplomacy, but of party politics too. It was surely an offence against democracy that the principal opposition party supported and applauded the worst mistake by a British prime minister in nearly forty years. Even the Liberal Democrats seemed strangely hesitant, as if they feared being accused of opportunism for doing what was only right and reasonable. Had Paddy Ashdown still been their leader, he would have urged them to take the warpath.

Even on an argument of regime change, the costs of the war have been unacceptably high, both in terms of casualties and the global incubation of terrorism. The war party has been discredited. It is inconceivable that the Prime Minister could embark on the next military adventure in the American slipstream ('Sancho Panza to George Bush's Don Quixote' as Robin Cook described it) without being restrained by his colleagues in the cabinet and the House of Commons. In addition, I believe that the enfeeblement of political parties provides an opportunity for the individual citizen to make a difference, both inside and outside them, greater than at any time since World War II. Inside them, there is scope for a sort of benign 'entryism' – the phenomenon that occurs when a constituency association is taken over by groups with their own agenda. The agenda in this case is real democracy, a return to first principles and the indictment – if necessary the replacement – of MPs who have failed in their most basic duty of holding the executive to account. Their identities are no secret: the names are listed in the Hansard of 18 March 2003.

Beyond the stockades of party politics, the Independents are stirring. The most remarkable result of 2001 was the success of Dr Richard Taylor, who carried all before him in Kidderminster on a campaign to save the hospital. He prevailed against Labour and the Conservatives by a margin of 17,000 votes, the largest majority of any opposition MP in England. The three Independent essentials were all present: an unpopular incumbent, a good cause and a well-known candidate. But Dr Taylor was no celebrity politician. As a physician he had probably treated 12,000 of his voters. They trusted him. They re-elected him in 2005.

The medical analogy is useful. Independents are the Alka-Seltzer of the body politic. They provide a remedy when the parties of the status quo fail. So it was in Kidderminster in 2001 and Tatton in 1997. After the re-adoption and defeat of Neil Hamilton, the Tatton Conservative Association attracted many new members determined that such a fiasco should not happen again. I never expected them to thank me for it, but I helped to restore the party's constituency fortunes.

Party politicians regularly complain that they are held in such low esteem because of a malevolent press campaign against them; the government's own henchmen in the media, like John Lloyd of the *Financial Times*, join in this doleful lament. They protest too much. That is not how journalism works. An honest politician isn't newsworthy – at least, we haven't got to that point yet – but a corrupt politician is.

The remedy is simple. If our elected representatives wish to be trusted more, they could always try behaving better. For a start, at government level, they could forswear pre-emptive warfare as a policy option. As MPs, they could look more to their standards than their privileges; they could be more scrupulous over conflicts of interest, more frugal in their expense claims, less hospitable to millionaires seeking influence or high honours, less cavalier in the treatment of those (like Elizabeth Filkin) whose task it is to regulate their conduct. In short, they should see themselves as others see them. The central issue is public trust in public life. It always has been; and in principle, nothing has changed since Edmund Burke analysed the 'present discontents' of the 1770s: 'The great and only foundation of government is the confidence of the people.'

So it is today. The people have a right to enjoy such confidence, and the politicians a duty to restore it.

Celebrating the Heroes of Democracy

DAN PLESCH

> Have we not an equal interest with the men of this
> nation, in those liberties and securities contained in the
> Petition of Right and the other good laws of the land.
> *Women's Petition to Parliament 1649*

Freedom is under attack from extremist fundamentalists who
would run our lives according to ancient texts and from
governments that talk about democracy but abuse it both at
home and abroad. In the end we may find ourselves unable
to act to break the escalating cycle of violence, imprisoned in
a web of CCTV surveillance, detention without trial and reporting
restrictions. We take our freedoms for granted. In forgetting to
treasure them we risk losing them.

When soldiers prepare for battle they are often inspired by
their regiment's historic victories. We need to draw similar
inspiration from those who won the political battles that
established the freedoms we now enjoy. Unfortunately, we know
too little about them to be encouraged. The British government
and the media keep going on about the need to defend
democracy, but it is like asking people to support a football
team when they are told nothing about its past glories. We
hear more than enough about 'The Royals' but nothing about

125

'The Democrats'. We have to look back to our ancestors in the eras of Charles I, Napoleon and Victoria. Almost by chance I discovered a family history of democratic activism in the mid-nineteenth century that has helped guide my own political work today.

Without this cultural memory, we cannot draw strength from the successes of previous generations in preparing for future challenges. In other areas of national life, past events such as the Battle of Britain strongly influence the way we think about what we should do today. Today we need to defend democracy, but it should come as no surprise that we have difficulty rallying a unified team spirit when we lack a sense of our democratic heritage. This lack of democratic history amounts to a loss of memory. We need to rebuild our memories to better understand and tackle the future. We should create a new branch of the heritage industry to celebrate our democratic heritage as much as we do our military and regal history. The whole panoply of heritage must be brought to bear to greet the visitor and to educate our children and ourselves. There can be democracy trails and walks, blue plaques, experiential museums, re-enactments, son et lumière, memorials, postage stamps, exhibitions – all perhaps co-ordinated with a new web-portal linked to others overseas. All this might lead to the opening of a new international museum of democracy to commemorate the eight-hundredth anniversary of Magna Carta in 1215, just ten years away.

The heritage deficit
Britain is a nation that celebrates its past like no other. The country's museums, memorials and historic events are a matter

of pride, and rightly so. They form an important part of the nation's sense of identity. They are also a prominent part of a tourist industry generating billions in income for the country and projecting an image of Britain around the world. Our democratic heritage is hard to find amongst the plethora of historical attractions even though the country is world famous for its democracy. The House of Commons is often referred to as the Mother of Parliaments. Its offspring can' be found in the United States constitution and in parliaments around the world. But visitors and immigrants to Britain are surprised how little there is on show to celebrate these achievements. There are exceptions such as the People's History Museum in Manchester and statues of Oliver Cromwell and Winston Churchill outside Parliament. But London is mostly populated with statues of dukes and generals. The celebration of Churchill's defence of democracy leaves him unjustly isolated as the main champion of the democratic cause in Britain's heritage.

There are no prominent memorials to the Parliamentary cause of the 1640s, let alone to the Levellers. Nor to the Chartists, the Suffragettes or even Simon de Montfort, the man credited with assembling the first House of Commons in the thirteenth century. There is no national museum of democracy. There is no British equivalent of America's 4th of July or France's Bastille Day, which celebrate the people's liberation from tyranny. Even the memorial to Magna Carta at Runnymede was built by the Americans.

Television and the cinema provide a procession of royal and imperial histories but ignore the people who gave us the freedoms we enjoy today. And they gloss over the tyranny that underpinned the reigns of so many monarchs and of the British

127

Empire itself. It seems almost in bad taste to mention how badly the poor and political and religious dissenters were treated in times past. Their role in overcoming oppression and creating the democratic values we cherish has been ignored.

In France, by way of contrast, the revolution is celebrated and the tyranny of the Bourbon kings made clear. In Britain we learn much of the savage use of the guillotine in the Terror of the French Revolution. Books like Baroness Orczy's *The Scarlet Pimpernel* and Charles Dickens's *A Tale of Two Cities* have been turned into films showing the awful fate of the French aristocracy at the hands of the revolutionaries. But in Britain we hear little of the tyrannical behaviour of these self-same aristocrats towards the people, and nothing of the massacres perpetrated by the aristocrats to crush previous rebellions in France. For many years there had been revolts against arbitrary laws and taxes imposed by France's Bourbon kings. These had always been suppressed with great savagery by whichever Louis happened to be absolute ruler at the time.

This amnesia about the brutality of the pre-democratic era is even more marked when we look at British history. As well as celebrating what the Tudors, Victorians and other monarchs did *for* us, we might look at what the Tudors and Victorians did *to* us. For wealthy men who went to the Church of England, life was fine and they enjoyed political rights. But if you were female, Catholic or Methodist, for much of Britain's history you had few rights at all. Women could not own property after marriage until the mid-nineteenth century or vote as of natural right until 1928, two inhuman restrictions that seem unimaginable today. Right up to the middle of the nineteenth

128

century people were executed for minor offences such as stealing bread. Until 1948 businessmen had two votes in local elections, one in their own right and another for owning a business.

The changes, when they did come, did not come easily. A history of the Chartist movement written in 1854 by the Sunderland doctor R. C. Gammage is punctuated with accounts of arrests, imprisonment and deaths in gaol. And this was at a time when the idea of one man, one vote was supported by only a handful of Members of Parliament.

Unsung heroes

I have chosen examples of unsung heroes from the time of Charles I, from the era of the Napoleonic wars and from Victorian Britain. My examples are not intended to be a comprehensive history of democracy, or even a comprehensive list from British history – there are none of the barons who forced Magna Carta of 1215 from King John, nor any of the Prime Ministers who in the end put voting rights into the law in the later nineteenth and early twentieth centuries. Neither have I described those figures who are allowed a brief mention in our history, but are never accorded the prominence they deserve as trail-blazers: Wat Tyler and John Ball and their revolutionary rhyme, 'When Adam delved and Eve span, Who was then the gentleman?' Nor do I discuss the early trade unionists or the Suffragettes. I have selected people who are, I think, virtually unknown outside small groups of enthusiasts and academics, but whose achievements were great.

Equal rights: the Leveller men and women – Thomas Rainsborough, John Lilburne and Katherine Chidley
The English revolution of the 1640s created the first republic in a major European state. The Civil War arose as a result of a confrontation between King Charles I and Parliament. Charles was seeking to abolish Parliament's right to control direct taxation of the people and establish the sort of absolute monarchy that the kings of France and other Continental monarchs were in the process of creating. In Parliament itself a strong Protestant – Puritan – element pressed in turn for greater rights for Parliament. The Civil War produced many deaths and a radicalization of the people and especially of soldiers who wanted to have equal political rights with the wealthy.

The republic was led by Oliver Cromwell, but shortly after his death, the monarchy was restored under Charles II in a settlement that limited the power of the King and gave taxation and other key powers to Parliament, but the deal also denied political rights to most people.

There had been a strong popular movement for equal political rights not just for men but also for women. The high point of the new democratic movement came in the late 1640s and was associated with the Leveller party. At the same time there was a myriad of religious and political groups arguing for and publishing many different points of view. The Levellers had strong support within the Parliamentary Army and thus were able to ensure that their ideas were given serious attention by the Parliamentary leadership. One key debate between their leaders, Cromwell, and other members of the Council who governed the Parliamentary Army happened in 1647. This took

130

place that October at Putney, outside London, at a crucial point in the Civil War. The King had been defeated and the victorious Parliamentarians began to debate both how he should be treated and what the new political framework for the country should look like. Thomas Rainsborough, a Leveller MP, argued:

> I think that the poorest he that is in England hath a life to live as the greatest he; and therefore truly, Sir, I think it's clear that every man that is to live under a Government ought first by his own consent to put himself under that Government; and I do think that the poorest man in England is not at all bound in a strict sense to that Government that he hath not had a voice to put himself under.

The reply he received from General Ireton, the leading general after Cromwell in the Parliamentary Army, was scathing. Ireton argued that only people with property mattered and, as for the rest, the fact that they were born in England gave them no standing. People had no innate or natural rights in England simply because they were English. His view won for the next two hundred years in England, though for a shorter time in America, France and a few other countries.

The Leveller manifesto, *An Agreement of the People*, is the first clear statement of democratic principles in the English language. It calls for votes for all adult males, the supremacy of Parliament, freedom of religion and the abolition of church taxes. Their work was accompanied by a strong movement for female emancipation, led by some of the wives of the leading male Levellers.

One leader, Katherine Chidley, was a successful business-woman in her own right. She and a reported ten thousand other Leveller women delivered a petition to Parliament in 1649 which declared: 'Have we not an equal interest with the men of this nation, in those liberties and securities contained in the Petition of Right [this was Parliament's statement against the King], and the other good laws of the land.'

In political terms, the achievements of these people eclipse those of the King who came after them – Charles II, whose principal claims to fame are not getting executed and shagging anything in a skirt. However, if you punch 'Tourism, London, Putney Debates' into the Internet you will be lucky to find half a dozen entries, and most take you to the local museum of the borough of Wandsworth, where the debates struggle to be noticed alongside such epoch-shattering matters as the Surrey Iron Railway and Building the Suburbs. So I set out for St Mary's church in Putney with my wife, Lindsay, and nephew Jethro, to see how this great moment in world history is remembered.

And there on the gates of the church is a sign where the parish priest, the Reverend Dr Giles Fraser, states: 'Famously, St. Mary's was the venue for the Putney debates where Cromwell and his army laid the foundations for modern democratic politics', though the battered A3 laminated notice and the rather small type do not quite seem to rise to the occasion. There is no Leveller museum featuring a re-enactment of the debates between Cromwell and the troops, no 'world hero' figurines of Lilburne and Chidley, no 'Democracy Started Here' neon signs along the High Street, not even a 'The Leveller' pub opposite the church. Jethro pointed at a green across the way and suggested a democracy theme park. And why not?

132

Overthrowing imperial slavery: Toussaint L'Ouverture
My next choice of unsung heroes comes from the era of the French Revolution, Wellington and Napoleon. My hero is Toussaint L'Ouverture, the successful leader of a slave revolt on the Caribbean island of Santo Domingo, now Haiti.

We hear much about Spartacus, the slave leader who fought the Roman Empire in Italy 2,000 years ago, and whose revolt was crushed, leading to crucifixion for him and his followers. But although Toussaint also died at the hands of his enemies, he had already won the greatest victory ever achieved by slaves and made himself into one of the great generals of the Napoleonic era. His country has been independent ever since.

To understand his achievement you have to consider the place and times he lived in. The sugar trade from the Caribbean to Europe was hugely profitable. England, France and Spain repeatedly fought for control of the islands during the eighteenth century, and the trade itself was of comparable importance to the economies of Europe as is the importation of oil from the Middle East today. The sugar was produced on slave plantations in conditions of savagery that are hard to comprehend.

The slave revolt led by Toussaint broke out in the aftermath and in imitation of the French Revolution of 1789. Initially welcomed by the revolutionary leaders in Paris, the slave armies had to fight off attacks by the Spanish and British Empires and then, after an attempt to reintroduce slavery by France, an army sent by Napoleon himself. The most readable account of Toussaint's success is to be found in *The Black Jacobins*, a very political biography written by C. L. R. James in 1963.

In the middle of the wars freeing Haiti, Toussaint evicted the British General Maitland, but concluded a treaty favourable to both sides. The *London Gazette* of 12 November 1798 noted: 'No event has happened in the history of the present war of more interest to Great Britain than the treaty which General Maitland has made with the black general Toussaint upon the evacuation of Santo Domingo.'

His military achievement is described in J. W. Fortescue's *History of the British Army*, written between 1899 and 1906. Fortescue tersely comments that: 'England's soldiers had been sacrificed, her treasure squandered, her influence in Europe weakened ... The secret of England's impotence for the first six years of the war may be said to lie in two fateful words, St Domingo.' The importance of this part of the war is neglected in most modern histories, airbrushed out of history. To be polite, the omission is a simple self-absorption of European historians with the familiar battles of the Peninsular War and Waterloo; to be blunt, it is simple racism to deny the achievement of black slaves in defeating every army the European empires could find to send against them. Fortescue's explanation for the fact that this episode – and Maitland's agreement to withdraw from the island – had been forgotten, is clear:

> The bare notion of an agreement with a negro, much more with a chief of insurgent negroes, was an abhorrence to every white man in the West Indies. The proceeding therefore was bound to gain him the enmity of every planter in the British tropical possessions, of every West Indian proprietor or agent in England or elsewhere, of every naval and military commander, of every Emigrant and every royalist.

134

Much is made of the role that disease played in defeating the Spanish, British and French forces sent to suppress the revolt, but Fortescue makes clear that the successful Spartacists won with military skill. His account is punctuated with such phrases as 'Toussaint bore down with sudden swiftness and overwhelming strength'; Rigaud, 'the mulatto chief, with astonishing industry and labour, had constructed military roads on every side, so that the natural defences of the place had been broken down.'

After the British defeat came the French Empire of Napoleon, bent on restoring French ownership and slavery where possible. They too wasted men and treasure, and as a result Napoleon abandoned all his plans in the Americas, agreeing to sell the Mississippi valley to the US. Toussaint and the revolutionaries in Haiti had first been greeted as comrades by the revolutionaries in Paris, but Napoleon had other ideas and sent a force of over twenty thousand troops to the island, either to trick the free blacks back into servitude or, if necessary, to conquer them. Napoleon's general succeeded in capturing Toussaint through a trick, but this only increased the determination of Toussaint's colleagues and soldiers. Napoleon's order for the campaign is quite broadly instructive as to how 'realist' politics can be conducted.

As a society we should pay attention to the heroism of a general of the Napoleonic era who was fighting for freedom as we already do to Wellington, Nelson and Napoleon himself, who were all fighting for political systems that denied human rights to the subjects of their empires.

135

Freedom of the press: James Watson, Henry Hetherington and Richard Moore

A free press is a vital part of a free society. And yet until the middle of the Victorian era, the press was not free in England. It was heavily taxed with the express purpose of preventing people without money from reading. Reading would produce knowledge and knowledge a population that made political demands. Such repressive instincts still exist in the world. Much to my surprise I heard exactly this view expressed recently by a young Mexican lawyer as we sat on the sidelines of a football match. After I politely enquired how things were in his country, he blurted out that 'democracy sucks' and went into a diatribe as to how for years the government had kept people ignorant, but now, stupidly, they had been given education and were making political demands.

In England, hundreds went to prison for flouting the tax on printing. The same group were also responsible for producing the People's Charter.

But I should declare my interest. Richard Moore and James Watson were ancestors of mine. Both worked for decades for democratic rights in England, but even within the family their efforts had almost been forgotten. One Chartist turned historian of the movement wrote of Moore: 'His name is not prominent in histories, yet to him, with Hetherington and Watson, more than to any other men, we are indebted for a free press in England.'

In early and mid-Victorian England there was a prohibitive tax on printing the news. This was designed to stop the poor from becoming educated. Those who flouted the law as Hetherington did in particular were imprisoned. Moore founded and became Chairman of 'The Association for Promoting the Repeal of the Taxes on Knowledge' which counted amongst its members leading radical Victorians such as Richard Cobden and John Bright. He was also amongst the first signatories when the Charter was first published in 1838.

Two hundred years after the Levellers, British men and women were still having to demand the natural rights that we now take for granted. Momentum for political reform had gathered pace in England in the aftermath of the American and French Revolutions and in 1832 a Reform Act was passed. The history of the campaign for this reform has been eloquently described by Edward Pearce in his recent book *Reform!* But the 1832 Act still kept the vast majority of men and all women from voting. In response to the failure of the Reform Act to emancipate normal people a new political movement began. It drew up a Charter in the Leveller tradition, drafted by William Lovett and James Watson. The Charter caught on and millions of people signed the petitions to Parliament. The Chartist movement continued until the late 1840s but it was another fifty to seventy years before even general voting rights for men were established.

The Chartists feature in our history books, but not in our heritage. Surely those who wrote the Charter might be celebrated. I have had passed down to me the cards printed to mark James Watson's death in 1874. These cards record his birth in Malton, Yorkshire, his home in Burns' Cottage, Norwood and his shop on Paternoster Row outside St Paul's Cathedral. By happy chance the redevelopment of Paternoster Square has included a grand column with blank spaces awaiting inscription. What better use than to inscribe the names of those who gave

137

us our freedom to vote and to print what we like. The new
square lends itself to all sorts of imaginative activities to draw
in those already bound for the cathedral.

Perhaps the Newspaper Publishers' Association could hold
an annual event in conjunction with the BBC and other
broadcasters to celebrate those who established the free press.

The impact of ignorance about our democratic history
To defend and strengthen our freedoms we must commemorate
those who gave them to us, just as we honour those who
fought in war to preserve them.

Government and other organizations should work together
to create a range of connected and mutually reinforcing
initiatives. Bank holidays should be designated to celebrate the
story of how we won our freedom before the law, our right to
free speech and the right to elect our government. They might
be called Magna Carta Day, Leveller Day or Suffragette Day.
Each should become a focus for educational and civic activity.

An annual series of special stamps should be created
featuring leading democratic campaigners. There is no shortage
of candidates. Several could be chosen each year.

The citizenship component of the new national curriculum
should place a greater emphasis on historic events and
milestones, including Magna Carta, and the special importance
of the fact that in England men were free before the law, when
for centuries the norm in most of Europe was that men were
serfs. British education should also do more to show the
emergence of the Commons in the seventeenth century as a
source of resistance to absolute monarchy; the Leveller call for
universal suffrage; the growing pressure for reform in the

138

eighteenth century; the successful export of democratic ideas to North America and later to the Dominions; the Chartist movement and the rise of the trade unions in the nineteenth century; and women's suffrage and the final removal of property qualifications in 1928. In further and higher education prominence should be given to the history of democracy, both academically and by celebrating the contribution to democracy made by past graduates. It is possible to take a degree in sports science or philosophy but I know of no degrees in democracy.

There is a great opportunity for the arts to make a contribution. National museums and galleries should stage special exhibitions and new permanent features. These might highlight the revolutionary politics of poets such as Samuel Taylor Coleridge, John Keats, John Milton and Percy Bysshe Shelley and of writers such as Mary Wollstonecraft and Thomas Paine. The National Portrait Gallery could give greater emphasis to democrats. The Public Record Office's exhibition of police files on radicals from the eighteenth century is a good example of neglected but exciting material that could be turned into popular historical drama.

We should build an international museum of democracy that would feature how Britain's democratic heritage influenced and was influenced by events in other countries. It could have much of the grisly appeal of existing museums such as the London Dungeon, because execution, beating, imprisonment and transportation were all meted out as punishments to early democrats. Schoolchildren could engage in games in which they could see what would have been done to them in previous times for speaking and acting as they do today – whether in criticizing the Queen, having to pay an exorbitant sum to buy anything printed or even shoplifting.

Local museums, government and associations should make more of people from their area who made a contribution to this part of our history. These have often been forgotten. For example, Ware in Hertfordshire hosted a key Leveller convention in the 1640s; other gatherings sought equality for women. The demands of these conventions were rejected by those in power for nearly three hundred years, and advocating what was on the Leveller agenda was a criminal offence until the nineteenth century.

It may be said that the British are already too immersed in their history and should spend their energies looking forwards rather than forever backwards. It may be said that public money should not be spent on celebrating obscure malcontents who had little respect for law and order. But so long as public money is spent on history we should rescue from obscurity those who created today's laws and order. How can we nurture a sense of democracy in a country that celebrates its monarchs and ignores the first people who wished to be citizens rather than subjects?

It will be important to provide a non-party-political approach and recall ancient rights of freedom as well as the more recent advent of universal suffrage. 'People do not appreciate what they are given, only what they have gained through their own efforts.' This adage has a lot of value, and it certainly informs much of contemporary government policy. It may even be true of democracy: deprived of knowing the achievements of their great-grandparents in winning democracy, people can much more easily see it as something of a handout rather than a precious jewel dearly won. A remedy presents itself.

More than three million Britons signed the People's Charter in the final major campaign of 1849 and, although the Charter failed, its core programme became adopted by the Liberal and Radical parties and passed into law as male suffrage for the middle and lower-middle classes in 1867 and 1884 respectively. In the early 1900s the movement for votes for women – the Suffragettes – attracted similar support.

Following the natural course of events, the descendants of the millions of Suffragettes and of the Chartists of 1848 now make up most of the population. It would make a wonderful national project for schools and colleges in conjunction with the government departments of education, culture and constitutional affairs to search out all such ancestors to whom we owe our rights today. Tragically, until 1950 Parliament burnt all the petitions that it received, so finding out about our democratic ancestors will entail a rather more complicated search through the archives of national and local associations and newspapers than simply examining the petitions of the time.

In the coming years there are a number of anniversaries that can focus the creation of a national celebration of our democratic heritage. The year 2005 marks the centenary of the Reform Acts of 1905, which deserve rather more celebration than the bicentenary of the Battle of Trafalgar. And 2015 is the eight-hundredth anniversary of Magna Carta – a suitable date to open an international museum of democracy.

The imaginative celebration of our democracy will help us strengthen our freedoms and provide the basis upon which we can renew our democracy for the future. Participating in running the country should seem as normal as placing a bet.

YOU'RE HISTORY!

Both need good judgement and luck and can soak up as much study as you want to put in.

I am lucky because I have in my front room a cabinet made by one of the early Chartists. When I think that change is too difficult, that I can just turn on the telly and leave it to others, there are Moore and Watson asking whether my problems are greater than theirs – when they could not vote and got thrown in jail for publishing untaxed news. There are millions of others who are being denied the example of their similarly heroic ancestors. Role models, we are told, are crucial to moral development. We must resurrect out democratic ancestors as role models for the future.

Further Reading
D. Plesch, *The Beauty Queen's Guide to World Peace*, (London: Politico's, 2004), from which this piece is drawn.

Website
www.danplesch.net

Cinema in Control and Conscience: Moviemakers from 'Double V' to McCarthyism

EVAN HEIMLICH

Washington's mid-twentieth-century involvement in Hollywood not only provided the political baptisms of Californians Richard Nixon and Ronald Reagan, but also yielded heroes of social progress. Moviemaking came to the fore as a racial minority and a political minority of Americans each fought stigmatization as 'Negroes' and 'Communists'. Carlton Moss countered defamation with *The Negro Soldier*, and the Hollywood Ten resisted the criminalization of dissent, each by asserting their freedom of speech as moviemakers.

Ever since President Woodrow Wilson in 1915 famously called *Birth of a Nation* 'history written in lightning', Washington has aimed to channel the movies' power to shape the public. During World War II, Washington manipulated Hollywood's scripts, used Hollywood stars and movies for propaganda, and even produced its own movies.

Why have the movies mattered? American movies matter not only for their simple dominance of the world's screens from World War I through to at least the 1950s. They matter firstly because cinema developed a new, common language of global modernity as it emerged. Thus, as America's pioneering

143

domination of international business, the Hollywood movie industry led the twentieth century's corporate stabilization of markets. A stabilized market of moviegoers became 'the public'. As Hollywood cinema has shaped people's sense of 'publicness' itself, mass culture has become more of a battlefield, through propagandist struggles over movies. These struggles would mark America's transition from World War II to the Cold War.

But first, as America entered World War II, in February 1942 President Franklin Delano Roosevelt ordered the imprisonment of about 100,000 innocent Japanese Americans without trial, thereby grossly violating the Bill of Rights' 5th-Amendment guarantee of due process of law. Notwithstanding this travesty, from 1943 to 1945 Washington tended to salute the Bill of Rights. Soon Washington was even championing racial tolerance.

As a result of such policies, in 1943 Washington produced a movie, code-numbered OF-51: *The Negro Soldier*. This movie's release significantly advanced a racial minority's right to speak through the movies.

By 1944 President Roosevelt, envisioning the dawn of a new, post-war day, called for augmenting the Bill of Rights with a 'Second Bill of Rights'. Roosevelt's State of the Union address – which, Cass Sunstein notes, shaped the Universal Declaration of Human Rights – portrayed 'external threats as a reason to *broaden* the class of rights enjoyed by those at home'. Roosevelt called for security, including 'moral security'.

Washington's wartime policies and rhetoric buoyed Hollywood on a rising current of co-operation with the war effort. But after victory in World War II came the Cold War, with which Washington's divisive current swelled to power. During the McCarthy Era, America's conservative leaders and their

144

supporters narrowed the protections of the Bill of Rights, to make more of their political opponents increasingly vulnerable. As the proving ground for its campaign of intimidation, Washington targeted Hollywood.

As if the imprisonment of about 100,000 Californians – for the 'offence' of Japanese heritage – somehow had helped defeat the fascist threat abroad, Washington's response to the Soviet threat featured an attack on another swath of Californians. Washington now portrayed a severe, national threat from 'Communists and sympathizers' particularly in Hollywood.

By 1947 James Agee perceived the stakes of this domestic conflict. In *The Nation*, Agee predicted that the civilization in which he lived 'will destroy itself either by failure to shut out enough of its enemies, or by definitively violating its own nature in its primordial efforts to defend itself, or by shutting out, along with some of the more conspicuous of its enemies, all those who might conceivably preserve within it some last flicker of humanistic sanity.' Today – as authorities increasingly use 'security' measures to secure their own control of their domains – social critics cite these same high stakes.

During World War II, America's war against external threats – German, Italian, and Japanese fascists – dovetailed with the goals of some champions of domestic social progress. Leaders of African America worked to bring a 'Double V' – not only victory abroad, but also victory over racist oppression at home. Because Hollywood movies had long tended to abuse, slander, mock, sideline, and/or omit blacks, the NAACP (National Association for the Advancement of Colored People) had been lobbying Hollywood studios to alleviate the movies' rampant

145

racism. But Hollywood resisted calls for it to tamper with its formulas pandering to the markets it already had stabilized. Then, as Japan and Germany were giving racism a bad name, as it were, Washington increasingly aimed to highlight America's tolerance, by portraying blacks in a better light. Thomas Cripps's magisterial *Making Movies Black* reveals the historical developments in which wartime necessities emboldened American moviemaking.

During World War II Hollywood produced a few movies opposing fascism abroad, but tiptoed around the issue of racist intolerance at home. On the need for domestic social change, Washington took the lead.

To ease its deployment of African-American troops, and as an antidote to divisive propaganda from Japan, the US Army produced a movie. Japanese propaganda was actively attempting to discourage blacks – who constituted 10 per cent of the US Army – from fighting 'the white man's war'. This tactic exploited existing unrest on the part of both blacks and whites. The Army's own surveys revealed that bitter, racial resentments 'impaired' the Army, in particular, the Army's own segregation and discrimination against blacks was hindering its training, morale, and deployment of troops. But, rather than tackling the oppressive policies, Army leaders aimed a pro-Negro movie or two at improving the Army's race relations, at least until the war was won.

Carlton Moss, a young, well-connected black producer, had lobbied Washington to make a pro-Negro movie. In 1942 Washington's Office of War Information (OWI) tapped him to write *The Negro Soldier*, and involved both the NAACP and Hollywood. Thanks mainly to the work of Moss, who also starred in the movie, *The Negro Soldier* emphasized the respectability of blacks' role in US society.

As Japanese warplanes strafe Hawaii's Pearl Harbor, on a burning battleship a black sailor leaps into the seat of a fallen, dead gunner, and fires on the attackers. With the leap of a heroic black actor to the centre of the silver screen, this scene in the forty-minute docudrama advanced African Americans' portrayals in the mass media. Towards countering Hollywood's wholesale defamation of African Americans, Carlton Moss asserted his freedom of speech.

As *The Negro Soldier* portrayed service and courage, opportunity and respect, it re-enacted the heroism of one black man, messman Dorie Miller. Dorie Miller's story had leapt from the deck of the USS *West Virginia* to America's black press, to the white press, to the silver screen. Because the US Navy had restricted all black sailors to posts in food service rather than combat, Miller's heroism came to symbolize new promise for America's social progress. Reviewing *The Negro Soldier* in *The Nation*, James Agee told his readers that for many viewers of this movie, 'the screen presentation of the Negro as something other than a clown, a burnt-cork Job, or a plain imbecile, will be more startling and more instructive than we are likely to imagine.'

Though it did not challenge segregation at all, nor even challenge racism directly, still this movie achieved Washington's primary goals and more, largely because of who released it. *The Negro Soldier* proclaimed itself 'presented by' the Signal Corps, and proudly bore the eagle logotype of the US Army. The Army's own studies showed that the great majority of black and white servicemen welcomed *The Negro Soldier*, and moreover reported that their own racial regard improved after watching it. So during 1944 and 1945 the Army showed it to all new recruits. Eventually OWI released copies of *The Negro Soldier* for civilian distribution.

Though *The Negro Soldier* played in less than half as many commercial theatres as did newsreels or Hollywood's feature-films, its other networks of distribution helped to change the role of movies. In those days home viewing was not an option, and few libraries had begun collecting movies. But after the US Army established some movies' respectability in education, school libraries began to archive and offer copies of *The Negro Soldier* and other movies. Subsequently movies in schools inspire and teach billions of teachers and students. In significant ways *The Negro Soldier* (OF-51) made a difference.

As social conservatives frowned on implications that the Bill of Rights applied equally to all Americans, one complained that *The Negro Soldier* epitomized the '"cult of equality" that had mushroomed in federal agencies during the war'. Yet overall, Carlton Moss himself 'ended the war feeling OF-51 had led white people to ask "What right [do we have] to hold back people of that caliber".'

Meanwhile during 1942 and 1943 an adaptation of Hollywood's war-movie genre had emerged, bringing to the screen Hollywood's new and improved stereotype, in a more prominent role for the black man: the lone, token black amidst a white circle of heroes. Then came further progress. After audiences had welcomed *The Negro Soldier* – the first Hollywood-style movie made primarily to deliver a social message – in its wake Hollywood itself dived into the waters the Army had proven safe. Hollywood launched a cycle of

148

melodramatic 'message movies' with themes of anti-racism and anti-anti-Semitism, including *Crossfire*, *Pinky*, and *Gentleman's Agreement*.

But in Washington, to replace the fascist enemies on the Right, leaders substituted a new enemy on the Left. As leaders demonized the Soviet Union, anti-fascism yielded to ferocious anti-Communism. Now Americans on the Left could no longer ride on wartime anti-fascism. Riding high on Cold War anti-Communism came the conservatives.

Pressure co-ordinated from Washington threatened Hollywood studios. They could have withstood Washington's pressure by itself, but the studio bosses feared threats, by organizations including Christian groups, to boycott certain studios' movies. As *Variety* reported, Hollywood dropped plans for more '"message pictures," like hot coals'. California Republican Richard Nixon suggested what kind of movies Hollywood should make: though anti-Communist movies consistently failed to attract enough audience for profitability, nevertheless the studios obediently produced more than fifty of them.

Hollywood became chilled to the bone by fear of the US Congress's HUAC – the House Un-American Activities Committee – and its collaborators. Larry Ceplair and Steven Englund, authors of *The Inquisition in Hollywood: Politics in the Film Community, 1930–1960*, tell how HUAC's inquisition focused on Hollywood screenwriters.

To avoid becoming targets for direct persecution, across America leaders of the Left, including labour unions, almost entirely capitulated and collaborated with HUAC. This Cold War regime lasted more than a decade, until Richard Nixon lost the

149

dead-heat 1960 presidential election to John F. Kennedy. Yet all through these decades, pockets of resisters struggled to affirm their rights. One such resister was Dalton Trumbo, a screenwriter.

While it awarded a medal to Carlton Moss, Washington geared up much worse treatment for Hollywood's vanguard anti-fascists, including Trumbo and other top screenwriters. Because they had struggled against fascism for years before the US declared war on the Axis, their preparation had enabled them to spur America's anti-fascism with movies such as *The Master Race* (1941), *Sahara* (1943), *Destination Tokyo* (1944), *Thirty Seconds Over Tokyo* (1944), *Pride of the Marines* (1945), *Hotel Berlin* (1945), and *Crossfire* (1947). But after the switch to anti-Communism, Washington prepared to bully these screenwriters who had fought fascism too early, and too lastingly, for Washington's liking.

On 21 September 1947, the House Un-American Activities Committee subpoenaed forty-three Hollywood moviemakers, including nineteen targeted as left-wingers, to testify in Washington. The nineteen were diverse 'activists, not career revolutionaries or ideological martyrs'. They plotted no violence or sabotage, neither were they spies. All but three were screenwriters. And most had been involved with the Communist Party of the USA (CPUSA). America's realignment from anti-fascism to anti-Communism cut them out, but their involvement with the CPUSA had not made these moviemakers any kind of criminal. American law had considered the CPUSA a political party. It was legal. In many Hollywood communities of the late 1930s, supporting the CPUSA was an accepted political option. The CPUSA's supporters had not witnessed the totalitarian atrocities of Stalin, but had seen the atrocities of American capitalism especially during the Great Depression. During World War II, the Soviet Union was a key American ally, not an enemy.

Hollywood's CPUSA supporters were not endangering the security or freedom of the United States. But HUAC's attack on them did indeed harm the United States and the world. Domestically, the regime stifled dissent in the electronic mass media. More broadly, the struggle over Hollywood claimed major territory for authoritarianism itself, from what had seemed the mainland of popular expression. These setbacks have hurt democracy and freedom in the world.

HUAC subpoenaed and infamously asked witnesses, 'Are you now or have you ever been a member of the Communist Party?' HUAC also violated trade unionists' rights by demanding that witnesses reveal their memberships in the Screenwriters Guild or other trade union. Worse, the Committee demanded that witnesses not only disclose their group affiliations, but also accuse associates by 'naming names'. Those they identified would then face the same persecution as subversives.

Hollywood's bosses collaborated with HUAC: any witness whose testimony failed to satisfy HUAC, the studios would blacklist from further employment in the movie industry. Each targeted witness had to choose: become an informer, or face the blacklist and a charge of 'contempt of Congress'. They decided to accuse only HUAC itself.

While America forsook its Bill of Rights, these first Hollywood targets of HUAC stuck to their plan and stuck together for the next three years. Their legal defence cited the first guarantee of the Bill of Rights – the First Amendment to the US Constitution – which says, 'Congress shall make no law ... abridging the freedom of speech ... or the right of the people peacefully to assemble'.

Stars who allied themselves with Hollywood's new Committee for the First Amendment included Lauren Bacall, Humphrey Bogart, and Katherine Hepburn. But HUAC's leading collaborators among Hollywood bosses – notably Cecil B. DeMille, Walt Disney and Ronald Reagan – forced such allies to recant their public support.

HUAC's Hollywood targets swore their loyalty to the movie industry, to their employers, and to the United States of America. They argued that 'freedom of association remained a sacrosanct right of political minorities in [the US], regardless of historical conditions'. Lester Cole pledged his allegiance to the flag of the United States of America, and to the republic for which it stands, adding, 'I further solemnly swear that I will continue to resist, with all my strength, under all pressure, economic and social, the current drive to subvert [the Pledge of Allegiance], in spirit if not in letter, to read: "I pledge allegiance to [HUAC], and to the anti-democratic forces for which it fronts; one nation divided, with fear and insecurity for all." ' After the first ten of these witnesses declined to give Yes or No answers to HUAC's questions, HUAC cited them for contempt of Congress.

When the Hollywood studios announced they would dismiss and blacklist these ten employees, America heard the axe fall. Liberals in Hollywood and across the US withdrew from the struggle against HUAC, turned against 'The Hollywood Ten', and distanced themselves from any dissent. The very few prominent Americans who openly and steadfastly supported the Ten included Helen Keller, E. B. White, Arthur Miller, and

Albert Einstein, in addition to a smattering of East Coast academics and a handful of Congressmen. News media outlets extensively self-censored dissent. Main exceptions came from anti-HUAC editorials in *The Washington Post* and *The New York Times*, and from James Agee in *The Nation*, who wrote of the Ten that 'I cannot imagine how any self-respecting man could, under such circumstances, hold Congress otherwise than in contempt.'

Subsequently HUAC shelved the Hollywood hearings for what would be four years. Denied further work in Hollywood, some of the Hollywood Ten departed for Mexico, France, or England, where they found work. A few, including Dalton Trumbo, used front-men and pseudonyms to sell scripts at 90 per cent discount on Hollywood's black market.

After crushing the Left's vanguard in Hollywood and across America, HUAC and its collaborators pressed onwards to garrote others who opposed the conservative agenda. Liberals and labour unions had not succeeded in their appeasement. HUAC throttled them. In the meantime the Ten went to Congress, then to court on charges of contempt of Congress.

The Hollywood Ten pleaded 'not guilty'. They also sued the studios, which had breached employment contracts and conspired to blacklist the Ten. To raise funds and public awareness for the anti-censorship campaign, the Ten toured widely, and even made a short movie, *The Hollywood Ten*, which governments and the studios suppressed both in the US and abroad.

Howard P. Eberharter, Democratic Congressman from Pennsylvania, suggested that the purpose of HUAC was 'not to destroy an existent subversive threat in Hollywood, but to intimidate and control the movie industry'. California Democratic Congressman Chet Holifield revealed that 'the issue is whether we believe in the basic principles of a government by law, or whether we turn, in the cowering fear of the moment, under the pressure of hysteria, to the variable judgment of scared men.'

It was no contest. HUAC's Chairman, Purnell Thomas, had characterized the Ten's defence as 'fog about constitutional rights [and] the First Amendment', and indeed Congressmen overwhelmingly rejected that defence. In the case of Dalton Trumbo, Hollywood's leading screenwriter, Congressmen voted 240 to 16 to affirm his citation for contempt. The charge then went to court.

There each of the Hollywood Ten argued that HUAC's questions 'violated the rights reserved to the defendant under the first, fourth, fifth, ninth, and tenth amendments to the Constitution to be protected from official inquisitions that can compel disclosure of his private beliefs and associations.' But as American public opinion already judged all 'Communist Reds' as war criminals, so the courts convicted the Hollywood Ten. It seemed that the United States had suspended its Bill of Rights in a cold fog of war. Although it had not declared the war, nor martial law, Washington soon requisitioned concentration camps for projected overflows of alleged Communists.

The Ten appealed to the Supreme Court. Unfortunately, within three months, Justice Murphy and Justice Rutledge both died, and President Truman stacked the deck against the Court's remaining liberals by appointing Sherman Minton and Tom Clark. Minton became an opponent of civil liberties. Clark had directed the wartime internment of Japanese Americans.

The Hollywood Ten did not triumph in any of their legal

fights. Each served a one-year prison term. Yet, during that year, some of the movies they had already made continued the struggle on their own momentum. In particular *Crossfire* – from the director and producer team of Edward Dmytryk and Robert Adrian Scott – became a profitable, award-winning movie.

Then, after ridding Hollywood of the Ten, Reagan, DeMille, and other anti-Left leaders in Hollywood closed ranks. In 1948 they formed the Motion Picture Industry Council (MPIC): as Ceplair and Englund document, MPIC aimed to 'publicize the efforts of the film industry to purge itself of "subversives," "clear" repentant Communists, and heap vituperations on any HUAC witnesses' who declined to testify against themselves or associates.

During the early 1950s as the Cold War intensified, so did the US government's suppression of domestic dissent. In March 1951, after its four-year hiatus, HUAC resurged to Hollywood with a flood of subpoenas. This time HUAC assailed not only the movie world, but also the industries of theatre and music, radio and television. The head of the Southern California chapter of the American Civil Liberties Union, Eason Monroe, later wrote that 'these were the years of the slow steady purge – out of employment, out of community organizations, out of public posts of one sort or another, [and] out of political candidacies – of anyone who either had in his own personal record membership in the Communist Party or associated groups, or was a member of any family in which these relationships were characteristic, or who had [such] friends, or who had ever attended a meeting, or who read the wrong literature, or for any reason at all'. HUAC's late-1940s victory over Hollywood had yielded this terrible momentum.

In promoting mass hysteria, HUAC already had capitalized on the popularity of news about Hollywood. Now HUAC tapped a new medium: it consolidated far-reaching power by broadcasting – live on television – these 1950s show trials. HUAC coached co-operative witnesses on how to perform. 'The key to a successful appearance – i.e., one that guaranteed continued employment – was the prompt recital of the names of a few dozen Hollywood Reds.' For witnesses who aimed to become good informers but could not name enough former comrades, HUAC provided a list to memorize and deliver.

Hollywood's full capitulation emboldened HUAC to mount major assaults on other professions. Sailors and steelworkers, assembly-line workers and electricians, lawyers and social workers, scholars and teachers all suffered systematic suffocation of dissent. The show trials of hundreds of citizens – framed as a defence of patriotic loyalty – had set the stage for massive action behind the scenes, where the regime destroyed citizens' livelihoods with no pretence of due process.

HUAC, having cast suspicion on wide swaths of the citizenry, shared with American employers the names of sixty thousand specific employees whom the government suspected of insufficient loyalty. The employers of about ten thousand dismissed them, citing HUAC's suspicion as the cause. For most of the rest of the targets, the disfavour resulted in harassment, denial of job applications or promotions, forced resignation, or dismissal on false pretexts. Such collaboration by employers made the blacklist a powerful tool of control.

The regime attacked non-citizens, too, including Charlie Chaplin, a British citizen who had been living and working in the US for forty years. In 1952 Chaplin, bearing a re-entry permit, departed the US for London, where his latest movie was premiering. After he had set sail, Washington revoked his re-entry permit and banished Chaplin, whose *A King in New York* (1957) later satirized HUAC.

Of those remaining in Hollywood, some blacklisted screenwriters survived by writing for television. Abraham Polonsky, Walter Bernstein and Arnold Manoff wrote uncredited scripts for the CBS historical series 'You Are There', highlighting Socrates, Galileo, Joan of Arc, and the first Salem witchcraft trial. Ring Lardner, Jr., one of the Hollywood Ten, co-wrote 'The Adventures of Robin Hood' series.

The successes of some blacklisted screenwriters eventually brought down the blacklist itself. Dalton Trumbo started and finished that struggle.

First, his front-man took credit – and the Academy Award – for Trumbo's original story for *Roman Holiday* (1953). Three years later another triumph brought a turning point when a screenwriter named 'Robert Rich' won the 1956 Academy Award for *The Brave One*, but actually there was no such screenwriter: it was a pseudonym of Dalton Trumbo's. When persistent rumours focused on Trumbo as author, he appeared on television talk-shows where he publicly challenged the legitimacy of the blacklist.

The following year, the blacklist blocked credit on another Academy-Award-winning screenplay: the actual screenwriters of *The Bridge on the River Kwai* were Michael Wilson and Carl Foreman, both in exile in London. Then in 1959, insiders knew that the blacklisted Nedrick Young had co-written the anti-racist movie starring Tony Curtis and Sidney Poitier as convicts chained at the wrist: *The Defiant Ones.*

157

Finally when Kirk Douglas produced and starred in *Spartacus*, and Otto Preminger produced and directed *Exodus*, both hired Dalton Trumbo to write their screenplays. In January 1960, Preminger defiantly revealed to the press that he had employed Trumbo. By openly listing Dalton Trumbo's name in their credits, these two movies broke the back of the Hollywood blacklist.

A few of the Hollywood Ten continued screenwriting successfully for the next decade or two. 1962 brought two landmarks. One was *Lawrence of Arabia*: co-written for the screen by Michael Wilson, it won seven Academy Awards including Best Picture. Another was a movie based on the novel *Brave Cowboy* by wilderness defender Edward Abbey, again starring Kirk Douglas, and written for the screen by Dalton Trumbo: *Lonely Are the Brave*. In 1970 Ring Lardner, Jr. scripted a movie satirizing the Korean War, which launched the landmark television series of the same name, *M*A*S*H**. Fortunately, with the rise of insuppressibly broad dissent against the Vietnam War, political currents freshened. HUAC's surviving opponents, including Trumbo, witnessed the end of HUAC in 1975.

Later Dalton Trumbo wrote, 'If the Ten weren't heroes, what were they? They were, quite simply, 10 men who chose in that particular moment and situation (although not necessarily in all other moments and situations) to behave with honor.' They insisted on the guarantees of the Bill of Rights and stood firm. They defied tyranny. As Trumbo said through his *Spartacus*, 'Just by fighting them we won something. When even one man says "No. I won't," Rome begins to fear. And we were tens of thousands who said it.'

In the spirit of Spartacus came Trumbo. Meanwhile in the

post-war period, tens of thousands had begun protesting segregation and stigmatization of African-Americans.

With unprecedented depth and reach in the 1940s and 1950s, America's cultural discourses interwove foreign policy with realignments in domestic struggles over racism, liberties and rights. Some culture-workers managed to exert needed leverage.

Because no power ever can win cultural struggles ultimately or completely, efforts like those of Carlton Moss or Dalton Trumbo can alter the flows of power. In struggles between repression and the exercise of rights and freedoms, who else in the crux will meet the challenge with honour?

With this essay the author takes
the torch passed to his forebear,
Aaron Kimmelman,
who died during its composition.

Further Reading
Most of this chapter borrows from the following two engaging histories:

Larry Ceplair and Steven Englund, *The Inquisition in Hollywood: Politics in the Film Community, 1930-1960*, (Chicago: University of Illinois Press, 2003).

Thomas Cripps, *Making Movies Black: The Hollywood Message Movie from World War II to the Civil Rights Era* (Oxford: Oxford University Press, 1993).

Websites
This chapter also draws from the following eight websites.

159

F. X. Feeney, 'Odd Man In: The Legacy of Dalton Trumbo',
  Written By, February 2002; reprinted at
  www.wga.org/WrittenBy/0202/trumbo.html
Dan Georgakas, 'Hollywood Blacklist', from Buhle, Buhle, and
  Georgakas, eds., *Encyclopedia Of The American Left*,
  (Chicago: University of Illinois Press, 1992); reprinted at
  www.writing.upenn.edu/~afilreis/50s/blacklist.html
'History Websites: Cold War', portal at
  www.spartacus.schoolnet.co.uk/REVhistoryCOLD3.htm
Victor Navasky, 'McCarthy's Secret Show', *The Nation*, 26 May
  2003; reprinted at
  www.thenation.com/doc.mhtml?i=20030526s=navasky
Ellen Schrecker, 'Blacklists and Other Economic Sanctions' and
  'The Legacy of McCarthyism', from *The Age Of McCarthyism:
  A Brief History With Documents* (Boston: St Martin's Press,
  1994); reprinted at
  www.writing.upenn.edu/~afilreis/50s/schrecker-blacklist.html
  www.writing.upenn.edu/~afilreis/50s/schrecker-legacy.html
Cass R. Sunstein, 'We Need to Reclaim the Second Bill of
  Rights', *The Chronicle of Higher Education*, Volume 50, Issue
  40, Page B9; reprinted at
  www.law.uchicago.edu/news/sunstein_roosevelt.html
'Dalton Trumbo' website produced in Finland by Pegasos,
  1999); at
  www.kirjasto.sci.fi/trumbo.htm

Additional Resources
Dalton Trumbo's approach to struggle depended on wit and
humour, which his letters best convey. For inspiration and
illumination, see Christopher Trumbo, ed., *Additional Dialogue:*

The Letters of Dalton Trumbo, a digital audio download.

For a scholarly account of American culture, foreign policy and anti-Black racism, in addition to Cripps see Christa Klein, *Cold War Orientalism: Asia in the Middlebrow Imagination, 1945–1961* (Berkely: University of California Press, 2003. See also Mary L. Dudziak, *Cold War Civil Rights: Race and the Image of American Democracy* (Princeton: Princeton University Press, 2002).

To read for yourself how HUAC confronted Langston Hughes (a great writer and an African-American leader of culture) and his work, see the transcript of his HUAC testimony, on pages 973–998 of the following pdf website, produced by the government of the United States:

http://a257.g.akamaitech.net/7/257/2422/06amay20030700
/www.gpo.gov/congress/senate/mccarthy/83870.pdf.

For an annotated list of movies see Glenda Pearson, 'The Red Scare: A Filmography', website produced in Seattle by the University of Washington, 1998, at
http://www.lib.washington.edu/exhibits/AllPowers/film.html.

Evan Heimlich researched culture and supports inclusion of minorities in education in the US and in Japan. See:
http://evanheimlich.blogspot.com

Time to Make War History As Well

SCILLA ELWORTHY AND CAROLYN HAYMAN

The world is far from peaceful. But the nature of conflict is changing. For perhaps the first time ever, the nineteen conflicts recorded by the Stockholm International Peace Research Institute in 2004 – those causing over 1,000 deaths in any year – were all classified as conflicts within states. Only three were less than ten years old – the conflict against Al Qaeda, the conflict in Iraq and the conflict in Darfur, Sudan.

On the plus side, the overall number of conflicts is declining, slowly. And large areas of the world – most of the European Union, the Caribbean, much of Latin America – seem to have 'grown out of' settling conflicts with the use of force.

On the minus side, civilians are increasingly the victims, whether through excessive and uncontrolled bombing in Iraq, or mutilation and abduction in Uganda and the Democratic Republic of Congo. And global sales of weapons are increasing.

Against this background, what are the prospects that over time we could make war history?

The importance of local peacebuilding
Einstein put his finger on the issue almost 100 years ago when he said 'Peace cannot be kept by force – it can only be achieved

163

through understanding.' Unless the cessation of violence, where peacekeeping force may be needed, is followed by active peacebuilding at all levels of society, violent conflict is always likely to break out again. This is why 16 out of the 19 conflicts logged in Stockholm are over ten years old. In fact the latest research suggests that there is a 44% chance that even where there is a ceasefire, conflict will re-ignite within ten years, unless cycles of violence have been stopped by active peacebuilding.

What is active peacebuilding? It is the determination of people local to the conflict, with or without assistance from outside, to deal with the root causes of conflict, to create dialogue between different parties, and to raise awareness of how conflict arises and who has an interest in prolonging it. It includes initiatives to create security, reduce the number of weapons in circulation, reintegrate people, often children, who have been fighting back into their communities and offer opportunities to make a living other than through fighting.

If conflicts are increasingly within rather than between states, then the role of local people is crucial. There are literally thousands of initiatives, spread across all the major conflict areas, where people are risking their lives to bring about this kind of change. Here are five examples.

Theological dialogue with Al Qaeda
When Judge Hamoud al-Hitar announced that he and four other Islamic scholars would challenge Yemen's Al Qaeda prisoners to a theological contest, Western anti-terrorism experts warned that this high-stakes gamble would end in disaster. Nervous as he faced five captured, yet defiant, Al Qaeda members in a Sanaa prison, Judge Hitar was inclined

164

to agree. But banishing his doubts, the youthful cleric threw down the gauntlet, in the hope of bringing peace to his troubled homeland. 'If you can convince us that your ideas are justified by the Koran, then we will join you in your struggle,' Hitar told the militants. 'But if we succeed in convincing you of our ideas, then you must agree to renounce violence.' The prisoners eagerly agreed.

Now, two years later, not only have those prisoners been released, but a relative peace reigns in Yemen. And the same western experts who doubted this experiment are courting Hitar, eager to hear how his 'theological dialogues' with captured Islamic militants have helped pacify this wild and mountainous country, previously seen by the US as a failed state, like Iraq and Afghanistan.

'Since December 2002, when the first round of the dialogues ended, there have been no terrorist attacks here, even though many people thought that Yemen would become terror's capital,' says Hitar; '364 young men have been released after going through the dialogues and none of these has left Yemen to fight anywhere else.'
(James Brandon, *The Christian Science Monitor*, 4 February 2005.)

Ending violent conflict in Mandera, Kenya
Conflict recently flared up in Mandera, in northern Kenya, for a complex mixture of reasons including electoral boundary changes, spill-over from the Somali conflict in terms of clan rivalry and arms, and competition for resources. Over sixty people have died to date, with women and children being particularly targeted, and thousands of people have left their homes.

The government responded by deploying extra security

165

personnel to keep the warring sides apart, and the Kenyan and Ethiopian presidents have met to map out strategies for cross-border security and curbing of small arms trafficking. However, for there to be a lasting peace, work needs to be done at community level to develop early warning systems and mechanisms for resolving disputes without resorting to violence.

The conflict has similar causes to conflict in the 1990s in the neighbouring province of Wajir. Here a remarkable woman, Dekha Ibrahim Abdi, started by bringing women together from different clans. Women had to commit that, even if members of their family were killed in the conflict, they would continue to work for peace. The project developed to draw in the clan elders and created systems to ensure that conflict was addressed by negotiation, and that early warnings of tension were acted upon.

With a small amount of resource, raised from Kenyan businesses and overseas sources, Dekha was able to fund travel, training costs and mobile phone talk time, in order to share the learning from Wajir with different groups in Mandera. The outcome was a crucial meeting attended by all the Members of Parliament in the district, government officials and community representatives, on 18 March 2005, which established the basic framework for action. On 19 March, elders from Wajir visited the community and gave condolence and listened to all sides' analyses of the conflict. The aim was to get an objective analysis of the problems.

Since April 2005 until the time of writing in June a fragile peace has held and there have been no more deaths from this conflict. But much more work is still needed.

Risking lives for peace in Colombia
Colombia has one of the most long-running civil conflicts in the world, with the ordinary population caught between the violence perpetrated by the army and by the guerrillas. As a response to this impossible situation, thousands of displaced people have opted to form non-violent communities. After a series of workshops, usually with Church facilitation and very sober consideration, those who have formed these communities renounce co-operation with any armed group including those of the state, and concentrate on rebuilding their lives and farming.

The first such community, founded on Palm Sunday 1997, was San José de Apartadó. This community – and those that have followed – has been permanently harassed. Its leaders have been threatened; drivers taking the community's crops to markets have been intimidated; and several times paramilitaries have attempted to mount an economic blockade. Shockingly, 10 per cent of its members have been killed – 130 in total.

This is despite international support from organizations such as Peace Brigades International and from the Church. Systems of violence are so entrenched – especially in a country like Colombia that receives more US aid than any country outside the Middle East – that any non-violent initiative that attempts to break the cycle of violence will have to be prepared to pay a high price. Despite this they are persevering – what better choice is there?
(Adapted from *Campaigning Power and Civil Courage* – a discussion paper by Howard Clark.)

Building a culture of peace in Afghanistan
Co-operation for Peace and Unity (CPAU) was established in
1996 to develop local capacity for peacebuilding in Afghanistan.
Their work programme is varied – district level training on
working with conflict, peace education in refugee schools in
Pakistan and in Afghanistan, research on Islamic Scriptures on
peace and publication of a peace curriculum from Grades 1–12
in school. One of their core activities is to encourage the
development of peace committees in towns and districts.
These typically involve a wide cross-section of different
groups – women, religious leaders, young people, businesses,
police, the army – with the aim of developing holistic
strategies to prevent violent conflict and resolve disputes
in other ways.

In 2002 CPAU held a one-week training event for a
peacebuilding community. They had expected 35 participants
but more than ninety had turned up, taking their own time
and money to attend from surrounding areas. On the first day
the participants were very wary of the trainers and wanted to
know who they were, where their support came from and so
forth. By the end of the workshop they had agreed to set aside
a space for a Peace Committee to meet once a week.

Three or four of the participants were local commanders who
have anything from 3,000 to 4,000 armed men under their
command. By the end of the week the commanders were
discussing how they could disarm men and use them to
support community development, peace and environmental
improvements. CPAU have returned at intervals to coach and
support this community.

Controlling arms in El Salvador

In 1995 the war in El Salvador had been over for three years, but the huge number of weapons in private hands had led to an escalation in violent crime. Roughly 21 people were being killed every day, a higher figure than during the 12 years of civil war. El Salvador had become the most violent country in Central America and the government had decided to put the army back on the streets. According to one report 'There was talk of the return of death squads and the politicization of criminal gangs, in effect the restarting of civil war.'

A group of businessmen formed MPCD, the 'Patriotic Movement Against Crime' and decided to respond to the situation by replicating an initiative that had worked in the Dominican Republic. They were motivated partly by self-interest, as their trucks were being hijacked by heavily armed gangs, putting the lives of their staff at risk. They instituted a weapons surrender programme, whereby people were given immunity to carry arms on the way to handing them in at the cathedral in the centre of the capital. This collection point was chosen to dissociate the process from the military.

In return for handing in their arms they were given food vouchers worth $100 – not direct compensation as the weapons were worth more in many cases, but a 'token of appreciation for their support of a more peaceful society'. $60,000 worth of vouchers were given out over the first weekend, despite the group having raised only $4,500 for the project. By the end of the second weekend they had given away vouchers worth $103,000. In the end, over the next four years they carried out twenty-three separate sessions, and

169

collected over 10,000 weapons. Although this is a small number in relation to the total number of weapons in circulation, an independent think tank noted 'the MPCD initiative has had a psychological as well as practical impact in El Salvaldor; the perception that a weapon is necessary for self defence has diminished.'
(Adapted from *War Prevention Works*, see Further Reading.)

These kinds of activity are growing, as more and more people are trained in peacebuilding techniques, and form networks where they can learn and be inspired by other people's examples. Dekha Ibrahim Abdi told us that she was first prompted to take action in Wajir by hearing a story of how a Dutch family hid Jewish refugees during World War II. And the militia commander in Afghanistan who became a commander for peace made his decision inspired by a similar story from Colombia.

What can the West do to support local peacebuilding?
As well as the spread of learning, other conditions need to be in place to make active peacebuilding widespread and effective. Let's just focus on four: resources, good governance, sanctuary and control of arms. These are all areas where we in the West need to act. And everyone can do something.

Resources
Firstly, we need to recognize that just as waging war takes resources, so does waging peace. By comparison, it's a bargain. For example, the Humanitarian Liaison Centre in Kirkuk, in northern Iraq, provides an opportunity for people who have

been damaged by conflict to tell their stories and be helped to gain redress. 'I have to reach people before they pick up a gun and take things into their own hands,' says Sami Velioglu, who founded the Centre. The Centre's existence provides a small check on the behaviour of both the Coalition forces and the Iraqi National Guard. It costs less than £50,000 per year to run. A network of a hundred Centres across Iraq would help significantly to promote citizens' security, at a cost of less than £5 million per year.

There is a particular need for rapid response funding, for situations like that in Mandera, where the killing is beginning and needs to be nipped in the bud. Here a rapid grant of £5,000, together with funding from local Kenyan businesses, enabled a violent situation to be turned around.

At the moment most peacebuilding initiatives are small scale. But imagine the impact if there were the resources to scale them up, as suggested above. Imagine the difference if there were academies for peace on the same scale as military training establishments, and standing peacekeeping forces ready to move in and defuse tension and protect civilians as soon as the first signs of violence appeared.

Good governance
It would be unrealistic, indeed Pollyanna-ish, to believe that the worst human instincts of greed and aggression will ever disappear. The point of good governance is to control them, so that abusive behaviour is noted and punished. Ultimately this can only come from within, and many people in many countries are paying a high price at the moment for their efforts to hold governments to account.

Western corporations and governments undermine these efforts every time they:

- GIVE BRIBES, INDUCEMENTS OR INCENTIVES TO LOCAL POLITICIANS.
- Attach conditions to aid, such as the requirement to charge school fees, or privatize utilities, which are not in the interests of local people.
- Refuse to sign up to transparency initiatives which allow local people to see how much revenue their governments are receiving from natural resources, and therefore influence how these are spent.
- Do deals on natural resources, such as the European Union's purchase of fishing rights from Guinea Bissau, which take resources out of the hands of local people and channel them to the government.

When people are brave enough to challenge oppressive governments they put their lives at risk. That's why sanctuary is so important.

Sanctuary
A young man – let's call him Joseph – in the Democratic Republic of Congo worked as an aide to a local chief. He had been a trainee priest and was well educated. When the army started abducting local 14 year-olds – the boys to fight, the girls as prostitutes – he wrote to complain, on behalf of his community. He was arrested, tortured, and then sent to a prison from which people left only to be executed or sent to fight. Fortunately one of the senior prison staff recognized Joseph, and smuggled him out to the UK, where he sought asylum.

Since then, most of the people arrested with him have been murdered. His uncle and father are in hiding. Three warrants for his arrest have been issued and presented as evidence in his asylum claim to the British Home Office. Despite this evidence the British government insists that there is no evidence that his human rights will be violated if he is returned to the DRC, and his appeal for asylum has failed.

Providing sanctuary for those who speak out against oppression is one of the strongest ways that we can positively contribute to good governance. We need to take pride in this opportunity that we have, and spread understanding of the heroic nature of genuine asylum seekers, and of what they have achieved. We also need to join up UK immigration policy with policy on development and conflict.

Control of arms

In a world where violent conflict is almost entirely within rather than between countries, it follows that much military expenditure is on weapons that are or could be used against a government's own citizens. The controversial sale of Hawk aircraft to Indonesia, which were then used against East Timor, is just one of many examples.

This makes the arms trade increasingly illegitimate. Good governments do not control their citizens by force, but by consent. For countries that have recently emerged from conflict, there may be a case for strengthening the army to maintain the security that is a pre-condition of active peacebuilding. But the focus of security needs to move rapidly to civilian institutions such as the police and justice system, whose need for weapons is much less.

173

The UK cannot present itself as a force for peace and development in the world while spending around £900 million of public funds each year actively promoting one of the world's top three arms export industries (source: Campaign Against the Arms Trade). Nor should we be giving aid to countries that, if they cut their military budgets, would be more able to fund vital services such as health and education out of their own resources. Take Burundi. According to the United Nations Development Programme, Burundi spent 7.6 per cent of its gross domestic product (GDP) on military expenditure in 2002, but just 2.1 per cent on health in 2001. By comparison, in 2003 the UK spent just under 7 per cent of GDP on health, and about 2.5 per cent on defence.

Where next?

We can sit back and say that war is an inevitable feature of human society. Or we can notice than in many areas this is no longer true (and in some it has never, or seldom, been so) and use the lessons learned to do something to bring it to an end elsewhere.

There is an exciting possibility, right now, to define and promote Millennium Security Goals that would start to take us along the second road. These would stand alongside the Millennium Development Goals (MDGs), which have a target date for achievement of 2015, and to which all 191 members of the UN have signed up. MDGs set specific quantifiable targets for such things as 'eradicating extreme poverty and hunger by a) reducing by half the percentage of people living on less than one dollar a day and b) reducing by half the proportion of people who suffer from hunger'. They can be

174

applied, country by country, in a partnership between
governments and providers of resources. So, for example, in
Liberia the MDGs are being used as a framework for national
recovery and reconstruction planning, and as a mechanism
for co-ordinating external assistance.

Increasingly we see that development and security are closely
connected – and while it is possible to point to countries with
good security and poor development, such as Tanzania, it's
hard to point to successful development without security. So
it's logical to start thinking about undertaking a similar process
to define, and get commitment to, Millennium Security Goals.

We don't yet know what these might look like – whether,
for example, they should focus on outcomes such as number of
civilians killed in violent conflict, or a reduction in the number
of countries under ceasefire where violence breaks out again,
or on process changes, such as the ending of the recruitment of
minors into the armed forces, or the introduction of training
in peacebuilding on the same scale as military training. They
will need to give due weight to the concerns of the West, for
example around international terrorism and cross-border crime,
as well as the concerns felt in conflict areas for greater
investment in peacebuilding, including the reintegration of
combatants, and control of small arms exports.

Despite these complexities, it is perhaps the best opening
we have for a mass movement, both here and overseas, in
support of peace. Making War History, though daunting, could
be at least as achievable as Making Poverty History. Almost no
single country has succeeded in abolishing poverty, while many
have turned their back on war.

We are talking here about a long haul – maybe 20 years to

see the first results. But what an achievement for 2005, if this is the year that the idea of Making War History is born.

Further Reading

Picciotto, R. *et al.*, *Striking a New Balance*, paper prepared for the Senior Level Forum on Development Effectiveness in Fragile States, January 2005; available on www.oecd.org

Hunt, S., *This Was Not Our War – Bosnian Women Reclaiming the Peace* (Durham, North Carolina: Duke University Press, 2004).

Peace Direct, *Unarmed Heroes: The Courage to Go Beyond Violence* (London: Peace Direct, 2004). Availablke from Peace Direct

Oxford Research Group, *War Prevention Works: 50 Stories of People Resolving Conflict* (Oxford: Oxford Research Group, 2001). Available from Peace Direct.

Website

Peace Direct: www.peacedirect.org

Islam: Clash or Dialogue of Civilizations?

AKBAR AHMED

'There will be a time when your religion will be like a hot piece of coal in the palm of your hand; you will not be able to hold it.' The Prophet of Islam was gazing into the future while he talked to his followers early in the seventh century in Arabia. 'Would this mean there would be very few Muslims?' someone asked. 'No,' replied the Prophet, 'They will be large in numbers, more than ever before, but powerless like the foam on the ocean waves.'

After September 11 2001, the prediction of the Prophet seems to be coming true. Islam has become as hot as a piece of coal for its followers. Let me give you an example of what has happened in my own family. One of my relatives was in the second tower of the World Trade Center on September 11. When the first plane struck its target, he rang his father in New Jersey immediately, to say that something terrible had happened and he was coming home. He put the phone down, and we never heard from him again. Can you imagine the horror of my relative's father? Like hundreds of Muslim families he suffered the loss of someone in the terrorist attacks. Like hundreds of thousands of Muslims he felt shocked and disgusted by the carnage. But Muslims like my relative suffer twice over, because this carnage was committed in the name

177

of our religion. And the suffering and the carnage is still continuing with attacks on the transportation systems in Madrid in 2004 and in London in 2005.

Yet many Muslims now feel themselves in the dock, accused of belonging to a so-called 'terrorist' and 'extremist' religion. The 'war on terrorism' President George Bush declared after September 11 threatens to stretch into the century. But, as a result of incessant attacks by well-known figures on the Koran, the Prophet and the customs and traditions of our religion, for many Muslims it appears to be a war against Islam. For many of us therefore, on both a global and personal level, this is a time of challenge and despair.

For better or for worse the twenty-first century will be the century of Islam. The events of September 11 saw to that. The hijackers of the four American planes killed not only thousands of innocent people. Their terrible act also created one of the greatest paradoxes of the twenty-first century: Islam, which sees itself as a religion of peace, is now associated with murder and mayhem.

Consider Islam today: there are about 1.3 billion Muslims living in fifty-seven states, and the Muslim population is growing fast. About 25 million Muslims live in the West – in fact, a third of all Muslims live in non-Muslim states. But Islam is the one world religion which appears to be on a collision course with its neighbours.

We know that for the first time in history, due to a unique geopolitical conjunction of factors, Islam is in confrontation with all of the major world religions: Judaism in the Middle East; Christianity in the Balkans, Chechnya, Nigeria, Sudan and sporadically in the Philippines and Indonesia; Hinduism in South

Asia; and, after the Taliban blew up the statues in Bamiyan, Buddhism. The Chinese, whose culture represents an amalgam of the philosophy of Confucius, the Tao and Communist ideology, are also on a collision course with Islam in China's western province.

Why is it that Islam now appears to be clashing with so many neighbouring civilizations? Perhaps because we are entering into what I call a 'post-honour' world. I think that the dangerously ambiguous notion of honour – and the even more dangerous idea of the loss of honour – propels men to violence. Simply put, global developments have robbed many people of honour. Rapid global changes are shaking the structures of traditional societies. Groups are forced to dislocate, or live nearby other groups. In the process of dislocation they have little patience with the problems of others. They develop intolerance and express it through anger. And this is not a problem unique to Islamic countries. No society is immune. Even those states that economists call 'developed' fall back to the notions of honour and revenge in times of crisis. President Bush himself spoke using the rhetoric of honour after September 11. Like a sheriff whose town had been hit by bad guys, he spoke of a great nation that had been attacked, and the 'fitting reply' that he would mete out. He used words like 'dead or alive'. He called the enemy 'a slithering snake'. Bush did not speak in terms of geopolitics, but in the simple terms of honour and revenge.

Besides, the traditional Muslim division of the world has collapsed: what Muslims once saw as the distinction between *dar al-harb* – the house of war, land of anarchy and disbelief and *dar al-Islam* – the house of peace or Islam in which they

179

could practise their faith and flourish, is no longer valid. In the last decades of the twentieth century the division has become largely irrelevant. Muslims can freely practise their faith and flourish in the United States and elsewhere; meanwhile they have been persecuted in Iraq. After September 2001, the distinction disappeared altogether. Muslims everywhere felt under siege. The entire world had become *dar al-harb*.

The events of September 11 appeared to push the world toward the idea of the clash of civilizations, but they also conveyed the urgency of the call for dialogue. We may not like words such as 'post-modernism' and 'globalization', but only with the compassionate understanding of other civilizations, through the development of the scholarship of inclusion, can we resolve some of the deleterious consequences of globalization. We need to address the increasing gap between the rich and the poor, and the growing sense of despair, especially in the latter. The tragic confrontation among the great faiths taking place in the Balkans, the Middle East and South Asia, the mindless cycle of violence, must be checked in this century through the dialogue of civilization. Long-term work needs to be started to build the confidence of communities. Serious and urgent rethinking is required by policy-planners and policy-makers in the corridors of power, not only in Washington, London, Moscow and Paris but also in Cairo, Islamabad, Kabul and Tehran.

There has been dialogue in the past. A thousand years ago in Muslim Spain, Jews, Christians and Muslims lived and worked together to create a glorious civilization, where libraries, public debate and learning flourished – and this at a time when the rest of Europe was stuck in the 'Dark Ages'. And five hundred

180

years ago in India, Akbar the Great ruled over a territory that encompasses modern-day India, Pakistan, Afghanistan and Bangladesh. A Muslim who was married to a Hindu princess, his reign ushered in a remarkable century of tolerance – each week he hosted meetings between leaders of all the faiths. I have even seen this wisdom in our own time, when Lord Carey, the former Archbishop of Canterbury, called together a similar meeting of religious leaders at Canterbury. Representatives from Christian, Jewish and the Muslim faiths gathered together to discuss our common goals, and how we could create peace and harmony in our troubled times. Such inter-faith initiatives continue.

The prophets of Judaism – and therefore of Christianity and Islam – were the first to think globally and conceive of a God transcending place and national boundaries and of humanity as a single moral community, the author Rabbi Jonathan Sacks, chief rabbi of the United Hebrew Congregations of Britain and the Commonwealth, reminds us.

Globalization – the interconnectedness of the world through new systems of communications – is one of the great transformations of history. It is giving rise to deep anxieties. We seem to be caught, in Matthew Arnold's words, 'between two worlds, one dead, the other powerless to be born'. We are in a double bind: 'Our technological powers grow daily, while our moral convictions become ever more hesitant and confused', Sacks contends.

Sacks asks the question relevant to all of us whatever our faith: 'What is it about globalization that makes us feel as if we were on a journey without a map, in a car that is out of control?' He emphasizes the traditional Abrahamic virtues –

humility, modesty, discretion and restraint – and notes that in our world people have little time for them. Furthermore, words such as 'duty', 'obligation', 'judgement' and 'wisdom' carry either a negative charge or no meaning at all. He points to the violence that is now endemic. He reminds us of the power of the word 'hope' or '*hatikva*'.

Hope is the faith that together we can make things better. Optimism is a passive virtue but hope an active one. In discussing the processes of globalization, Sacks notes the gap between the small number of exceedingly rich people and the large numbers living in developing societies. In 1999, the United Nations Development Programme estimated that the world's three richest individuals had more assets than the 600 million people who made up the world's poorest nations. The top 358 billionaires were collectively richer than almost a half of the world's population. One-sixth of the world population – one billion people – live on less than a dollar a day and cannot satisfy the most basic human needs.

The gods of globalization are not bringing a new faith but are allowing people to express their faith in new ways. These gods and goddesses are a product of globalization and yet they are rebels against it. They revel in the materialist culture that defines and drives the consumerism in society while expressing disquiet about the directions it is taking. Author Thomas Friedman argues in *The Lexus and the Olive Tree* that globalization is little more than a decade old and translated means 'Americanization'.

If we accept Friedman's definition, then it follows that the gods and goddesses of globalization will be from within American culture. It is notable that there are no Muslims among these gods and goddesses. There are a few non-Abrahamic and non-American figures – Gandhi is a remarkable exception, but an emaciated, half-naked, bald, toothless 70-year-old does not sit comfortably with those who worship at the altar of youth and physical beauty. Yet Gandhi's towering moral authority has created a global glow around him.

Gods and goddesses identified by commentators are more than just symbols in our times. Many of them represent substantial political positions and achievement. President John F. Kennedy and Martin Luther King Jr are examples. Both men succeeded in changing the way people look at politics, race and society.

I suggest a formula for the new millennium: if justice and compassion flourish – and are seen to flourish – in the Muslim world, if its rulers are people of integrity, and if Muslims are allowed to practise their faith with honour, then Islam will be a good neighbour to non-Muslims living outside its borders. And it will provide a benevolent and compassionate environment to those living inside them. It will continue to resist attempts to subvert its identity or dignity. Because resistance can take the form of a Muhammad Ali Jinnah, the founder of Pakistan who believed in human rights and fought within the law, or resistance can take the form of an Osama bin Laden who fights outside of it.

The profound poetry of Maulana Rumi, the great 'mystic', served as an important bridge between Jews, Christians and Muslims and is also found in mosques, synagogues and churches at the same time. Many would agree with the German poet Hans Meinke, who said that Rumi's poetry is 'the only hope for the dark times in which we live'. Dialogues, interactions, visiting each other and friendships are the only solutions for removing misunderstandings and bringing peace between the Islamic and western civilizations. I hope that one day we embrace this new formula, so that the whole world can become *dar al-Islam* – the house of peace.

Further Reading

Ahmed, A., *Discovering Islam: Making Sense of Muslim History and Society* (revised edition, London and New York: Routledge & Kegan Paul, 2002).

Ahmed, A., *Islam Under Siege: Living Dangerously in a Post-Honour World* (Cambridge: Polity Press, 2003).

Sacks, J., *The Dignity of Difference: How to Avoid the Clash of Civilizations* (London and New York: Continuum, 2002).

Conflict and Personal Liberty

TERRY WAITE

On September 11 2001 I stepped out of my house in rural
Suffolk and into my car. It was a warm sunny day and I looked
forward to driving through the country lanes to my destination
somewhere in the heart of the Lincolnshire countryside.
I arrived at mid-morning just in time for coffee. Sixty or so
delegates had assembled from various parts of the British Isles
to attend a Disaster Planning Conference. All were experts in
their own field, the majority of whom had responsibility for
co-ordinating services in their respective areas when disasters
of various kinds struck. Later in the day I was due to address
them on the subject of international terrorism. I had spoken
at such conferences before and it was good to meet some old
friends again and to chat about the state of the world. The
time for me to address the gathering arrived and I made my
way into the lecture theatre. I was just about to begin my talk
when someone hurriedly entered the room.

'Something very strange is happening,' he said, 'it seems as
though an aircraft of some sort has flown into a building in
New York. The situation is very confused at the moment but
it's all being shown live on TV.'

A number of delegates quickly left the room to telephone
their headquarters and I, in company with several others, made
my way to the gym where there were two or three large

185

television screens. We watched incredulously as the whole Trade Center tragedy unfolded before our eyes. At a certain point a gym club member walked in dressed in shorts and vest and clearly intending to take some exercise. 'Do you mind turning the sound down?' he asked. He mistakenly thought that we were watching a film rather than an actual event taking place there and then in New York. Who could blame him? On that mild September day little did any of us realize then that we were witnessing an incident that would reverberate around the globe and trigger massive changes in the political, religious, economic and judicial systems, not only in the USA but throughout the world.

I returned to a somewhat depleted lecture theatre as many members of the conference had to return to their districts to prepare landing facilities for passenger aircraft that had been ordered to abort their transatlantic crossing and return to Europe. International terrorism on September 11 2001 took on a whole new meaning for many. Truly the world would not be the same again.

Now, as I write, four years have passed since the day that shocked much of the world and seemed to virtually traumatize America. Alas, the death of some three thousand innocent civilians in the Trade Center was just the beginning of further slaughter. The President of the United States of America declared a 'war' against terrorism and later took his troops into a war against Iraq, an event that flowed like boiling lava from September 11, sweeping further innocents into oblivion. The Prime Minister of the United Kingdom, despite many urgings of restraint given by former diplomats and others experienced in Middle Eastern affairs gave his full support to

186

this action. Once again the leaders of the so-called 'free world' were travelling along the well-trodden road of warfare claiming that this was the road to peace.

There is no getting away from the fact that the Twin Towers incident was a terrible act that caused untold suffering to many. It was an act of international terrorism and as such engendered an aggressive reaction from the United States. It is not my intention to enter into a detailed discussion as to what constitutes a 'war' and whether or not one can wage 'war' against terrorism. That ground has been covered many times before in the past four years. What I will say, however, is that in my opinion, warfare is a crude, blunt tool that should only be used as a very last resort when all other means to deal with the issue have been tried and failed. I would go further and say that the so-called war against terrorism that has been raging in one form or another for the past several years has, in the main, been counter-productive and has handed a victory to the terrorist as increasingly our democratic freedoms have been eroded.

Not too long ago, I returned to visit Lebanon, a country in which I was held captive for almost five years. For over four years I was held in solitary confinement and for much of that time I did not have books or papers and only received a radio during the final few months of my detention. One evening I was listening to the BBC World Service in my solitary cell when I heard a familiar voice. It was the then director of Y Care, a development agency that I helped found in the 1980s. She said that she had recently returned to London from visiting Y Care-supported projects in Lebanon. One day her driver took her on a tour of Beirut. He stopped at a certain stage and pointed down a street. 'I can't go any further,' he said, 'but I believe Terry Waite is being held somewhere down there.' It was a strange experience to listen to this interview whilst still a hostage, but I was greatly encouraged by the fact that despite the problems, Y Care continued to work with the needy in that country.

On my first visit to Lebanon since release I visited Y Care-supported projects in the country. I went to a refugee camp where for many years Y Care has been sponsoring various educational programmes. The camp is huge and now is home to third generation refugees. I went along to meet a group of young people who were taking part in a programme designed to enable them to become computer literate. They were bright youngsters and clearly had made good progress. 'What about your future?' I asked. 'What do you intend to do when you have finished your studies?' They smiled, 'What future?' one replied. 'To get a job in Lebanon is virtually impossible as jobs go first to Lebanese citizens. We have no right of return to the place our grandfathers came from and how can we travel abroad when we are refugees? We are trapped here.'

That young man uttered the sentiments of thousands of displaced people in the Middle East and beyond. People who in different circumstance have one thing in common and that one thing is that they have no hope for the future. As I left the computer classroom I thought it remarkable that more young people did not join 'terrorist' groups. The simple point I want to make is this. War, as well as being a blunt instrument, fails totally to deal with the root issues underlying terrorism. It is comparatively easy to engage in warfare. It is complex and demanding to find the root causes and tackle them. The roots lie in many areas – refugee camps, international and domestic economic imbalance, political immaturity, ethnic and cultural conflict – the list goes on. You don't tackle issues such as these by blasting people off the face of the earth. It takes men and women of stature and intelligence to deal with root issues. In the political realm it requires statesmen and -women; individuals who are confident and committed enough to think beyond the next election and who have the wisdom and understanding that comes from making a real attempt to understand and appreciate cultures other than western culture. Admittedly western democracy has many attractive features and has brought benefits to thousands. It takes no intelligence whatsoever to recognize that it also has its dark side and we might say that it cannot, nor necessarily ought it to be, exported lock stock and barrel to all parts of the world. One cannot stick democracy on a country as one might stick a postage stamp on a letter. If some of the optimistic statements made by some British and American politicians immediately prior to the Iraqi war, when it was stated that the conflict would be concluded in a matter of weeks and the occupying forces would be showered with all manner of gifts, were statements that were truly believed then one can only despair at the level of understanding demonstrated.

As I indicated earlier in this chapter, September 11 set off a tsunami effect around the world the consequences of which continue. One of the most depressing has been the attempt to devalue the role of the United Nations in world affairs. In a moment I want to make reference to Guantanamo Bay and other places where terrorist suspects have been detained but before doing so let me say that I was in Washington prior to the Presidential election as a member of a small delegation who were raising concerns about Guantanamo and elsewhere. I happened to meet a friend of mine who is a descendant of the late Eleanor Roosevelt, wife of the former president. She expressed concern about the attitude of certain politicians in the USA. With reference to Guantanamo she said, 'I find it hard to believe that Eleanor sat down in this city with a group of people from different parts of the world and drafted what eventually became the Universal Declaration on Human Rights. To think that we have strayed so far from those principles is hardly believable.'

Despite protestations to the contrary, many throughout the world are convinced that the UN has been both side stepped and undermined by some of the post Twin Towers events. It can be argued that the UN is in urgent need of reform but it is only as healthy and effective as its member bodies will enable it to be. In the area of human rights and international law it is the only organization that is capable of commanding authority and that authority has been undermined by the rush to go to war for stated reasons which many have difficulty in believing. Even if the protagonists of war totally believed that they were embarking on a moral crusade they ought to have known that if you remove a dictator who has held down a country by force it is highly likely that the suppressed forces will be released and internal conflict will ensue which will be extremely difficult to control. Furthermore, it was said very clearly by many at the time that the invasion by a foreign force would act as a powerful recruiting ground for many disaffected young people and others from outside Iraq. It appears that this prediction has come true and we witness the ensuing carnage daily on our television screens.

190

Inevitably, war has a corrupting influence on those who participate in it and it is with this thought in mind that those who occupy positions of leadership within both the political and military realm must enforce the highest standards on those whom they command. The thoughtless talk of some politicians and the failure of military leadership has led to abuses that have done tremendous damage not only to the occupying forces but to the very concept of western democracy itself. It may well be that only a small number of servicemen and -women behaved in reprehensible ways but one might ask where the leadership was when these indignities and brutalities were being committed. In the minds of many, the occupying forces are seen as being at one with Christianity and the damage done to inter-faith relationships is massive. Perhaps the only realistic way to view the situation is to be totally frank and make the recognition that this whole conflict is about power and the desire to maintain power by the most powerful country in the world and its allies. If that recognition is made then all morality can go out of the window, as it appears to have done in certain quarters.

The destructive eruption following September 11 has not only penetrated the armed forces but also struck at the very roots of democratic freedom itself. The arguments will continue until the cows come home as to in which particular category terrorist suspects should be grouped. The plain fact is that on the basis of suspicion alone men (and it is believed a few women) have been detained, and in some cases have been subject to processes that ought to have no part whatsoever in the behaviour of a so-called civilized nation.

Let me give another personal example. Years ago I was

detained by a group of hostage takers in Beirut because they *suspected* me of engaging in dubious political activity. They blindfolded me and kept me in poor conditions without any contact whatsoever with the outside world. Furthermore they subjected me to physical and mental abuse during a lengthy period of interrogation. Had I not been able to convince them of my innocence I would not be walking free today. What, I ask myself, is the essential difference between the methods deployed by my captors, who were labelled as terrorists, and those of the authorities that detained suspects in Guantanamo Bay and elsewhere? They were detained on *suspicion* and treated in a manner that no civilized nation ought to condone for one moment. One must also make reference to the widespread belief that in some circumstances evidence that has been obtained under duress (or, to use a more powerful term, 'torture') has been used against suspects. Such measures should have no place whatsoever in any society that claims to respect the rule of law. The dangers of using such methods are obvious and must be outlawed.

I firmly believe that one does not fight terrorism by adopting the methods of the terrorist. When one does that the terrorist has won a major victory for he has succeeded in undermining some of the fundamental values of our society, values that have been hard won through bitter trial and experience. The process has seeped through to the United Kingdom where men have been detained in Belmarsh Prison by legislation rushed through by politicians seemingly anxious to maintain public credibility. I don't doubt that some politicians genuinely have the public interest at heart, nor do I doubt that it is possible that some of those detained are truly dangerous men. However, it must be stated loud and clear that the avoidance of due process leads us into deeper difficulties and that all who value freedom and fair dealing must speak out when they see due process being eroded. I have little doubt that the 'Special Advocates' procedure adopted to deal with such cases has been operated by men and women of integrity. However, the whole procedure is based on trust and the plain truth is that because the public has been subject to so many deceptions in the past years, trust in government and in our institutions is at an all-time low. The Special Advocates procedure was adopted to deal specifically with cases involving national security but recently it has been applied to a case where national security is not an issue. Once the undermining of due process has started there is no telling where it will lead.

Our connivance with the war against Iraq is, in my mind, linked with the seeming shallowness of thought that appears to be part and parcel of our Parliamentary decision-making today. To ordinary members of the public, such as myself, it seems that decisions are taken without any genuine concern or understanding for the long-term consequences of such decisions. The moral framework of the nation is shaky to say the least and it is little use political leaders lecturing the young on morality when their conduct on the wider stage is so dubious. As a member of the Church I am obliged to say that, although individual members have spoken out against some of the matters to which I have referred, the Church as a body has hardly been shouting from the hilltops about these issues.

In case any critic of this chapter might want to accuse me of displaying an anti-western bias, let me say first of all that it is my belief that as a member of a free society one has the responsibility to look at the beam in one's own eye first. Having lived and worked in most parts of the world I am not ignorant of the defects of others. I recognize that there are states that are utterly corrupt. I know there are many evil dictators and brutal regimes. I am aware of the economic imbalance in many Arab states and elsewhere. However, I do not believe for one moment that the wrongs of this world are going to be resolved by warfare or economic dominance by one nation over another. We have to learn to grow into a world community where difference can be celebrated rather than being seen as divisive. To enable us to progress in that direction we need men and women of stature who will be able to demonstrate compassionate wisdom and political acumen that brings hope to those in despair. It is likely that such men and women will have been forged in the crucible of suffering and through that experience will have learned that suffering need not destroy. They are the ones who can bring hope to this world and enable us to regain the moral dignity that is an essential part of our heritage as human beings.

What Price Imprisonment?

DAVID RAMSBOTHAM

At the time of writing, the prison population of England and Wales has just reached yet another new record – 75,550. This marks a rise of 25,000 in the ten years since the author was appointed Chief Inspector of Prisons in 1995, 15,000 in the years since New Labour came to power in 1997. England and Wales now top the statistical league table in a number of dismal areas. At 142 per 100,000 people, we have a higher percentage of our population in prison than any other country in Western Europe. At over 5,000 we have more life-sentenced prisoners than the rest of Western Europe put together. Sentences in England and Wales are markedly more severe than in any other country in Western Europe.

Thankfully we do not yet match the statistics for the United States of America. Here over 2 million people are in prison, or 668 per 100,000 of the total population. This amounts to a quarter of all the prisoners in the world. A distinguished American criminologist has stated that, when those immediately affected by imprisonment, such as families, are included, this effectively amounts to the marginalization of the bottom 20 per cent of the population. The problem with this is that imprisonment then begins to eat into the next 20 per cent and so on.

When considering how people can make a difference to imprisonment, it is important to have some idea of the scale of the operation in the first place. The understanding of numbers must be linked to an understanding of what these figures actually mean. Who are the people that make up this 75,550? What part of the population as a whole do they represent?

The first thing to be said is that there is no such thing as a criminal class in this country. During the time that the author inspected prisons he found a cabinet minister, officers from all three Armed Forces, ministers of religion, police officers, probation officers, social services workers, doctors, nurses, barristers, solicitors, university and school teachers, businessmen, children, pensioners, mentally disordered, disabled and foreign national prisoners.

It is often said that there are three types of people in prison, the bad, the mad and the sad. Of these the wholly bad are by far the smallest number, despite what some of the extreme elements of the media would have people believe. Instead of every prisoner being a combination of mass murderer, paedophile, arsonist, fraudster and armed robber, a maximum of 15 per cent of the prison population, can safely be put into this category, of whom less than 100 in total are regarded by the Prison Service as needing to be held in what are called Close Supervision Centres because of the evil that they represent to the conduct of imprisonment wherever they may be held.

A survey carried out by the Office of National Statistics and published in October 1998, showed that 70 per cent of all those in prison were suffering from some form of personality disorder, a figure that was increased when substance abusers were added to the total. This does not mean that those

196

numbers are sectionable, under the provisions of the Mental Health Act, but that there is something that is measurable – and treatable – that affects their behaviour.

The sad include many of these people, including those who, until the recent past, would have been held in the old asylum system. They also include many homeless, unemployed and in too many cases unemployable people, who continuously commit minor crimes that guarantee them a home in a prison rather than having to live rough. The Prison Service refers to these people as 'poor copers', meaning that they cannot cope with life 'on the outside'. The question of whether prison is the right place for such people must surely then be asked.

What then is the purpose of imprisonment? Is it to contain the bad, providing a place of punishment? Is it to contain the mad, providing a place of treatment? Is it to contain the sad, providing a place of refuge? Is it to deter people from crime by the way in which it contains prisoners? Is it to prevent further crime by those committed to it, by the way in which it treats prisoners? The fact that there are so many questions about its purpose is indicative that, in many respects, its true purpose has not been clearly defined, which makes it difficult to judge the success or failure of its current conduct.

This purpose is best examined against current practice and historical fact. There have always been prisons, gaols, bridewells and penitentiaries in this country, used to hold offenders until they were tried and sentenced. As sentences were usually capital or corporal, subsequent confinement was usually short. These prisons were 'local' in that they existed in every locality in the country and were paid for by local taxes.

When the parish poor laws were amended in England in

sixteenth-century Elizabethan times, Houses of Correction were added in every county. These were also paid for by local taxes, but existed to hold vagrants and vandals, and also debtors. At the same time transportation, to the American colonies, was substituted for some capital offences. After the American War of Independence, this was changed to Australia, until 1856 when it said 'no more'. By this time a new category of prison was being added to the system – what were called 'convict prisons', paid for by national taxes and containing those awarded long sentences.

As one of the deliberate measures taken to relieve the rural population of its heavy tax burden in the years of agricultural depression following the various Corn Laws, these two types of prison were nationalized in 1877, under what was called the Prison Commission. The nearest analogy to this is a Next Steps Agency, in which the Commissioner, Director or appointed Head is given a directive and a budget, for which they are accountable to a Whitehall ministry.

It is the author's firm belief that all today's problems stem from that decision. The needs of unsentenced and short term prisoners differ markedly from those of the long term. Putting both together in the same prison, particularly at a time of limited financial resources, inevitably means that there will have to be compromise between them. Compromise is bound to be less effective than concentration on one or the other. Go, today, into what is still called a local prison – one that exists to serve courts by holding those remanded for trial near enough to that court, and delivering them on time, when required – and you will find an incredible mix of prisoners. Life sentenced, long, medium and short term sentenced, unsentenced, sentenced but not convicted, immigration detainees and asylum seekers, sex offenders, mentally disordered, drug addicts and, in some, children and young offenders. What is the governor of such a prison meant to do with and for his or her prisoners?

Immediately before New Labour came to power in 1997, the Prime Minister declared that he intended to be 'tough on crime and tough on the causes of crime'. Nothing wrong with that, except if he thought that he was addressing his call to the criminal justice system, which includes prisons, he was talking to the wrong people. The causes of crime – poverty, unemployment, social neglect, lack of education etc. – exist in society. The criminal justice system – courts, police, prisons, probation – cannot tackle these causes. That is a rallying cry to all of us. Society as a whole has to tackle the causes.

He went further by issuing a unifying role to the criminal justice system, which does not look like a system at all. When observed closely it looks more like a series of warring tribes, competing for ever diminishing resources, apparently ignoring the fact that it would be much more effective if all the parts worked together.

The aim given to it was again simple and clear: 'To protect the public by preventing crime'. Again nothing wrong with that, except that it was given to the wrong people. The criminal justice system does not prevent crime. It clicks in when a crime has been committed. Police investigate, courts sentence and prison and probation services administer that sentence.

However, if that were adjusted to read 'To protect the public by preventing re-crime', or 're-offending', then that would be a sensible purpose. Currently 58 per cent of all adult

199

prisoners, 68 per cent of all prisoners aged between 18 and 21 and 78 per cent of all prisoners aged between 15 and 17 re-offend within two years of release. In cost terms, crime costs in the order of £60 billion per year of which re-offending costs £12 billion. The Prison Service costs £2.5 billion. Such a re-offending rate cannot possibly be regarded as anything other than a dismal return on the money spent. If the purpose of imprisonment is agreed to be 'to prevent re-offending', what should it be required to do with and for prisoners?

This is very clearly described in the Prison Service's own Statement of Purpose, written in 1983. 'It is our duty to keep secure those committed by the courts, to treat them with humanity and help them to live useful and law-abiding lives in prison and on release.' In the Army the author was taught that there should only be one aim and here there are three. Therefore an alteration of the word order is suggested: 'To help prisoners to lead useful and law-abiding lives, in prison and on release, with the qualifications that they must not be allowed to escape and must be treated with humanity.'

This then requires three sequential actions by the Prison Service:

Firstly it must establish just what it is that has prevented an individual from living a useful and law-abiding life, which has resulted in a crime and a prison sentence.

Examination of the reasons for lack of law-abiding will include the crime itself – murder, sex-offending, armed robbery, fraud for example – together with mental impairment, substance abuse and a whole variety of social factors. Examination must include risk – to the prisoner, to other prisoners, to staff and to the public.

Examination for the lack of usefulness should include five separate areas. Firstly education, and a detailed assessment of ability or lack of it. Dreadful statistics about poor educational ability abound – 65 per cent of all adult male prisoners have a reading age of less than eight years old; 30 per cent of young offenders have literacy and numeracy standards lower than that expected on entry to primary school aged seven. Examination should not only be of whether they can read and write but why they cannot. Learning difficulties abound, and unless examined in detail, much time will be wasted trying to educate those who cannot respond to the method of teaching. Dyslexia is often cited; low IQ, seeing and hearing difficulties and others must be treated with equal care.

Secondly, work skills, or lack of them. Eighty per cent of those received into prison were either unemployed at the time, or lacked any qualifications. Everyone should be put through an aptitude test to determine their capabilities. These should then be harnessed.

Thirdly, social skills – a term that covers a multitude of problems. HM Young Offenders' Institution Hyde Bank, in Belfast, runs an admirable course for its young offenders entitled 'Learning to Live Alone'. Bearing in mind how many prisoners do live rough or alone, all should be made able to look after themselves – cooking, painting and decorating, basic plumbing and electrics, home economics, coping with the welfare system. Add to this the numbers who are fathers or mothers of children, but have neither been parented nor are capable of being parents themselves.

Fourthly comes health, both mental and physical. The main mental health statistic has already been quoted. In 1999 the

201

government estimated that there were some 2,500 'Dangerously and Severely Personality Disordered' (DSPD) people in the country, of whom 400 were in the Special Hospitals – Broadmoor, Rampton and Ashworth – 700 somewhere in the community and 1,400 in prison. All needed the same treatment. Those in Special Hospitals received the best. Those in the community might be under psychiatric supervision. Those in prison received nothing and indeed the evidence suggested that the conditions in which they were confined frequently made them worse. Of the 75,550 in prison, all except 30 will be released. The release of the severely mentally disordered is therefore clearly a public health issue, even more so than the release of any other prisoner, as the sensationalizing of further crimes proves.

Physical health is also an issue as the numbers in prison include many with blood-transmitted viruses, such as HIV or hepatitis C, resulting from substance abuse. In addition, a particularly virulent form of tuberculosis has been brought into the system, not only by prisoners from Eastern Europe, but also by some rough sleepers. The degree of muscular-skeletal and other disorders is also indicative of the 'outside' lifestyle of prisoners.

Lastly, substance abuse. Eighty per cent of all prisoners are abusing some form of illegal substance at the time of reception into prison. In ideal circumstances, every one should be tested at that time, and those who test negative separated from those who test positive. Negative ones can be awarded certain privileges, in return for random, voluntary drug tests in the future. Positive tests can be further examined, to determine the severity and type of problem. Detoxification and further treatment can then be given. It is unfortunate that this only happens in one or two prisons. The remainder only test those who say that they have a problem. As a result the Prison Service is, once again, failing to protect the public, because it is not doing all it could do to stamp out the abuse.

Once these assessments have been made, a plan can be designed for every individual prisoner, based on the severity of the cause and the time available to treat it. The aim should be to turn such work into a full, purposeful and active daily programme, for each individual. It is interesting that suicides and drug use are lower in prisons in which prisoners are kept active. Such a programme, which tires as well as challenges, is the best possible antidote to the frustration and boredom that are behind all too many of the incidences of both. At present far too many prisoners spend all day locked up in their cells doing nothing. Not only is this likely to lead to suicides and substance abuse, but it is also failing to protect the public by tackling the likelihood of re-offending.

Finally the plan must be implemented. The author has long thought that the best analogy for the role of prisons within the criminal justice system is with that of hospitals in the Health Service. Neither has any control over who comes in, but has to try to make them better, conscious that the process will not be completed in either hospital or prison, but will have to be continued in the community in the form of aftercare. That aftercare has to be planned and, unless the treatment is to be wasted, must be continuous from the moment that the patient or prisoner leaves hospital or prison.

To achieve this, it must make sense for every prisoner to be held as near to their homes as possible, so that those who will continue treatment can be involved with it from the start. It is said that the three factors most likely to prevent re-offending are a home, a job and a stable relationship, all of which are put at risk by imprisonment. The present policies which see 7,000 prisoners held more than 150 miles from home and 12,000 more than 100 miles, with millions of pounds per year spent on family visits, show that such sensible placing is not currently practised. The establishment of what he called 'community clusters of prisons', in which there were sufficient prison places to house all categories of prisoner from a particular geographical region – with the exception of high security, whose numbers do not justify more than a small number of suitable prisons – was a key recommendation of Lord Woolf's masterly inquiry report following the serious prison riots in 1990. Sadly, like all too many sensible recommendations concerning the conduct of imprisonment, it has not yet been implemented.

If it were, it would be possible to ensure that prisoners were sent to prisons in which the law-abiding or useful requirements could be tackled. At present every prison tries to do everything, which is unwise. Much is left undone, because of lack of resources, meaning that needs are not met. Again the author suspects that, had the purpose of imprisonment been properly thought through, such introductions would have followed the logic.

And how will this be brought about? It will only happen if politicians make it happen. The problem is that, at present, too many of them seem to think that the public only wants retribution: that prisoners should be locked up and the key thrown away because of who they are. It is said that there are no votes in prisons, which, of course there are not. Prisons are inanimate objects. The votes are in prisoners. Change to this approach will only come about if and when the public realizes that the present system, with its appallingly high re-offending rate, is failing both to protect them and to implement the given aim of the criminal justice system. Once that has happened, individual voters should question their candidates, from whatever party, asking what they are going to do about our failing prisons. Prisoners will be in, and released from prison, whatever party is in power, so this is not a party political issue.

Inevitably comes the question 'Can we afford it?' The author's answer to that is that we cannot afford not to do it. We do not want to marginalize any part of our population. Evidence – from America, because such research has not been carried out in this country – shows that if programmes, such as those outlined are carried out, there is a 30 per cent chance that the person will not re-offend. Aspirin is said to have a 4 per cent chance of preventing heart attacks, and think how much is taken. We can get more out of the £2.5 billion, currently spent on imprisonment if more were spent on rehabilitating prisoners than managing the management of offenders. It will take a bold person to instigate such an approach. But, as always, individual bravery is the key to essential difference.

Website
The Howard League for Penal Reform: www.howardleague.org

Showing solidacity: feeding the Jarrow marchers, 1936

'Places Without a Future': the Jarrow March and the Great Depression

WILLIAM FRAME

This chapter is about unemployment and poverty in the depressed areas of Britain in the 1930s. It examines the public reaction to the troubles of the small town of Jarrow in north-east England, where unemployment in the mid-1930s reached the figure of 80 [er cent. Jarrow came to prominence following a series of reports in the press in 1934 highlighting unemployment and living conditions, and the town became a motif for the seeming abandonment of large sections of the country to poverty and hopelessness. The role of the media was critical in reporting events in the industrial North, a part of the country that most well-off people in Britain knew little about. Critical also was the determination of the townspeople to campaign for new industry to provide employment. This determination culminated in 1936 with a march from Jarrow to London to petition Members of Parliament for action to promote regeneration. The publicity surrounding the problems of Jarrow did much to expose the dependence of industrial populations on arbitrary decisions made by big business, and provided a counter to the Government's view that employment was solely a matter for the free market. In the longer term the Jarrow March became symbolic of the effects of large-scale unemployment in the 1930s, and was central to the development of regional policy in post-war Britain.

Jarrow is situated on the south bank of the river Tyne, a few miles east of the major city of Newcastle. In medieval times it was famous as the site of the home monastery of the Venerable Bede (died 745), author of the *Ecclesiastical History of the English People*, a major source for the early history of England. The industrial revolution saw the spread of shipbuilding along the banks of the Tyne, and in the nineteenth century Jarrow became a prosperous shipyard town, building merchant vessels to support Britain's dominance in world trade. Palmer's shipyard was the centre of the town's economy, directly employing several thousand men and indirectly supporting numerous local businesses. Following World War I shipbuilding went into decline in the UK as foreign competitors emerged to challenge British dominance in both trade and the building of merchant vessels. Palmer's, like many other British firms, limped through the 1920s perpetually on the brink of bankruptcy. The collapse of world trade in the economic blizzard of the Great Depression resulted in the final closure of the yard. The end came in the summer of 1934 when Palmer's was acquired by National Shipbuilders Security Ltd (NSS), a private firm representing a cartel of British shipbuilders and backed by the Bank of England, which existed for the purpose of closing down redundant firms so as to bolster the market for those remaining. NSS operated a scorched-earth policy, demolishing the yards it acquired and banning the vacant site from being used for shipbuilding for forty years. This policy was carried out in Jarrow leaving the town without its dominant employer, and thousands of men out of work with little or no hope of finding alternative employment.

For many in Britain it seemed by 1934 as though the country had weathered the worst of the Depression, with the beginnings of renewed prosperity being seen in the South East and Midlands. In 1934 unemployment dropped below three million for the first time since 1930. However, economic growth in some parts of the country masked continued stagnation elsewhere, where the collapse of markets for traditional industries such as coal, steel and shipbuilding left whole populations bereft of hope for the future. In March 1934 *The Times* sent a special correspondent to report on conditions in Britain's industrial North East. The result was a series of articles under the title 'Places Without a Future', which examined the human cost of the Depression in the Durham coalfields. The first article stated 'there are parts of Durham where one feels, strongly and sometimes angrily, that London has still no conception of the troubles that affect the industrial North':

In London and the South, for every 86 men working there are 14 men out of work. In the whole county of Durham, no small area, for every 63 men working there are 37 out. In the south-west of the coal field, around Bishop Auckland, for every 42 working there are 58 out. In Jarrow, a formerly prosperous shipyard town of 32,000 inhabitants, for every 25 working there are 75 out. These places are helpless.

The National Government, a coalition of the Conservative Party and a small number of Labour and Liberal politicians, was committed to recovery through a restoration of business confidence and rejected regional policy as a diversion from this aim. In the week the first article was published the

209

Chancellor, Neville Chamberlain, found himself giving a speech in the North East of England. He wrote to his sister: 'I certainly did feel rather sorry for myself having to go to Newcastle just before the Budget, for Tyneside is not sharing much in the recovery and it was rather difficult to find the right note of sympathy without undue optimism.' The Government believed that the only long-term solution was for younger people to migrate to areas where work was available and for the populations in the older industrial regions to decline. Its sole regional policy was the Industrial Transference Act (1928), which aimed to help unemployed workers migrate to other areas in the UK and the Empire. This policy accepted both the permanent unemployment of older industrial workers and the gradual de-population of the regions. Even if successful it meant the abandonment of whole areas to poverty and unemployment for a generation.

The publication of *The Times*' articles resulted in a public demand for action to resolve the plight of industrial workers in the stricken areas, and challenged the Government to bring forward a more active response to unemployment. The existence of poverty often elicits as a first reaction an attempt to apportion blame. Is the person poor because of personal failures or because of circumstances beyond their control? We are all familiar with the success of Charles Dickens in highlighting the unfairness and inhumanity of the Victorian industrial system. By depicting the hopelessness inherent in the situations of the poor he exposed the unfairness of the view that poverty arose from indolence. In 1934 hopelessness was the key factor in reports of the plight of the derelict areas and led to a widespread call for action. It was also important that these

210

reports were validated by their appearance in *The Times*, a newspaper widely regarded as the voice of the British political establishment.

The public outcry in 1934 over conditions in the North East and other distressed areas seemed for a time to have brought hope to Jarrow. Within weeks the Government had appointed investigators to report on conditions in the North East and other derelict areas. By the end of the year it had passed the Special Areas (Development and Improvement) Act, with Commissioners appointed to oversee substantial funds aimed at alleviating the distress. The Commissioners were able to use their funds to invest in development works with the aim of encouraging industry and reducing unemployment. Sir Malcolm Stewart, the Commissioner for England and Wales, spent much time lobbying private firms to encourage them to locate new factories in the Special Areas. Money was also spent to develop the infrastructure, and a scheme was planned for a new deep-water harbour between Jarrow and South Shields.

There was also a substantial public response to the plight of the regions, including a plan by Surrey County Council for the 'adoption' of Jarrow and establishment of a fund towards which the people of Surrey were encouraged to subscribe. This was based upon the help given by British towns to shattered areas of France and Belgium after the Great War. The appeal proved popular and by the end of 1935 £30,000 had been raised. The leading figure was Sir John Jarvis, High Sheriff of Surrey and a businessman with interests in publishing and ironworks, who aimed to bring work to Jarrow rather than to expect the unemployed to migrate South. At the end of 1935 he bought the *Olympic*, sister ship to the ill-fated *Titanic*, for the price of

£100,000 and sold it to a Sheffield firm for the same figure on the condition that it be broken up in Jarrow. This led to the establishment of the Jarrow Shipbreaking Company. At the start of 1936 it was announced that money from the Surrey Fund would be used to start a factory making steel furniture on the site of the derelict shipyard.

While all of these ventures offered the hope of new work, the scale of unemployment in Jarrow meant that renewed prosperity could only come from the establishment of a major new industry to replace the closed shipyard. In late 1934 it seemed as if the work of Stewart, Jarvis and others behind the scenes had paid off when rumours were published in the press that an American steel magnate was interested in acquiring the Palmer's site to establish a modern steel works, which would employ many of the men whose careers had seemingly ended with the closure of Palmer's. The harbour created for the shipyard provided an ideal basis for the transportation of ore, and the existence of both substantial coal deposits and a skilled labour force were also major advantages. However, the negotiations dragged on and it was not until 1936 that the plan was officially announced. Like shipbuilding, the steel industry in the UK was stricken by overcapacity and outdated works, with the result that the industry was heavily cartelized and dependent on protective tariffs for its survival. In order to ensure markets for its steel the promoters of the new Jarrow plant had to come to agreement with the British Iron and Steel Federation. Many of the existing steel producers in the North East feared competition from a modern plant able to produce at a lower cost than their own works. In early 1936 the seeming completion of the deal had encouraged predictions in the press that within a year unemployment in Jarrow would be eliminated. Three months later the news broke that the steel works would not, after all, be going ahead. It had been blocked by the British steel cartel.

The collapse of the steel works scheme showed the weakness of the British government in dealing with the chronic problems of older industries. Protection from foreign competition had been granted to the steel industry on condition that a programme of rationalization be carried out to make the industry more efficient and competitive. Having granted protection the government was faced with a situation in which the fragmented nature of the industry meant that the more backward firms, faced with extinction if a rationalization policy were followed, could combine to prevent such a policy from being approved. The government was unwilling to intervene to enforce a rationalization policy and unable for political reasons to withdraw the tariff. Effectively this provided a blank cheque to the industry to manage its affairs in its own interests. The blocking of the Jarrow steel works showed the steel cartel in its worst light and exposed the failure of the government's policy of relying on the private sector to put its own house in order.

For the people of Jarrow the blocking of the steel works at the behest of one group of industrialists, coming hard on the heels of the closure of the shipyard at the behest of another, was too much. A deputation went to London to see Walter Runciman, the President of the Board of Trade, to demand action. Runciman, a shipping owner and supporter of business autonomy, refused to intervene and reputedly told the deputation that 'Jarrow must work out its own salvation'.

The result was that in July 1936 a decision was taken by the unemployed of Jarrow to march to London to protest against the abandonment of the town. There had been a number of such marches already in the 1930s, but the Jarrow March was distinctive on two counts. Firstly it had the endorsement of the town council and was organized under the name of the Mayor. Secondly, press attention focused on the problems of Jarrow and the efforts of the Commissioner for England and Wales, and also of the organizers of the Surrey Fund, to resolve them ensured that the march took place in the full glare of publicity. The local problems of Jarrow were projected onto the national stage and became emblematic of the failure of government or private sector to bring forward adequate solutions for the depressed areas.

The march was a response by the town as a whole to its predicament. It was planned from Jarrow Town Hall and the preparations supervised by the Town Clerk. The route was broken up into manageable sections and letters, signed by the Mayor, were sent out on official paper asking for the use of village and town halls as overnight accommodation. Two hundred men were selected from the much larger group who volunteered and each of them was vetted by the borough medical officer. Field kitchen equipment was borrowed from the local Boy Scouts, and subscriptions received from members of the local Rotary Club. On the day before departure prayers were said for the marchers in every church and chapel in Jarrow. The march began on Monday 5 October 1936 after a service presided over by the Bishop of Jarrow and attended by the Mayor and other leading town figures. It was planned to arrive in London for the start of the autumn parliamentary session, when a petition would be presented to the House of Commons.

Many of the marchers had served in the army during World War I and the march was conducted by army rules, with 50 minutes' walking and 10 minutes' rest in each hour. The weather in October was mixed and when rain struck conditions were grim with only cold food and tea to sustain the marchers. The march had been planned to gain as much publicity as possible and was accompanied by journalists all the way to London. Every night a public meeting was held at which Jarrow's Member of Parliament (MP), Ellen Wilkinson, and other leading figures addressed the local people. At an official level the march lacked support, with not only the National Government, but also the hierarchies of the Church of England, the Labour Party and the Trades Union Congress instructing their members not to provide help. However, human sympathy triumphed over official obstruction and help was provided to the marchers along the route, with most towns responding favourably to the plea for accommodation. Much of this was from within the Labour movement, for example in Leicester where the Co-operative Society's boot repairers worked all night for free to repair damaged footwear. Where the Labour council refused to help, as in Chesterfield, help was forthcoming from the Conservatives or the churches.

The marchers arrived in London on an overcast, rainy October day. Their shabby appearance and wet clothes provided a picture in miniature of the privations of people living in the depressed areas. At the House of Commons two petitions were presented. The first was from the people of Jarrow and contained over 12,000 signatures calling on the government to intervene to provide work. The second was from the other towns on Tyneside drawn up with the backing of the Mayor of Newcastle and supporting Jarrow's demand for work as an appeal for help for the whole region. It was signed by 68,000 people and expressed the view that 'Jarrow's troubles are our troubles'. This petition was supported by the northern group of MPs in Parliament and presented by Sir Nicholas Gratton-Doyle, a Conservative and the longest-serving Tyneside MP. The case was presented to MPs at a packed meeting in one of the committee rooms.

Although the march did not bring immediate help for the town, Jarrow was to find employment again in the late 1930s when a steel works was built to supply the re-armament programme before World War II. However, the greatest effect of the march was to come during the war and post-war years, when the British government became committed to full employment policies. World War II has been labelled 'the people's war' and undoubtedly popular memories of the 1930s were critical in establishing the post-war political consensus. Employment, health care and adequate housing were from 1945 onwards seen as responsibilities of government rather than matters to be left to market forces to resolve. The strength of popular feeling was such that it was believed for a generation that no party could win an election if unemployment rose to the scale seen in the 1930s. Many of the political leaders of the post-war period had witnessed the effects of regional unemployment in the 1930s and regarded a return to such a system as unacceptable. Ellen Wilkinson, for example, went on to become a minister in Attlee's post-war government. On the Conservative benches leading figures such as Harold

Macmillan, who had been MP for Stockton in the 1930s, also supported the political goal of full employment.

Since the 1980s much of the structure of the post-war consensus has been dismantled and full employment is no longer regarded by governments as essential to their political survival. A limited return to free-market principles has taken place, and the role of the state in the economy has been pushed back. As in the 1930s it is no longer thought desirable that the state should intervene in the decisions of private firms to promote employment. Nonetheless there remains a belief in politics and in the wider community that the Government has a role in promoting the well-being of the British regions. If direct intervention to bring employment is no longer regarded as viable, there is nonetheless a continued activity to promote the regions. Much has been done to attract business through improved facilities and cultural developments. In the North East the building of the Metro light-rail system has linked towns along the banks of the Tyne with the business and retail centres of Newcastle and Gateshead. Improved shopping, cultural and sporting facilities have done much to promote the region as a good place to live. Tourism has also become a major part of the regional economy, with visitors coming from around the world to visit the many heritage sites. This includes Jarrow, which remains famous as the home of Bede.

Almost seventy years on the Jarrow March retains an iconic status as the defining image of unemployment in the 1930s. If the issues it raised have not been solved in the way in which Wilkinson and other Labour leaders of the period originally hoped, they have not been ignored or pushed to one side in the way they were in the early 1930s. In this sense the problems

217

of Jarrow in the 1930s marked a genuine watershed in British politics. From this time onwards it was no longer acceptable for governments to abandon regions to their fate. While politicians continue to dispute the viability of different solutions few would seriously dispute that it was their responsibility to find solutions. Although commitment to regional policy has varied between parties and over time, all governments since 1945 have invested thought and money in developing strategies for the regeneration of stricken areas. The belief that Britain contains places without a future is no longer practical politics. For this the Jarrow marchers, and the public opinion that they mobilized, can claim much of the credit.

Reporters on the Line: Risk Taking and Conscience in the Former Soviet Union

BRUCE CLARK

I will never forget the moment when I learned that despite our worst fears, Andrei was more or less free, and more or less well, and very much alive. At the beginning of March 2000, I was flying back to London, relieved to be heading home after an exhausting but not especially hazardous reporting trip to the hot spots of the Balkans. I opened a newspaper to find out what was going on in the rest of the world, and within moments, I found myself shedding tears of relief and joy. My eye took in the familiar, scarred features of a colleague whom I had not, in all honesty, been sure of seeing again; and I learned of his release after six weeks of captivity and torment, orchestrated by the authorities of his own country who were determined to silence his irreverent, fearless and morally engaged style of radio journalism.

Andrei Babitsky is a Russian citizen who is employed by the American radio station Radio Liberty – but he has a lively, contrarian mind of his own that refuses to submit entirely to any earthly master. Since the war in Chechnya re-ignited in 1999, he has been one of the few Russian journalists to cover that conflict, in all its ghastliness, from a point of view other

219

than that of Russian officialdom. This independence of spirit
has made him one of the sharpest thorns in the side of a
Russian administration which has reaped rich political rewards
from a policy of relentless suppression, not only of armed
Chechen separatists but of the whole civilian population in
that unhappy corner of the Caucasus. While Russian officials
have tried to demonize Andrei as an active supporter of the
Chechen rebel cause, he is nothing of the kind; if he is an
active supporter of anybody, it is the little people – bewildered
Russian conscripts as well as distraught Chechen mothers and
children – whose lives have been darkened by an avoidable
conflict that has claimed tens of thousands of victims.

On 15 January 2000, Andrei was filing reports from the
Chechen side of the battle-lines as war was raging around
the territory's half-ruined capital, Grozny. Then he disappeared,
and Russian officialdom denied all knowledge of his
whereabouts, while implying that he had only himself to
blame for any mishap he might suffer. That was a bad sign;
it suggested that the authorities knew exactly where he was,
and harboured the darkest intentions towards him. There was
good reason to fear the worst: over the nine years since the
downfall of the Soviet system, at least a dozen Russian
journalists had paid with their lives for offending the powerful
– though the people they had challenged were usually local
tycoons, or personally corrupt generals, rather than the Kremlin
and its masters.

Two weeks later, the authorities changed their story. They
had in fact known all along where Mr Babitsky was, because
they had arrested him and indeed charged him with belonging
to an illegal armed formation. They then announced that they

had handed him over, under a deal that he had freely accepted, to some 'Chechen fighters' in exchange for some Russian prisoners. To add credibility to the story, they released some grainy footage of the handover; and then, a few days later, his radio station was presented with a video of a battered-looking Andrei, saying he was longing to rejoin his wife and children in Moscow but that 'circumstances' prevented him from doing so. All this smacked of a series of dirty tricks, and his colleagues grew even more alarmed when it became clear that the main group of Chechen rebels had not agreed to any sort of 'prisoner swap' with the Russian authorities, and that they (quite genuinely) had no idea where Andrei was. Fellow journalists quickly realized that if Andrei was now in 'Chechen' hands, he must have been transferred to a renegade group that was collaborating with Moscow. This was an ominous portent: on one hand, the Kremlin was discrediting Andrei by implying that he was, in effect, a camp-follower of the Chechen cause; at the same time, they had transferred him to a group of people who might well kill him, without it being obvious that the killing was done at Moscow's behest.

Some time in late February, I remember comparing notes on Andrei's case with some journalists in London who were either Russian or knew Russia well. We all came to the sombre conclusion that the authorities might well be planning to do away with him, and that he might be dead already; either hypothesis was perfectly consistent with the information we had.

As it turned out, Andrei had become too well known to be disposed of so easily. His case was raised by the US, British and other western governments at the highest level; it became part of the broader calculus of Russian-western relations. Most encouraging of all, at a time when the bulk of the Moscow media was meekly toeing the Kremlin line, a group of Russian news organizations and journalists made a collective protest on Andrei's behalf. At some point, it seems, the authorities decided that to keep Andrei prisoner, even by proxy, was more trouble than it was worth.

But they could not simply release him without losing face; something had to be done to make him lose face instead. So his renegade Chechen captors (presumably acting under Muscovite instructions) brought him in a car boot to the neighbouring Russian republic of Dagestan, where his real passport was taken away and he was given a false, Azerbaijani one with an Azeri name. Left with no other documents, he tried to check into a hotel in Dagestan with the Azeri passport, and was promptly charged with using counterfeit papers. But the worst of his nightmare was over. He was bundled onto a plane to Moscow and allowed to go home, although his movements were restricted and he was barred from leaving the country. That prevented him from accepting some of the prestigious invitations that began flowing into his tiny apartment on the outskirts of the Russian capital from various western cities. The parliamentary assembly of the Council of Europe, in Strasbourg, asked him to come to give evidence about the terrible human cost of the Chechen war; in the end he had to speak to them by video satellite link. Then the Vienna-based Organization for Security and Cooperation in Europe, a human rights watchdog whose member states include Russia, awarded him a prize for journalism, which he was unable to collect in person. But the moral victory was his.

222

Few of us in the news-gathering business were in any doubt that the authorities would, if they could, have silenced for ever Andrei's characteristic sing-song voice, which somehow commands attention by saying deadly serious things in a half-grave, half-mocking tone which leaves the listener perpetually uncertain whether to laugh, cry or do both at once. So on reading of his release, it seemed impossible for anyone who loved that voice not to cry with relief. A day or two later, he was interviewed on air by a Radio Liberty colleague who asked him delicately whether he had been tortured. He replied in his laconic tone that like everyone else who was sent to the Chernokozo detention centre, he had been beaten around the kidneys, leaving a pain that 'goes away after two or three days'; this did not amount to torture, he said, but he had heard the screams of people who were being subjected to excruciating pain.

When I first met Andrei in early 1990, he was a witty, rambunctious Muscovite – part of a group of young people who were restless, highly intelligent and easily bored. Even more than the others, Andrei was endowed with the streak of self-destruction that seems to be part of the atmosphere in Moscow, along with pungent cigarette smoke and the reek of badly refined petrol. His dark levantine features have been marked by a car accident in which his own carelessness played a part. Andrei's father was a well-known literary figure in Tajikistan in Central Asia; he bore the surname of his Jewish mother. Because of his parents' separation, much of his childhood had been spent in a boarding school of the harshest Soviet variety. That made him resilient, sharp-tongued and sharp-witted. But at some point in his childhood, he must have

223

been cared for by somebody with a basic sense of decency and humanity. To that extent he was luckier than most inmates of Soviet boarding establishments. He was probably the wildest of the disorderly youngsters, dabbling in freelance journalism and playing cat and mouse with the dying (but still occasionally vicious) Soviet authorities, whom I had met when I arrived in Moscow at the end of 1989. But there was plenty of competition.

My own situation, as I joined the Moscow corps in the headiest moments of Gorbi-mania, was also rather precarious. I had taken the huge professional risk of leaving a secure job at a well-known daily to work in Russia for a newly established Sunday paper whose chances of survival were deemed to be fragile at best. The paper had no permanent office in Moscow, and it seemed almost impossible to acquire one. So I was forced to migrate almost nightly from one cockroach-ridden hotel to another, telling myself it was all part of a rich journalistic experience that would help to enliven my news copy. If some young Russian bohemians, dabbling in opposition journalism and politics, took me to their heart, it was probably because I seemed a little more human (and fractionally closer to their situation) than my sleeker western colleagues, with their large apartments and chauffeur-driven Volvos. But in one huge respect, my circumstances were utterly different from any Russian's. Not only was I earning hard currency, which even in modest quantities seemed like a fortune in Russian terms; I was carrying a return ticket to the safety of London.

I remember sitting around with Andrei and his friends in chaotic, virtually unfurnished garrets whose stairways smelled of old cabbages and unwashed laundry. I remember Sasha, who is now a successful magazine editor; Mitya, an aesthete who

224

dabbled in verse and literary criticism; and Grisha who had been brought up a devout Communist and longed to find a new faith. In one particularly chaotic household of students in south Moscow, Andrei explained with a certain relish that his five flat-mates could not all eat at the same time, because they only had three dinner plates and two forks between them. In 1990 Andrei became an assiduous reporter of the proceedings of Russia's embryonic and often shambolic parliament, and I wondered what he found so interesting about the proceedings. Like a good professional news-hound, he almost always managed to find something worthwhile to report. But he later explained to me that the real attraction of parliament was its canteen, with its curling salami sandwiches and tiny pots of mushroom soufflé. At a time when the grocery shops of Moscow were simply empty, because the Communist retail system had collapsed and nothing had replaced it, it was prudent to take advantage of any source of edible, affordable food.

The day I arrived to take up my job in Russia was also the day of Andrei Sakharov's funeral. Almost the first thing I saw was a queue of thousands of people, waiting for hours upon hours in the snow, to pay their last respects to one of the few distinguished public figures who had been prepared to speak the truth when doing so carried a heavy personal price. I soon realized that I was in the most idealistic of countries, but also the most cynical of places; a world where – underneath a smokescreen of old-Communist rhetoric about equality, and new Communist rhetoric about reform and human values – almost everything and everyone was for sale. That made the few people who were not for sale, be they well-known dissidents or struggling journalists, doubly admirable.

225

But as the Soviet system teetered towards oblivion, most of its rulers were not Sakharovs or even Gorbachevs; they were bitter, narrow-minded old men who did not want to surrender an iota of their power or privilege and were prepared to act ruthlessly against any impertinent youngsters who defied their authority. A layer or two below the Politburo, cynical party hacks were preparing to sell off whatever sliver of privilege or bureaucratic access they controlled, for whatever it would fetch. Bribery under the Soviet system had been a limited, circumscribed affair; soon it would be spinning out of all control.

No wonder kids like Andrei were bewildered. My young friends had grown up in a world which, despite the stale rhetoric of revolutionary socialism, was designed to avoid change, to lock in old hierarchies; it offered a decent, dull life to those who were prepared to pay lip service to its oafish leaders and avoid protesting when their sons were recruited to fight in Afghanistan, or when brave voices of dissent were silenced. But suddenly that world was collapsing; only the young could see how fast the collapse was happening. To any intelligent youngster at that time, it was obvious that wherever truth lay, it did not lie with the hatchet-faced old rogues who were now in power. Mikhail Gorbachev had charmed and delighted the world with his attempt to reform the system in order to save it; but to impatient youngsters living inside the rusting cage, Gorbachev's promises were only a small variation on an outworn theme.

Young Soviet citizens sensed that whatever values were worth preserving, they were not the ones they had been taught in school. The old gods had died, so almost everything that the Communists had opposed – from casinos to Seventh Day

226

Adventism, from monarchist uniforms to private commodity exchanges – therefore seemed attractive and worth trying, at least once. In the twilight of Communism, a world that was designed to stay the same forever was changing so fast that today's certainties were tomorrow's forgotten absurdities. The pace of change would soon be so dizzying that only the young had any chance of keeping up; they had less to unlearn.

This was a more frightening situation than any westerners I knew had ever faced. At the height of America's youth revolution in the 1960s, rebellious Americans kids had chanted slogans like 'kill your parents'. But compared with the real, unavoidable dilemmas that these Muscovite youngsters faced, their American counterparts were silly, spoiled brats. Russians of Andrei's generation were facing real problems, not invented ones. Whatever they felt about the generation that had brought them into the world, they knew that their elders had no solutions to offer. Tomorrow would belong to the young or there would be no tomorrow.

When a regime, a power structure, a way of life, is clearly about to collapse, a number of responses are possible: people find release in eccentricity, in self-indulgence, in decadence, in self-destruction. In Andrei's circle, all these tendencies existed. But there was another possibility: to behave with wild, self-sacrificing idealism, on the ground that nothing else has any hope of succeeding. At the critical moments, Andrei always did that. During the August 1991 coup that brought down the Soviet Union, he was in the heart of the besieged White House, waiting for the tanks that might have come at any moment. In October 1993, when Yeltsin, the anti-Communist liberator, turned his tanks against the White House, Andrei's

227

sympathies swung to the other side: he understood that the repressive forces which he had opposed as a young dissident journalist were now serving new masters, and helping Yeltsin to crush his foes with all-too-Russian ruthlessness. So for several months, my reporter friend quarrelled with his radio station (which had taken a pro-Yeltsin line) and refused to broadcast. When war broke out in the north Caucasus, his moral compass told him that on those, far bloodier battlefields, Russia's future would be decided.

Returning to Moscow in the summer of 2000, I saw Andrei again and confirmed to my own satisfaction that he was still very much alive and still his old uproarious self. Everybody present drank too much vodka; in Russia it could not be any different. But suddenly, in the midst of the revelry, Andrei dug into his pocket and gave me a tiny, cheap metal cross. He told me (and I believed him) that he had taken a handful of crosses from the stall selling trinkets at Grozny's only functioning church, shortly before he tried leaving the city and was instead taken into captivity. He also told me that during his darkest moments, when all his other possessions had been taken away, these crosses had sustained him. That is not a small thing for a person who has endured captivity, beating and a high risk of death to say.

Somewhere in his dissident days in the late 1980s, Andrei had become an Orthodox Christian. At that time, being baptized was a fashionable, anti-Communist gesture, but with Andrei it had obviously gone deeper. In some ways it is hard to think of him as a religious person. Andrei is not a puritan or an ascetic in his manner or personal behaviour, and he never will be. But in another sense, he was a bearer of crosses, and supremely

228

entitled to wear one round his neck. Deeply touched,
I immediately hung his present round my neck. To my
great chagrin it fell off and disappeared a few months
later. Then it occurred to me that I was not worthy to
wear it; only Andrei was.

The Media's Fault?

JOHN SIMPSON

We live in a world where the means of communication are so sophisticated and swift that they can stir up violent emotions almost instantly in some of the least advanced countries in the world. As a result policies are destroyed, buildings are torched, and people killed even before the initial report can be verified.

On 9 May 2005, the US magazine *Newsweek* printed a paragraph that read: 'Investigators probing interrogation abuses at the US detention center at Guantanamo Bay have confirmed some infractions alleged in internal FBI e-mails that surfaced late last year. Among the previously unreported cases, sources tell *Newsweek*: interrogators, in an attempt to rattle suspects, flushed a Koran down a toilet and led a detainee around with a collar and dog leash.'

The item, with its reference to the mistreatment of the Koran, was spotted by someone on the Arabic-language television news channel al-Jazeera and broadcast as a news report.

Since then, there have been violent riots in at least six areas: Afghanistan, Pakistan, Egypt, Sudan, the Palestinian territories and Indonesia. A dozen or more people have died.

A spokesman for the Pentagon in Washington put the blame squarely on *Newsweek*. 'People are dying,' he said. 'They are burning American flags. Our forces are in danger.'

Strong accusations

The pressure was on *Newsweek* to retract its report. The magazine checked with its source – a senior US official – who confirmed that he had come across references to the mistreatment of the Koran in the results of a US investigation into the mistreatment of prisoners at Guantanamo.

But he was no longer certain that they had come from the specific report he had originally named.

These are not even the first allegations that US guards and interrogators have desecrated the Koran in order to frighten prisoners or humiliate them.

On his website the respected US authority on the Middle East, Professor Juan Cole of the University of Michigan, carries a despatch from the Italian news agency Ansa on 18 August 2004. It quotes accusations from former Guantanamo prisoners that a Koran was thrown into a toilet.

Perhaps these specific allegations are true, and perhaps they are not. But people tend to believe them, because there have been so many other allegations of deliberate anti-Islamic acts from Guantanamo, Afghanistan and Iraq – of prisoners being forced against their religious convictions to shave their beards, and even to eat pig-meat.

The shaving clearly happened: there is pictorial evidence for that. As for the forcible feeding of pork and bacon, and the desecration of the Koran itself, these things have not been proven. But such reports are instantly believed across the Islamic world.

So should *Newsweek* have reported the Koran allegation, given its inflammatory nature? It looks very much as though

232

the magazine's editors had no idea that it would be taken up so widely, or cause so much trouble.

And what about al-Jazeera? Should it have rebroadcast it, knowing how fiercely the allegation would be received by Muslims around the world?

Media under fire

The weakness of the story lies, as the Pentagon spotted immediately, in the vagueness of its sourcing, though *Newsweek* was perfectly clear that the source was an official who had seen the detail about the Koran in an official report.

With hindsight, perhaps, the magazine would have been more comfortable if it had had more details. But it did not try to deceive its readers about the story.

Yet since this was by no means the first time that allegations of the desecration of the Koran by US guards and interrogators had emerged, *Newsweek* may not have been as concerned as it might otherwise have been.

What about al-Jazeera's part in the affair? Well, if news broadcasting is about telling people what is of interest to them, then the station was only doing its job – even if that job is something which the UK and US governments often dislike and suspect (a leading adviser to the White House habitually calls al-Jazeera 'the enemy'). All al-Jazeera did was to report what *Newsweek* was saying.

It is hard to avoid the inference that the people who are really to blame are the men and women who have abused their prisoners, not those who have reported allegations about the ill treatment.

What happened in prisons like Guantanamo, Bagram and

YOU'RE HISTORY!

Abu Ghraib after 2001 has done serious damage to the United States and its allies: not just the dwindling number who still have troops in Iraq, but the new governments in Iraq and Afghanistan.

Do not blame the news media for this. Instead, all the effort needs to go into convincing the world that the abuse has stopped, and will never be allowed to start again.

Further Reading

John Simpson; *Strange Places, Questionable People*, London, Macmillan, 1998.

— *A Mad World My Masters, Tales from a Traveller's Life*, London, Macmillan, 2000.

— *News from No Man's Land: Reporting the World*, London, Macmillan 2002.

— *Days from a Different World – A Memoir of Childhood*, London, Macmillan, 2005.

Genocide: the Violence and the Silence

CIARÁN QUINN

In August 1941, but two months after Germany's surprise attack on Soviet Russia, Winston Churchill spoke by radio broadcast from London: 'The aggressor ... retaliates by the most frightful cruelties ... whole districts are being exterminated ... literally scores of thousands – of executions in cold blood ... upon the Russian patriots who defend their native soil. Since the Mongol invasions of Europe in the sixteenth century, there has never been methodical, merciless butchery on such a scale ... And this is but the beginning. Famine and pestilence have yet to follow in the bloody ruts of Hitler's tanks. We are in the presence of a crime without a name.'

The unnamed crime was not new but what was different was that this was 'the only time in history an entire industrial infrastructure, a whole industry was turned into factories of death, the systematic attempt to wipe out one people and its culture off the face of the earth' (Rabbi Jonathan Sacks, interviewed by David Frost). In 1933, Adolf Hitler and the Nazi regime came to power in Germany fuelled with the polemics of a racist rhetoric that expounded a German (Volkesdeutsche) ethnic supremacy and pursued a policy of persecution – later extermination – of those it viewed as an underclass, as virtually or actually subhuman. By 1945, the final weeks of the war in

Europe, as Allied forces from the West and Russian from the East crushed Nazi and Axis forces to overrun Germany and Poland, horrors worse than war confronted soldiers, journalists and civilians who walked into ghettoes, labour and concentration camps. There they met with men, women and children in the thousands, demoralized, many emaciated or diseased or near to death, wandering amidst the loss and carnage of kin or kindred. The Holocaust left a litany of devastation that cost many millions of lives: 6 million European Jews (including 1.5 million children); 6 million Polish citizens (3 million both Polish and Jew); 7.5 million Soviet civilians (3.2 million prisoners of war; 2 million Soviet Jews from the areas of former Eastern Poland, Belarus, Ukraine and Russia proper); Romani (East European gypsy groups); other non-ethnic groups, such as those suffering from birth defects, learning disabilities or insanity; homosexuals, prostitutes and communists, and others – all as part of 'Aryan' eugenics.

Listening in on Churchill's speech in 1941 from the US was Raphael Lemkin – Polish-Jew, lawyer and refugee – who had been living in neutral Sweden, monitoring, compiling and analysing reports on German occupation policies. Lemkin lost over sixty of his relatives in the Holocaust. In the preface to his book, *Axis Rule in Occupied Europe*, in 1943, he gave name to the crime, paralleling homicide with his new term – genocide. In 1948, the Convention on the Prevention and Punishment of the Crime of Genocide was adopted by the UN General Assembly and came into effect in January 1951. The Convention (in Article 2) defines genocide as 'any of the following acts committed with intent to destroy, in whole or in part, a national, ethnical, racial or religious group, as such':

236

(a) Killing members of the group;
(b) Causing serious bodily or mental harm to members of the group;
(c) Deliberately inflicting on the group conditions of life calculated to bring about its physical destruction in whole or in part;
(d) Imposing measures intended to prevent births within the group;
(e) Forcibly transferring children of the group to another group.

What was horrific tragedy was now also a crime. What is encouraging is that since the trials at Nuremberg and Tokyo, courts and a corpus of law can and do implement safeguards for peoples and individuals from abuses perpetrated by their own governments. What has changed for humanity worldwide is, when 'man's inhumanity to man' erupts, both the plea and the plaintive have a recourse other than to the state, the nation, the ideology, religion or ethnic group that cause their plight. But the reality is that only two members of the Security Council, France and Taiwan, signed the Convention in 1951. The USSR signed in 1954, the UK in 1970, China in 1983 (replacing Taiwan on the Council in 1971) and, belatedly, the US in 1988. Four decades of dalliance has meant that only since the 1990s has this convention proved effective.

Does history teach us anything? Two nations, Germany and Japan (accused of war crimes, not genocide), have dealt with their darkest moments in very different ways. Germany, since World War II, has conceded 24 per cent of its traditional territory to Poland and Russia. Japan has conceded only the

237

small southern Kurile Islands, north of Hokkaido, which Russia had seized in the final weeks of the war and still disputed; claims by the original indigenous inhabitants, the Ainu (Utari), are ignored by both nations. In 1958, Germany established an investigative office (still in operation) at Ludwigsburg that has charged 100,000 and convicted 6,500 individuals of Nazi crimes. In 1958, Japan released from Sugamo Prison all remaining war criminals, razed the prison in 1971 and built Sunshine 60, Tokyo's tallest building, in its place, shadowing a rock inscribed 'pray for eternal peace'. Testaments to the Holocaust in Europe lie within the scars and ghosts of buildings preserved, as at Auschwitz, and more than fifty-six Holocaust museums worldwide, while the content of school history textbooks in this respect was decided upon in negotiation with France, the Netherlands and Poland. In Japan, the most visible memorials to a wartime past are the Hiroshima Peace Park and the Atomic Bomb Museum in Nagasaki. References to Japan's aggressive expansionism in East Asia in school history textbooks has become a source of tension between Japan and its nearest neighbours, in particular the phrasing or omissions relating to the Nanjing Massacre (December 1937; 200,000–300,000 dead, 80,000 raped) and 'comfort women' (women forced to serve in military brothels in Japanese-occupied countries). While repeated visits by Japanese prime ministers to the Yasukuni Shrine ('peaceful nation shrine') where nearly 2.5 million Japanese and former colonial soldiers are enshrined, as well as fourteen Class A war criminals – *Shōwa junnansha*, Martyrs of Showa – controversially enshrined in 1978, have only served to exacerbate already strained diplomatic relations. Yet both Germany and Japan today are not only leading economies and democracies, but epitomize how the world can triumph over the worst of tyranny.

This is the goal with which prosecutors approach suspected genocidal cases. The International Criminal Court (ICC), established in 2002 at The Hague as a permanent tribunal, has begun to prosecute individuals for genocide, crimes against humanity, and mass murders; 97 countries have ratified or acceded to the ICC statute, a further 42 have signed but not ratified (September, 2004), and notably both the US and Israel who signed initially have since withdrawn their signatures. Ongoing tribunals – the International Criminal Tribunal for the Former Yugoslavia (ICTY) at The Hague and the International Criminal Tribunal for Rwanda (ICTR) at Arusha, Tanzania – have made successful convictions in their efforts to bring about justice and reconciliation for victims. Courts should be independent – politics and the judiciary are not meant to mix – yet these tribunals are dependent on goodwill and the willingness of nations and leaders to co-operate.

Is the alternative, then, to let countries deal domestically and individually with cases of genocide, as in the case of the Truth and Reconciliation Commission (TRC), set up in Cape Town in 1995, which has very successfully recorded and reached out to victims and perpetrators of human rights violations through years of oppressive apartheid? The answer appears to be no. In Rwanda in 2004, ten years after the 1994 genocide, 100,000 people, young and old, languish in jails across the country in unhealthy and overcrowded conditions awaiting trial. Only 11,000 cases have been handled to date and the government's decision in 2001 to set up localized village courts – *gacaca* ('on the grass') – electing

239

lay judges to hear testimony, has not led to a single trial and will not reach international judicial standards; nationwide with up to as many as 600,000 cases projected, it is proving unmanageable. And as a new tribunal is now set up in Cambodia, it might seem as ironic as Al Capone being caught for tax evasion that Pol Pot, leader of the Khmer Rouge which caused the deaths of 1.6 million people between 1975 and 1979, should in 1998 die of a heart attack, but not in prison. To 'bring to justice' implies not only fair and correct court procedures but catching the criminal in question.

Our promises to ourselves are unkept. The world had said 'never again' in 1948, only to watch it happen again and again. The statistics are stark and startling. In the twentieth century genocide, ethnic cleansing and mass murder killed an estimated 170 million people, more than all the wars of the century combined. Genocide is the world's worst human rights dilemma; despite the UN's guard and aspirations it remains relatively unchecked, with monitoring at times amiss and the mass murders and massacres continuing.

We should seek no panacea. We lack the institutions internationally to predict and prevent genocide. Often once action is taken, atrocities have already been committed. The caveat is the filibuster that courts require proof, reports take time and recommendations require resources for implementation; the immediacy of the emergency leaves lives lost in the piles of files, shimmering in the haze of a heated debate. Where is the recognized rapid response force, the international 'SWAT' team, regular unit or coalition with a proven track record to cope with massacres? The Geneva Convention, 1948, provides statutes but no blueprint; legislation on genocide is a landmark in human rights but a milestone too far away from its intended destination. The legacy of the last half-century in saving lives from massacres should be deplored as a litany of flaws and failure. Entrusting such matters to the UN and relying upon its resolutions in times of crisis has proved inadequate. It is sometimes tempting to think of the large amphitheatre of the General Assembly and the Security Council as a place where good men do nothing while evil triumphs. But it is also where damage is done deliberately when members obstruct, ignore, veto, or abstain from motions of urgency. Condemnation is rife but rectitude is rare.

East Timor (Timor Leste) speaks volumes for what goes wrong. On 28 November 1975, East Timor unilaterally declared independence from Portugal. Nine days later, Indonesia invaded under President Suharto, claiming the need to stem pro-Chinese communist influences and, by playing Cold War politics at the end of the US/Vietnam War, annexing East Timor without objection from the US or neighbouring Australia. During the 27 years of ensuing occupation 100,000–250,000 of the initial 1975 population of 600,000 were killed. Ironically, Australian peacekeepers were the first to arrive to restore order after anti-independence militias and elements of the Indonesian military went on a killing spree (leaving 1,400 dead and 250,000 displaced) in 1999 when the East Timorese, voting on a UN-supervised referendum, sued for independence from Indonesia. East Timor – our newest nation, our poorest people – may be forced to sell itself short on restitution. The Truth and Friendship Commission set up jointly with Indonesia grants amnesty and immunity from prosecution for atrocities in trade for truth. Indonesia has refused to extradite suspected

241

defendants; a special tribunal was set up there, trials were
highly politicized (possibly to avoid prosecutions internationally
by the UN) and all 16 defendants walked scot-free. Have
both countries put national self-interest ahead of universal
principles of justice? Jose Ramos-Horta, Timorese foreign
minister and joint Nobel Prize Winner for Peace asks with
realism: 'Are we going to be playing the role of Don Quixote
and run against the winds of justice, or play the role of
Lilliputian judges to chase every villain in the world?'
(*International Herald Tribune*, 11 May 2005).

Quixotic indeed is this maze of allies and alliances, wars
and warfare. There is the illusion that we are all 'citizens of
the world' while, in fact, we are but citizens of countries who
pick and choose their friends and agreements; being tight-lipped
or a non-signatory may be one of the best ways of literally
getting away with murder. The top five countries profiting from
the arms trade are the five permanent members of the UN
Security Council, accounting for 88 per cent of reported
conventional arms exports in what is arguably one of the most
unregulated industries worldwide. And yet it is our $2-a-day
denizens, two billion of the world's poorest people, that are
most at risk from violence. But even more alarming is the
strained malaise of weapons of mass destruction, nuclear
weapons in particular, which can cause genocide at the press
of a button, and in the face of which the only advice given
seems still to be 'duck and cover'. In 2002 there were an
estimated 20,000 nuclear weapons in the world. Although the
Nuclear Nonproliferation Treaty (NPT), opened for signature
in 1968, has proved highly successful, the five major nuclear
powers – once again the five permanent members of the

Security Council – maintain a monopoly, preaching but not practising nuclear abstinence, with no clear ethical explanation for the distinction between the 'haves and have-nots'. Meanwhile other nations – including Israel, India, and Pakistan – which are non-signatories are free to pursue their own testing and stockpiling near areas of regional conflict. Uranium enrichment, which the NPT permits for fuelling power stations, is also very close to what is needed to develop a nuclear warhead. A further 40 countries may have the potential to make the bomb. North Korea or Iran may have already done so. How hard will it be for the UN, the Security Council or others to dissuade a voice raised in anger from their use?

In a genocidal emergency whom do you call? Swift, direct intervention might appear to be the best option. However, calling upon a country to mobilize its forces turns out more often than not to be a disaster, since nearly always it is the nation's own military and police that carry out the genocide or consort with militias. Is intervention by international forces the credible deterrent? The controversial US-led invasion of Iraq, the largest foreign intervention of recent years, comes with a plethora of problems with potential genocidal implications. The problems are manifest – the legitimacy of intervention, issues of sovereignty and territorial integrity, nation building, possible abuses, exit strategies – and agendas that cannot but be informed by the fact that Kuwait and Iraq between them sit on roughly 20 per cent of the world's known oil reserves (Saudi Arabia a further 25 per cent). International forces should not be mustered ad hoc from whoever is willing but from whomsoever is appropriately required. The when, what and how of military action are thin tightropes that should be

243

pulled taut in legality, intelligence and understanding before troops tread them. Walking in the shadow of a gunman into hostile, volatile environments can escalate further violence. On the other hand, the UN made many resolutions on Iraq but remained irresolute. The stringent economic sanctions imposed on Iraq after the Gulf War, an attempt in part to force the Iraqi regime to comply with UN weapons inspectors, are estimated to have caused 400,000–500,000 infant mortalities among the under fives during 1991–8 (UNICEF report, August 1999). The world has yet to learn how to cut the Gordian knot.

US forces in Iraq and Afghanistan are over-stretched at present in the name of democracy. Should we set up, as Dr Gregory Stanton (Genocide Watch) urges, a 'UN standing, volunteer, professional rapid response force that does not depend on member governments' contributions of brigades from their own armies'? Articles 43–48 of the UN Charter provide for a permanent command structure – never created – under which a standing army could be established; this is a step too radical in global governance and bites off the hand that funds you. The UN has over 66,000 military personnel and civilian police serving in peacekeeping operations, over 4,000 international civilian personnel and over 8,000 local civilian personnel, with 103 contributing countries operating at present in sixteen missions worldwide, and has suffered more than 1,900 fatalities since 1948. The figures look impressive, suggesting that things are being done – and they are. Each peacekeeping operation has a specific set of mandated tasks, sharing common aims in striving to alleviate human suffering and, in a third-party capacity, to create conditions and build institutions for self-sustaining peace. In both Bosnia and

Rwanda peacekeeping forces froze or failed to act and the UN, the US and the world looked on and did little as people died; returning thereafter to keep the peace. Proffering paper cranes after the atomic bomb has dropped is an appalling indictment on how thin the veneer of conviction to prevent genocide can be.

Bosnia-Hercegovina, in October 1991, made a declaration of sovereignty and in February 1992 forwarded a referendum for independence from Yugoslavia which the Bosnian-Serb minority (32 per cent) boycotted. Soon after, Serbs and Bosnian Serbs attacked Croats and Bosniaks to tear the republic apart along ethnic lines and withhold areas that favoured a 'greater Serbia'. A war erupted and in 1992–3 Europe suffered its worst genocide since 1945. By the end of the war in November 1995, signalled by the Dayton Agreement, an estimated 200,000 had died, with 20,000 missing; 2 million more had fled. Serbian military units had massacred tens of thousands; a new term, 'ethnic cleansing' in the English language, had made its debut. Richard Holbrooke, US Assistant Secretary of State, described the debacle as 'the greatest failure of the West since the 1930s'. Who was responsible for the Balkan brutalities? Ultimately, ultra-Serbian nationalism incited by demagogues such as Slobodan Milosevic (now on trial at The Hague) and Radovan Karadzic (still at large) may be to blame. Yet the global village also kept its shutters down for too long: the response from world leaders was tardy, measures taken to halt the slaughter shoddy. On 2 August 1992 Roy Gutman in *Newsday* broke the story of death camps in northern Bosnia; the next day an official from the Bush Administration faced a media barrage and stated that the government had been aware of their existence; the day after that another official stated that they had not been aware of any camps. If governments had known of the camps and acted earlier who knows how many lives might have been saved; estimates say some 35,000 Muslims died in the first few months of the Bosnian war. But there were politics to be played, three months before a presidential election, and the spectre of Vietnam still haunted the corridors of Congress and the Pentagon. When, on 6 August 1992, our eyes met with images on television (via a British ITN report) of emaciated men, sunken-cheeked and hollow-eyed, behind the wire in a camp at Omarska, northern Bosnia, it was as if we were watching 'the drowned ... an anonymous mass ... of non-men ... in silence ... One hesitates to call them living: one hesitates to call their death death, in the face of which they have no fear, as they are too tired to understand' (Primo Levi; *Survival in Auschwitz*, 1993, p. 90). Bullets weren't wasted; at Omarska men wasted away, kept near to starvation in a terror of unrelenting cruelty and degradation – a rot. It had happened again. It was only then, faced with the likelihood of an outraged American public, that President Bush (senior) began to talk of the need for international observers and UN humanitarian aid. When the decision was given, finally, to dispatch American troops it was to a different starving population – in war-torn Somalia (Mark Danner, 4 December 1997, 'America and the Bosnia Genocide', *The New York Times Review of Books*).

The war got worse. Fulfilling election promises in 1992, the new president, Bill Clinton, issued an ultimatum, deploying NATO forces to bombard Serbian ground positions. However, a Muslim–Croat alliance failed to stop Serbian attacks on Muslim towns in Bosnia that the UN had designated as 'Safe Havens';

246

six towns were under UN supervision by May 1993. Despite NATO limited air strikes on Serbian forces, UN peacekeepers were taken hostage and held as human shields. Then, in July 1995, Serb forces under General Ratko Mladic (indicted by the International Criminal Tribunal, 1996) invaded Srebrenica, a 'Safe Haven'. Dutch UN peacekeepers allowed Serbs to walk in and pick out Muslim men and boys aged between 12 and 60. The Red Cross now lists 7,079 dead and missing at Srebrenica. In November 1999, the UN released a highly self-critical report stating that 'Through error, misjudgment and the inability to recognize the scope of evil confronting us, we failed to do our part to save the people of Srebrenica from the Serb campaign of mass murder.'

In Rwanda, on 6 April 1994, the airplane carrying Habyarimana, President of Rwanda, and Ntaryamira, President of Burundi, was shot down as it prepared to land at Kigali, the capital. This was a catalyst that contributed to a catastrophe. Hutu militias went on the rampage to drive out ethnic Tutsis and moderate Hutus. Civil war and a massacre ensued. A hundred days later – with around 10,000 people dying each day – 937,000 lay dead and 250,000 had been raped. The slaughter only ended when the Tutsi Rwandese Patriotic Front under Paul Kagame invaded from neighbouring Uganda and a Tutsi-led government took power.

Were the 'ancient animosities' between a lighter-skinned ruling Tutsi minority (15 per cent) and a darker-tanned Hutu majority (85 per cent) solely responsible for hurling everyone into such horror? Or was Rwanda overtaken by the ills of Africa: debt-induced poverty, mismanagement, the haemorrhage of a soul-destroying slave trade, the implications attendant upon the carving-up of a continent and of colonials leaving newly fledged nations to grapple with political delineations which may be antithetical to ethnic and territorial realities – the population of the Congo, Rwanda included, was halved, leaving 10 million dead between 1880 and 1920, under the Belgian King Leopold II.

Although it looked like nobody had noticed, actually the 'international community' had turned a blind eye. General Roméo Dallaire, United Nations Assistance Mission for Rwanda (UNAMIR) commander, learned of the shipments of 500,000 machetes to arm Interahamwe (Hutu) guerillas at their training camps. On 11 January he faxed the UN headquarters in New York seeking authorization to confiscate the caches; his request was refused, the explanation given being that he would be exceeding his mandate. Instead the Security Council voted in favour of a US-led motion to pull out all of the 2,500 UNAMIR troops; Dallaire maintains that his troops could have saved lives by the thousands – or more. To the US and other nations the debacle may have looked like just another failure to intervene, to judge the situation, to take action, but in fact 'The decision was not to act. And at that we succeeded greatly' (Philip Gourevitch, 'The Triumph of Evil', Frontline Documentary, PBS). Promises to protect were broken and blame lies in part with 'people like me, sitting in offices day after day' (President Clinton, speaking with regret about the Rwanda genocide, 26 March 1998, Civic Center, Cape Town). A series of massive population displacements, a nagging Hutu extremist insurgency, and Rwandan involvement in the First and Second Congo Wars in the neighbouring Democratic Republic of the Congo continue to hinder Rwanda's recovery.

One wonders when the killings – 80,000 murdered, 180,000 dead from hunger and disease, 2 million displaced – in Sudan will cease. Since early 2003, in the western region of Darfur, civilians of the same ethnicity as members of two rebel groups, the Sudan Liberation Army (SLA) and the Justice and Equality Movement (JEM), have been subjected to state-sponsored terror and a systematic scorched earth policy. Indiscriminate aerial bombardment in north Darfur, in particular, and the violent attacks of the 'Janjaweed' – militia forces recruited from Arab nomadic tribes – have left a blighted land fallow and empty. The UN took five months to debate whether or not genocide had occurred in Darfur, reaching the conclusion that it had not, in a report released on 25 January 2005. Although the report does state that ethnic cleansing and war crimes have occurred, giving the clear precedent for action internationally, we are still left with the lethargy of a slow action replay, watching as hundreds of thousands of refugees spill over into camps in neighbouring Chad and as humanitarian aid arrives without heeding the medical adage 'prevention rather than cure'. The world still stands idly by but 'We cannot say we didn't know, and we cannot say there was nothing to be done. We must act – unless we plan on mixing tears with our popcorn all over again, as we settle down sometime in 2015 for a screening of a new, acclaimed movie: Hotel Darfur' (Jonathan Freedland, *Guardian*, 30 March 2005).

Genocide is a rare crime, an emotive issue – highly charged. To be accused of it is to sit in the dock indicted of the intent to wipe out a part of humanity – 'dead as a dodo', as Lewis Carroll put it in *Alice in Wonderland*. But, although the 'crime of genocide' is a legal concept, it was conceived in response to a moral imperative and is about people and pain. As we sit down to Thanksgiving dinner, should we forget those from Arctica to Antarctica who were wiped out, systematically and inadvertently, by war and disease (smallpox, influenza, and measles) during the colonization of the Americas by European settlers (and others) since the time of Columbus? Estimates of the pre-contact 1492 US/Canada population range from 1.8 to 12 million, but four hundred years later only 237,000 descendants of the indigenous populations remained: it took only four decades for the native people in post-conquest Mexico to be reduced from 30 million to 3 million. Schoolboys on both sides of 'The Pond' were fed a diet of Caesar's *Gallic Wars* as a model for manhood for over two hundred years and barely considered the death toll of a probable 1 million Gauls – victims of Caesar's ethnically based aggression. Even today our 'Books of the Dead' still tend to commemorate the Unknown Soldier, rather than the unknown civilian.

The crimes of genocide are both chronic and acute and our collective DNA pool has lost a genetic marker or two of late. There remain some rare biodiverse gems of race, culture and language within and outside of Africa, but for the remaining 350 million indigenous peoples, 50 million of whom are rainforest dwellers, the situation is precarious: in 1500, there were over 1,000 different tribes in Brazil and now there are only 215. There are habitats denuded, hidden from history – mass graves but no bodies – and undocumented because crops and profit, multinationals or farmers don't document or leave room for the hunter-gatherers from whom we are all descended. In 2002 the government of Botswana drove all the Bushmen out of the Central Kalahari Game Reserve, their ancestral home for 20,000 years, an event that went unnoticed while the world media made headline news about a handful of white farmers being evicted from their lands in neighbouring Zimbabwe. Although it is not genocidal, lack of interest and neglect may lead us to watch the world's oldest surviving people, possibly the most direct link back to our most recent common female ancestor, 'Mitochondrial Eve' who lived some 150,000 years ago, soon disappear.

So, should we just put a penny in the rusty tin for the blind beggar or should we really address the issues? The dilemma is that genocide is a crime for which the body of evidence must conclusively prove that the veritable intent was not to decimate but to annihilate. Silence conceals truth. The mute or muzzled are not only the victims but those who deny. Successive Turkish governments have rejected the charge of genocide for the large-scale massacres of Armenians caused through their forced displacement by Turks in 1915–17 (with an estimated 750,000–1,000,000 dead), despite this being the second most-studied probable case of genocide, now acknowledged by a small but growing group of countries. Denial might consist of questioning or ignoring facts, or of claiming inadvertence such as famine, migration and disease, or of rationalization based on economics and inter-racial conflicts, or of blaming the victims, or of arguing that genocide doesn't define the crime ... The heart-rending reality, however, is that although we may take months or years to indict or to convict, we can never staunch the ebb and flow of bloodstained events – but at the very least their history will be 'an argument without end' (Pieter Geyl), forever scrutinized and never forgotten. The one evil worse than mass murder and genocide is having to walk away powerless in the aftermath, knowing that, so long as the judge is forced to proclaim 'silence, silence in court', it will happen again.

Further Reading

Harff, B., *Early Warning of Communal Conflict and Genocide: Linking Empirical Research to International Responses* (Boulder, Colorado: Westview Press, 2003).

Power, S., *'A Problem from Hell': America and the Age of Genocide* (New York: Basic Books, 2002).

Totten, S., W. S. Parsons and I. W. Charny, eds, *Century of Genocide: Critical Essays and Eyewitness Accounts* (2nd edition, London: Routledge, 2004).

Websites

Human Rights Watch: www.hrw.org
Genocide Watch: www.genocidewatch.org
Refugee Action: www.refugee-action.org

Change – and North Korea: Is Aid Really Making a Difference?

KATHI ZELLWEGER

'Why are you doing this?' (This meaning giving aid to the North Korean people.) 'That terrible regime will never change or collapse,' they continue, 'if you continue to give aid.' Such is a fairly typical beginning of conversations relief workers engaged in Democratic People's Republic of Korea (DPRK) relief efforts face among friends, colleagues and acquaintances.

Not that surprising of course. If you think of North Korea, unflattering images immediately appear: hungry children, starvation, disease and poverty, weapons of mass destruction, refugees, human rights crises, a gloomy economy, isolation, control – all negative pictures. Other accompanying and complicating images might include South Korea's reconciliation and engagement policy with the North, or President Bush branding North Korea as part of an 'axis of evil'.

So it was that ten years ago, in the spring of 1995, I set foot for the first time on North Korean soil, at a time when library shelves on the Korean peninsula were packed with books about the South, and almost bare of any material about the Northern part. So, ill prepared, but with an open mind, I began to absorb the workings of a totally different society, and became fascinated by an absorbing experience, one far removed from the mainstream.

253

The food situation at that time was already precarious, but the devastating floods that came in the summer of 1995 proceeded to wipe out the harvest and food stocks, culminating in large-scale famine. And it was not only natural catastrophes. With the break-up of the Soviet Union, North Korea had lost its friends and the centrally planned command economy began to fail. The DPRK government, despite its fervent guiding ideology of self-reliance, for the first time in its history asked for humanitarian assistance from the international community – and for almost all of the decade since then governments, UN agencies and a number of non-governmental organizations (NGOs) have been providing such support. The needs are manifold: food, medicine, clothing, clean drinking water, school materials, fertilizer, plastic sheeting and hand tools – to name just a few.

We all know that human suffering arouses strong emotional reactions of concern and compassion, but depending on the nature of the disaster, it can also bring about feelings of helplessness and anger – dilemmas for the outside observer but even more so for the aid worker on the ground, who must deal with host governments, donors and beneficiaries and is often faced with the daunting task of prioritizing aid programmes because there is never enough assistance for all who need and deserve it.

From the onset, humanitarian aid and communist regimes make strange partners – and North Korea is no exception, with the added complexity of being part of a divided country. Thus, while South Korea, Japan, the US, the EU and some other governments tend to make decisions regarding the provisions of aid according to their own political agendas, North Korea remains eager to restrict direct contacts between donors or aid workers and the ordinary North Koreans, who are the aid recipients. A North Korean official once put it bluntly, stating that 'humanitarian aid is sugar with poison' while aid from South Korea is viewed as almost 'an obligation within the family' since the South has the ability to produce more than just what is required for its own needs. Therefore, while international NGOs working in this isolated country are, like anywhere else in the world, guided by the principle of 'concern for people in need', they nevertheless often face almost insurmountable dilemmas. The advice given to them by those aware of the complexities of working in North Korea is simply: 'Soldier on.' For the international press the problem of no access exacerbates the task of describing a situation to the rest of the world, to a public that has a mostly negative view of North Korea, so that often 22 million people, ordinary people who happen to be the residents of North Korea and who struggle for survival there, are forgotten and left without a voice. NGOs raising money for North Korea struggle with this too because of the media projecting an image that is not conducive to giving amongst the wider public.

During my nineteenth trip to North Korea in 1998 I wrote a diary; the entry for 17 September reads:

The last stop of three days in the field leaves a very lasting impression. The patients in Kaesong city's pediatric hospital are all malnourished to some degree and some of them have other medical conditions also. The 50 or so children that we see range in age from one week to 13 years. The director, Dr Han, who has worked there for 10 years tells us that there were no malnutrition cases until three years ago and that now most malnutrition occurs in children under three. However, many of the children that we see are aged between 8 and 13, and are malnourished. They look somehow neglected and apathetic and there are no relatives with them unlike the younger children. We can't help wondering where these children have come from and what their future is.

Some of the children are receiving glucose and water through naso-gastric tubes or intravenous lines. The solution bottles still bear labels (including Fanta and mineral water), telling us that they have not been sterilized. Lack of food is not the only problem – the children also have diarrhoea, which Dr Han tells us is a result of dirty drinking water. At present three to four children are dying each month and this is very credible – many of the children appear so weak that it's hard to imagine how they will survive the harsh Korean winter.

The desire to present visual images to our donors and friends is nevertheless not strong enough to enable us to point a camera at mothers and their hungry children – they too have their dignity. Despite the fact that we have three cameras between us we have no photos of Kaesong Children's Hospital, except the photo images in our minds.

Dr Han pleads for increased help and is open in his admission that the hospital could not cope without it. We leave Kaesong Children's Hospital, lost in thought – not only are we thus affected: our Korean colleagues were also obviously moved by the visit. The journey back to Pyongyang is a quiet one. Our thoughts are full of frustration, sadness and anger and an overriding sense of helplessness – where do we go from here and what is the most appropriate way for our charity, Caritas, to help?

Today, the situation has improved slightly, but it is a fragile, unsustainable recovery with a need for aid agencies to shift from relief to more long-term development assistance. Without addressing the root causes of the problem, people will somehow – and in part thanks to relief aid – survive or keep afloat, but without a chance to develop and grow. That presents a grim picture for the future.

But there is hope too. Walking around Pyongyang, but also in other parts of the country, one can see that people have become used to seeing foreigners and now even show some curiosity. 'Where are you from?' asked a teenager in his blue and white school uniform, practising his first English language skills. Aid beneficiaries are also surprised to find that strangers come from afar to offer help. Moreover, aid has called for linkages with North Korean officials at national, provincial, county and village levels and the relationships thus established have grown over the years, showing an increased openness to discussing and addressing issues. Not all of the issues though: from the continuing flow of defectors from the North, knowledge about human rights violations, the existence of labour camps, oppression and discrimination has become available in the media. Some of this information cannot be confirmed or verified; some appears to be credible; some of it is doubtful, and distinguishing the wheat from the chaff is often impossible. Nevertheless, human rights abuses are a great concern and cannot be dropped from an aid worker's agenda.

To the questions: what is poverty? what is suffering and distress? who decides? there are some answers available. Sixty to seventy per cent of the North Korean population depends on rations from the Public Distribution System. But ordinary civilians are getting food rations of only 750–1,000 calories a day, half of the UN's standard daily intake for refugees sitting in camps, and just over a third of the calorie level for people who are working. Chronic malnutrition remains the fate of the majority.

Only a small group of people that have access to foreign currency from foreigners through business, aid or party connections can live well, but still even they cannot escape an environment with a depleted infrastructure: bad roads, erratic electricity supply and poor water and sanitation facilities.

Aid is critical: providing food, medical care and basic education is a direct and tangible means of supporting human dignity. The people here are hungry, but not only for food. The authorities keep a tight lid on information and officially only national news is available: no international newspapers, magazines, television programmes, no Internet, no email services, no mobile telephones – all reminiscent of China during the Cultural Revolution (1967–76).

We, the visitors, have a hard time finding out how ordinary people think or how they view their own situation. But here and there, in locations near the border, radio messages received from China offer a glimpse of the outside world to them. The increased number of visitors to the country, the small international humanitarian and diplomatic community living there and more North Koreans travelling abroad are all puncturing the bubble of the tightly controlled system.

Contrary to popular knowledge, in the past few years North Korea also began moving towards opening its doors and working on economic reforms. Reform is always a difficult process and particularly for an isolated country like the DPRK. Measures taken are gradual; change is only creeping in. The cradle-to-grave security is disappearing and ordinary people are given more freedom and therefore responsibility. Receiving a salary instead of coupons for daily necessities and food rations makes an immense difference.

The newly established all-purpose markets, whose existence was unthinkable even five years ago, are packed with people, shoppers and, even more so, curious onlookers without money – but interested in finding out what is available there. In fact, almost anything can be purchased – fruits, vegetables, spices and herbs, rice, maize, noodles, flour, edible oil, chocolates, biscuits, sweets, cigarettes, Cuban cigars and all sorts of drinks, all of this mostly from China, competing with local goods. Meat, seafood and fish vendors are less busy; it is all a matter of cost, as is the case in other non-affluent societies. The washing machines, refrigerators, pirated DVDs, computers, shovels, new and second-hand bicycles displayed, remain dreams for but a handful, especially visitors. The sales teams are all female, equipped with small calculators. The price is flashed at us non-Korean customers and the bargaining can start: clothing and shoes, belts, soap, lipsticks and underwear – all again from China. Garments with labels cut out originate from the 'village below' – meaning South Korea. So, the streets of Pyongyang have become more colourful, but it still remains the only country I know of where blue jeans are forbidden.

Small-scale entrepreneurship is bustling: from hair cutting to delivering wood, sewing, repairing bicycles or selling ice cream. Money instead of communist ideology, propaganda and devotion to Marshal Kim Jong II, is now the topic at family dinners or in the packed beer halls. People now have dreams, hopes and aspirations. But of course market reforms in any transition economy bring gains and pains, winners and losers. The new 'have-nots' are mostly industrial workers employed by big, but idle, state-run companies, living in dark, dilapidated apartment blocks without a garden or access to a piece of land on which to grow food. The average worker's salary amounts to one US dollar a day at current black market rates, or, to make it real, it buys you perhaps five kilos of rice. So among the most vulnerable are the children, the pregnant and nursing women, the sick and the old.

Without hesitation it needs to be stated that it is morally unacceptable to allow people to suffer and die on the grounds that aid will support a nasty government or its army. It must, however, be remembered that humanitarianism does not prevent famine. Aid is about saving lives; reducing human suffering; supporting the survival tactics of individuals who must change out of bare necessity and aid also opens channels of dialogue with governments. Although one of the most difficult tasks is to change a closed mind, as is the necessity of having the patience not to expect quick results but to support an often slow process, these are the realities in the DPRK. External pressure seldom has a favourable impact as real change has to come from within a society: *change imposed often results in change being opposed.*

In 2000, after travelling in the country for three weeks, I shared my impressions and observations with officials in Pyongyang and I was told it would be better not to use the word 'reform', just 'interesting change'. Now today reform is part of the daily vocabulary, along with many market economy terms and the fact of hundreds of North Koreans studying abroad. Originally, the first group of DPRK students I encountered had left Pyongyang with the proud attitude of 'we know it all'; by now that has become 'we know we have to learn a lot'. So that is genuine progress.

Opening up this economy simply cannot be done in isolation and it only works if the international community is willing to help. In North Korea's path to advancement, domestic reforms to increase production and profits are the first steps taken by internal measurements. Trade and investment with other countries, as well as the relief and development aid, will eventually lead to a long-lasting solution, provided that the political environment improves and the goal of denuclearizing the Korean peninsula is achieved.

In the meantime, guided by the principle of 'humanity tied to impartiality', aid workers not only bring aid to the poor to cover basic human needs, but also help to build bridges; encourage change; support training; bring hope to people and advocate on their behalf. But we must ask ourselves: Are we on the right track in the aid 'business'? The answer is that we constantly need to evaluate; to learn; to understand; to study the social and cultural contexts; to accept differences; to be cautious; and to try to do no harm, dealing with difficulties and frustrations and always putting our own prejudices behind us. It is a tall order and one that we must try to fill, if there is to be hope.

Those pictures not taken, of hundreds of children, all taut skin and bones sticking out, the ones I saw in that summer of 1995 in the North Korean institutions, still haunt me. I knew immediately that the majority I would never see again. For them it was probably too late: when the aid came, it would no longer be for them but for others.

So now the children I do see can smile again. Some aid has come: it is something.

We all realize that the situation in North Korea is tainted by international and national politics but humanitarian needs should override political considerations if we are to be true to our mission. Assistance must continue. But there are so many emergencies competing for funds and people tire of giving ...

Further Reading

Alexander De Waal, *Famine Crimes: Politics and the Disaster Relief Industry*, Villiers Publications, London, 1997.

Bruce Cummings, *Korea's Place in the Sun: A modern history*, New York, W. W. Norton, 1997.

Larry Minear, *The Humanity Enterprise: Dilemmas and Discoveries*, Bloomfield, CT, Kumarian Press, 2002.

Don Oberdorfer, *The Two Koreas: A Contemporary History* Reading, MA, Addison Wesley Longman, 1997.

C. Ford Runge *et al.*, *Ending Hunger in Our lifetime: Food Security and Globalization*, published for the International Food Policy Research Institute by The Johns Hopkins University Press, 2003.

Toni Vaux, *The Selfish Altruist: Relief Work in Famine and War*, Earthscan Publications, UK and USA, 2001.

Simon Winchester, *Korea: A walk through the Land of Miracles*,
London, Perennial, 2005

Websites
Caritas International: www.caritas.org
caritas – Hong Kong: www.caritas.org.hk
Relief Web: www.reliefweb.int

The Dregs in the Pot of Gold: the Irish Experience of Exchanging Dignity for Racism

ALAN TITLEY

We do not want to live in mutually unimaginable worlds.

The imagination is the spark that engenders empathy with others elsewhere. Others elsewhere live for us because we see ourselves in them. 'We' is everyone else, because 'we' have been there and if we haven't been there, we haven't been anywhere at all.

We have seen the future and it is the past. We have seen the past and it is not another country. We have seen the past and the present and the future and they are lodged in the imagination. The imagination is either big and expansive and smiling, or it is small and narrow and sour-pussed.

I walked the streets of London as a student looking for accommodation. I did see the sign in black and red and forbidding Gothic lettering: 'No dogs, no blacks, no Irish'. The woman who answered the door had a beautiful smile and a grin that bespoke more than just rent and profit. It wiped away to some place that I have never understood when I opened my mouth and she heard my ungarbled Irish vowels, my unsoftened consonants and my rhotic 'orrs'. As the Irish came third in the trinity, I often wondered if it would have been better to be a dog?

It must be similar in Ireland today for those who come to make their living there. Apologetic legislation requires that nothing as crude as 'No blacks, yids or dodgy eastern European types' need apply can be published. Despite this, it does not stop the late night radio chat shows, nor the street gossip, nor members of the Irish parliament hinting and nudging and nodding and winking and smiling and giving out signals that we are not any more the land of a hundred thousand welcomes, unless there are wads of fat dollars in your back pocket and your skin is a whiter shade of pale.

There is one great big sense in which all of this should be wondrously strange. The entire Irish national project was driven by the demon of dignity. There was always a lively understanding that if Ireland sought her freedom from the British Empire, then it was perfectly understandable that others should do the same. No group or gaggle – unless they have a direct line to God – can claim for themselves what cannot be claimed for others. All anti-imperial intentions spring from the rights of 'man' expressed both individually and collectively.

The great Irish democrat Daniel O'Connell opposed slavery on these very grounds before it became either diurnal or demagogic. The leaders of the Irish political revolution after World War I begged entrance to the Versailles Conference as that appalling war of carnage was supposedly fought for the freedom of small nations; and for many years the Irish political elite remembered that some nations were small, but some were much smaller than others. The Irish government tried to steer a neutral path when they entered the United Nations, although one foreign minister is reputed to have said that the Arabs and the Israelis should sit down and solve their disputes 'in a good Christian manner'. Another diplomat put it that Ireland was always 'between Iraq and a hard place'. In recent years, the Irish won a place on the Security Council, because, as President Mary McAleese put it, it was a country with a first world standard of living and a third world memory. It may be truer now to say that Ireland is a first world country with the practices of a third world government.

There is no problem now with that first world standard of living, at least for those people whose business it is to make money. There is a problem, however, with the third world memory. It is the snow of yesteryear, the bog-cotton blowing in the wind, the foam on the slush of the receding tide.

I met somebody a few years ago who in turn knew somebody who was alive during the great Irish famine of 1845–7. It was only yesteryear. Put out your hand and you can touch its cold fingers. The Irish countryside is littered with deserted villages and lush green grass fertilized by the bodies of those who perished from hunger. Irish America and Irish Britain live because millions of the Irish in Ireland died.

It was a devastation that the Irish did not want to remember. No other European country lost one quarter of its population in a period of five years. No other European country lost its language in two generations. No other European country chose to forget what it could not bear to recall. We developed generations of the unknowing, hugging the amnesia of the past in the hope of a better future.

There were bits and pieces, of course. The sun going down over Galway Bay, and the soft voices on the Old Bog Road, and Old Killarney Hats, and Two-Shillealagh O'Sullivan having it out with Darby O'Gill and the Quiet Man. We invented an identity of kitsch because we had trashed everything else and we put on the emotive aura of the hurt and the oppressed for the while that we needed it.

People of a certain generation in Ireland remember vividly the 'penny for the black babies' that they brought to school every week. We were not sure what those pennies were for except that they were pennies from heaven from us. We knew it had something to do with Catholic missionary activity, and also with the alleviation of poverty and the feeding of hungry mouths that had not the strength to look up. We paid and we knew that it was good.

We loved those black babies, but we loved them from afar. We knew that we could visit them, but we never dreamed that they could visit us. And we still love those black babies; but we love them in their prams. We 'oogle' at them and 'goo' at them and make lovely babbling noises. They have that chocolate skin that we pay fortunes to acquire every summer in 'Creet' [sic Crete] and in 'Ibeeta' [sic Ibiza] and in 'Sancho Panza', or wherever it is, but who cares because we fly there. And they have sparkling shiny teeth that no dentist could ever give you, and deep dark eyes inviting you to delve into the secret recesses of romantic Africa, and most of all they do not speak. Because when they speak they actually say things, and they say things we do not want to hear, and they say things that call up the ghosts from the nether regions that we have been trying to bury under prosperity and progress.

They call up our own famine, and our own emigration, and our own economic and political refugees. And these are things that we wish to dump in the garbage bin of the past. We desire a past washed clean in order to show ourselves in the bright shop window of the gaudy world. Even in the current quotidian present less than dense Irish politicians cannot see the contradiction between representing the case of illegal Irish immigrants in the United States and closing the door of charity on illegal immigrants of darker hue in Ireland. It is because they choose not to see it.

Even the Irish propensity for self-colonization should generate that smidgen of sympathy that should lead to greater justice and equality. Immigrants will normally attempt to abandon the baggage of their previous culture and integrate in their new surroundings as far as they can. They will retain some symbols and some signs and some wonders; or they may reshape an identity based on a dubious essentialism, even though their essentialism is often a defence against being wiped out and a device for staying intact. More than anything else, immigrants bring energy and drive and a will to succeed. Crossing the sandy desert holed up in the back of an airless truck is their equivalent of the Irish diaspora – being tossed on the briny ocean in the steerage class of coffin ships before being deloused and examined for physical and mental imperfections on arrival in Ellis Island, the gateway to the US.

The best are full of passionate intensity and the worst grow weak and wan at home.

The Irish myth prided itself on being non-racist, and we do need myths to survive and to guide. It may have been a necessary fiction, as all national movements require some element of moral difference in order to put long green grass between them and their former masters. If the British had treated their 'lesser' breeds with some contempt then we were not going to do the same. There is some evidence to show that the Irish missionaries did not have the same disdain for the 'native' populations as others did; but there is also evidence to the contrary.

The treatment meted out to minorities and to people with differences in the new Irish State was, at times, disgraceful. Orphans, unmarried mothers and travellers were shunned, or locked away, or segregated. The seeds of Irish racism were sown in the industrial schools for abandoned children, in the Magdalen Laundries where 'fallen women' were incarcerated and often left to rot, and in the camp sites where itinerants or tinkers smelled on the side of the lovely nice road or on the edge of the fancy neighbourhood even when it was only on the bottom rung of the greasy property ladder.

But it was a racism that was confined to our own, and what we had we could hold forth with them in whatever way we liked. And it was not based on the colour of the skin, but rather on some notion of moral weakness, and so it was deemed to be acceptable. Irish priests in the mission fields and Irish soldiers in the Congo displayed our love and our concern, and when the starving children in Biafra and Ethiopia appeared on our television screens in the 1960s and the 1980s respectively, we dug deeply in our pockets and congratulated ourselves on our generosity. But when the tide of human misery and necessity threw them up as naked strangers on our shore we averted our eyes, or said 'We do not know you! Go back to from where you came!'

In 2004, Ireland had a citizenship referendum. There had not been any discussion of citizenship in Irish political discourse for three generations. Up until that referendum anybody born in Ireland was automatically entitled to Irish citizenship. It was

a generous and a wholesome rule. The political elite proposed
a change that would not automatically confer citizenship at
birth. There was no overt demand for this as it was never a
public issue. The worst of the politicians – and in Ireland they
are just as venal, corrupt and crude as anywhere else – had
their ears to the dirty holes in the ground, and the grot in the
bus, and the armpit of the street corner, and the cesspool of
the squinting-windows town, and they heard the Alabama
whispers, and the plaintive bourgeois whine, and the pure
musings of a *terra blanche*. They were stealing our women, and
taking our hospital beds, and getting our jobs, and jumping
our queues, and sponging off the state, and organizing crime,
and financing scams and doing all those things that the Irish
never did to themselves. And anyway, there were just too many
of 'them' there.

It is the use of 'them' that was the most interesting. There
had been substantial immigration into Ireland for more than
ten years since the Celtic Tiger grew his claws and started to
growl. Much of this immigration was from other countries in
the European Union, and from the United States and Australia.
Ne'er a murmur was raised or heard about this immigration. It
was only when the skin became dark, and the hair tight and
curly, and the teeth as pearly white as Mack the Knife that the
racist skeleton began to rattle in the closet. The 'them' was
'the darkies', the different and the done-down.

Twenty years ago all of my students in a tutorial group
supported the anti-apartheid movement, loved Nelson Mandela,
and got angry if there was any suggestion that blacks were
inferior, or that ebony and ivory could not live in perfect
harmony; twenty years later all of my students in a similar

271

tutorial group, and I mean all, thought there were too many of 'them' in our country. Not 'racist', of course, just about citizenship. Nobody is racist, of course, it's just that they lower the price of property, and you'd better get born somewhere else. The referendum was carried by a majority of four to one.

After that, the deportations began. First of all they came for the men, and nobody said anything. And then they came for the families, and everybody kept their mouths shut. And then they came for the children, ripping them from their schools with their uniforms on and locking them in the big airplanes as they were taken away as deportees. This is what people voted for, and they knew it. It need not have been like that, but it was. The Irish government, when it has a choice between power and compassion, will always choose power.

It was not supposed to be like that. There was an Irish dream that was not the American one. There is always a dream that lives within a people that sustains them even if they sully and abuse it. Dreams, like nations, are abstractions, and abstractions have an arbitrary and porous quality about them. Whatever that Irish dream was it had something to do with dignity, equality and international solidarity on the civic front. It grew out of the famine and nurtured a new state. It was nourished by an artistic and cultural renaissance whose afterglow still lends light to the life of the country. Great literature, poetry, art, drama and music are never the product of hatred. Great art cannot be mean-spirited and small and sour and little-roomed. The Irish creation of their own imagination reached out to others as all imagination does.

There are lessons here for greater understanding and greater sympathy beyond what we can do for others in the economic

272

sphere. There are obvious issues of the abolition of debt, free trade and immediate relief from destitution on which I am not competent to add anything. It is true that when you are wounded your wound is the only reality. But there are issues beyond the economic that the Irish experience might illuminate for good or for ill, unless we presume that the only goal in life is the accumulation of lovely lucre and gaining steps on the property beanstalk to the castle in the sky.

The Irish have shed identities like a dog shakes off fleas. They swapped a linguistic for a religious one in the nineteenth century; then adopted political nationalism informed by a reinvigorated culture at the end of that century; statehood buttressed these identities until religion withered under the assault of secularism, a religion (or religiosity) hand in glove with the state which between them concealed scandals that eventually burst upon us; and political nationalism became suspect because of the conflict in Northern Ireland; communal goals have been eroded by the introduction of individualist capitalism as the highest ideal. What the Irish have not had for a long time is a sense of unproblematic nationality (as distinct from 'nationalism'), and they have never had a sense of civic duty or identity that transcends the mere paying of taxes, exchanges in the currency of thin public words and occasional participation in communal affairs.

The very fact of statehood, however, for all its faults, failings and embarrassments, has had a dramatic effect on Irish life. Statehood, undoubtedly coupled with education and democracy, rather than with ignorance and dictatorship, has made an immeasurable difference to people's lives. That immeasurable difference took several generations to work its way through.

It may take 60 or 70 years of independence, education and democracy for any state to gain enough confidence, to make enough mistakes, to laugh enough at itself, to forge enough inchoate belonging, to be finally successful in looking after its citizens without favour or fear.

Independent democratic states with an educated population do not have famines or mass poverty. Knowledge revolts against stupidity, and necessity demands a place at the table of the accessible. Irish political experience gives one example of the shadow of a model that can be looked at and embraced or discarded or half-hugged.

While smiling and open arms are as much a part of politics as any simple plan, wealth perfumed with charity is never enough on its own.

The difference is that the Irish political model, and most European models, were designed to serve the people; while the African political configurations were designed as shapes to fit into the maps of ex-colonial exploitation. The European nation state, at least in theory, was developed in order to exploit the resources of the people for the people. Democracy can only spring from some sense of a shared community, and that shared community is more awkward in states that were founded on arbitrary lines drawn on chancy maps by ignorant generals meeting at unknown points on wayward journeys.

There is a need for serious African engagement with their imposed political contours. One of the most puzzling African questions is their unwillingness to raise and address the issue of their colonial past as a colonial present; of their weird and arbitrary borders as determinants of the future. In truth these borders are as weak as a departing horizon and as watery as thin gruel. They are, in fact, the sublimation of European hegemony and their continuance will strengthen the grip of white supremacy in every facet of their lives.

The Irish cup of myth may be broken and its shards scattered on the complicated table of reality; but at least there was a cup to be broken. We do not even begin to imagine the African clay, using 'African' as an easy measure. When people say 'African' to me, I ask, do you mean Congolese, or Senegalese, or Nigerian, or Namibian? And when they say 'Nigerian', I ask, do you mean Yoruba or Tiv or Igbo, or Hausa, or Fulani? Because these latter are their normal pre-colonial units of living exchange, and just as cosmopolitan colonialists cannot wipe out the kinks and the twists of various kinds of 'national' culture, or wish them away in the trashing hall of all underclass difference, neither can we treat Africa as one unit, as one big black mashing tub out of which everyone emerges the same.

The Irish political and national experiment was originally designed to show that you should love your crooked neighbour with your crooked heart wherever he or she lived. There is no point whatsoever in clasping your own to yourself, if you do not support the rights of others to do likewise in their own way. The Irish political and cultural experiment was to rejoice in living in a coloured world of dappled things, determinedly twined and linked with everybody else. Smallness of sympathy and snootiness and superiority were never meant to be part of the plan. But they were, when we began to forget, and commenced to live in another world where we knew more and imagined less.

Part of the solution to the world's problems is imagining how it is; imagining with love and sympathy and passion. It is not just a matter of the way poverty is sustained, or of how it can be solved, or of why it is there. It is also a matter of re-imagining and repossessing from deep inside the heart, of reliving the pain that we all have felt. Many European countries are not capable of doing this even with the best will in the world because they have no memory of being the crushed, the underdog, the non-dignified. Even the most liberal and open and charitable brain raised in privilege finds it difficult to get down into the sump of the imagination and the horrors and frustration that dwell in the unequal and the dumb-voiced.

The imagination comes first, and then empathy, and then understanding, and then action; but the begetter of all of these is the imagination.

The Irish contribution should have been to show some of the way because those who cannot sleep have many real dreams. It should have been to re-imagine our immigrants as ourselves, because that is what they are and will be. It should have been to imitate their pain and their joy as we did our own. It should have been because we are an island nation that knows that the sea takes and the sea receives. It should have been that we should have known that there is no limit to greed and there are no borders to bigotry. It should have been that we should have known better. We should have known better, but we did not.

Further Reading
Garner, S., *Racism in the Irish Experience* (London: Pluto, 2004).

Kirby, P., Gibbons, L., and Cronin, M., *Reinventing Ireland: Culture, Society and the Global Economy* (London: Pluto, 2002).

Lentin, R., and McVeigh, R., eds, *Racism and Antiracism in Ireland* (Belfast: Beyond the Pale, 2002).

Ó Doibhlin, B., *Cosaint na Daonnachta* (Dublin: Coiscéim, 2004).

Rolston, B., and Shannon, M., *Encounters: How Racism Came to Ireland* (Belfast: Beyond the Pale, 2002).

Silent Suffering, Stoic Resistance: Human Rights Abuses of Women and Children in Latin America

KARI LYDERSEN

First, the men left.

Throughout Latin America, there came to be towns and rural hamlets populated by women and children and old men, with hardly any males of working age. That's because as free trade agreements and other global economic trends have made it harder and harder to make a living in their home communities, they have fled to cities, border regions or often the United States in search of work.

At first, the women stayed.

Their already hard lives became even rougher, surviving essentially as single mothers, struggling to handle all the duties of keeping families and communities together. Money would often be sent from the US. But as the epidemic of migration dragged on, many women stopped hearing from their husbands, who after so long away from home started new families in the US.

Now women are increasingly migrating to the US and elsewhere themselves – it has been called 'the feminization of immigration.'

They go with their children in tow ... and often, young children make the dangerous trip to a new land on their own.

Whether they try to stick it out in their home communities or set out in search of work, these women and children are suffering myriad and often overlooked human rights abuses brought on by this vast economically driven migration. Everything from the de facto denial of rights to sufficient nutrition, shelter and health care ... to more aggressive human rights violations perpetrated by police, military or private security forces acting directly or indirectly in the service of global commerce ... to gender-specific violations such as rape, sex trafficking and sexual violence.

In San Juan Polho, a small community in Chiapas, Mexico, not far from the site of the brutal Acteal massacre of 45 people in December 1997, women told me how most of the men had left in search of work or gone into hiding from violent paramilitary forces. The women who remained behind struggled to feed their children without even enough beans or corn. As in rural communities throughout Mexico, their lives had changed since NAFTA (the North American Free Trade Agreement) took effect in 1994. Since NAFTA obliterated most tariffs and allowed US-government-subsidized corn and other mass-produced crops to flood the Mexican market, Mexican farmers struggle to sell their goods for any profit at all. The community in San Juan Polho had it particularly bad since, as a town sympathetic to the Zapatista movement, they spent years under constant surveillance and threat from paramilitary groups and military soldiers at a base on the road just outside town. The residents of San Juan Polho would go for weeks at a time without being able to plant, tend or harvest crops for their own subsistence,

280

since they risked attack when venturing out to the cornfields. In 2002, five years after the massacre, the air was tense with fear and suspicion.

'Paramilitaries harass us when we leave the town,' said one mother, standing near a colourful mural of Zapatista women in bright dresses, black braids and smiling eyes peeking out from behind the handkerchiefs covering their faces. 'And the military harass people, especially the women. They're always drinking. Prostitutes go to the base, so our children are exposed to that.'

Since women typically take ultimate, daily responsibility for keeping the household together and caring for children, the stress of living in extreme poverty in places like San Juan Polho falls even more harshly on them than on men. Then when women decide to leave their communities in search of work and a better life, often with their children, they continue to face harsher conditions than men. Over the past decade many women from throughout Mexico and other parts of Latin America have headed for sprawling cities on the US–Mexico border to work in the maquila industry, which has grown exponentially since NAFTA (maquila – factory operating under free trade to allow duty-free export of finished products for sale in the US). Maquila zones in Guatemala, El Salvador and other Latin American countries also draw workers from the countryside and small towns. Initially maquilas employed mostly men, but women soon became the preferred workforce because of their small, nimble fingers and the fact that they are seen as easier to control and intimidate. Thousands of migrants from central and southern Mexico and other parts of Latin America have streamed up to the border to find work in maquilas, and they continue to do so even though many of these factories have now taken off for China where labour is even cheaper.

Maquila jobs are often the first work outside the home that migrant women have done, which in many ways is a positive development. But the working conditions are far from ideal.

At a wage of roughly US $5 to $10 a day, maquilas offer better pay than most other unskilled jobs in Mexico. But in border cities, this is still barely a subsistence wage, especially to support a family. Sexual harassment at work is a given, and rape or coerced sex by supervisors is widely reported. Employers don't want to hire pregnant women, since they'd have to pay maternity leave, so in numerous maquilas women report being forced to display their used sanitary napkins as proof they aren't pregnant. In many maquilas women are forced to work without adequate safety equipment and protective clothing, and they are regularly exposed to toxic chemicals and dangerous situations.

At the 'Delnosa' maquila in dry, dusty Reynosa, for example, women told me that when safety inspectors came they were told to hide certain chemicals and workers with raw throats from chemical exposure were locked in the bathroom. A young woman named Aneth Delgadillo described watching her sister die at age 23 of a brain haemorrhage, in what the family sees as a direct result of her long hours of overtime – up to 100 hours a week – without basic safety equipment at Delnosa, which undertakes contract work for General Motors.

'She never knew all this work would cause her harm,' Aneth said, sitting in the family's dim but immaculately scrubbed apartment, fingering her sister's old Delnosa photo IDs. 'With all the overtime she didn't have time to detoxify her body.

Workers are exposed to so many toxic chemicals. The protections in the plant are all to protect the product and the machinery, they don't care at all about us.'

In Ciudad Juarez, a major maquila city across the border from El Paso, Texas, concerns about workplace safety take a backseat to a more dramatic threat to women, a decade-plus epidemic of serial abductions and murders, characterized by rape and ritual mutilation. On a desert hillside next to fences made out of rusty box springs stand a solemn row of pink crosses adorned with plastic roses, casting forlorn shadows on the sand – monuments to some of the thousands of women disappeared and murdered in Juarez in the past decade, most of them employed at maquilas. Handmade missing posters with young women's faces are taped to poles around the city. Over 340 women have been officially logged as murdered in Juarez since 1993; hundreds more have been reported missing and never found.

Police, drug traffickers, a motorcycle gang, wealthy businessmen and others have been blamed for the murders. But more pressing than the question of 'whodunnit' is why the Mexican government and maquila owners haven't done more, sooner, to solve and prevent the horrific crimes. With increasing international attention, the Mexican government has finally taken some meaningful steps to address the femicide. But still the murders continue; at the time of writing in late May 2005 two bodies had just been found.

Mass murders of women are also happening in Chihuahua City not far from Juarez, Guatemala City and other Latin American metropolises, in virtual silence. In Honduras, El Salvador and Guatemala, many women have been raped and murdered and in some cases beheaded by violent street gang members deported from the US. Gangs like Mara Salvatrucha and Mara 18 were incubated in Los Angeles, Washington DC and other US cities, where the youth had immigrated at young ages and grown up. As strict immigration reform laws passed in 1996 are being fully implemented, many young men are being deported because of their gang activity, often to countries where they have no family or friends except other gang members. Many don't even speak Spanish.

These youths have become infamous for perpetrating human rights abuses like the massacre on a city bus in Honduras just before Christmas 2004. But in the bigger picture, they are victims themselves, cast adrift without resources or hope in limbo between countries and cultures. International human rights groups complain that as part of their war on these admittedly brutal gangs, Latin American governments are grossly violating the civil rights of youth. In Honduras, for example, teenage boys are imprisoned just for having tattoos that might signify gang membership. In Colombia, neighbourhood militias hunt down and extrajudicially execute suspected gang members with the tacit support of the government and police.

Along with providing a sense of belonging and, ironically, physical security, these gangs also often provide jobs, maybe the best jobs the youths will ever get. It's been debated exactly how organized and lucrative a role these gangs play in international trafficking of drugs, arms and other illicit goods, but clearly they make up part of the informal economy.

Throughout impoverished regions of Latin America, the informal economy is the most viable option for thousands of women and children. Child labour laws have no meaning here.

In La Paz, Bolivia, bright-eyed cousins Christian and Enrique, aged eight and ten, described to me how they spend hours a day after school and on weekends shining shoes to earn money to augment what their parents make selling vegetables and washing cars. They are among an army of prepubescent shoeshiners who work the wealthier parks and plazas of the city, dirty rags or black scarves covering their faces. This gives them a sinister appearance, but Christian explains that they actually cover their faces because they are ashamed of being poor and having to do this dirty work.

Just as people might erroneously think child labour is a relic of the industrial age, so too most people think slavery is only an embarrassing memory for humankind. But a surprising number of Latin American migrants are in fact working in slavery in the US, not to mention slavery situations that exist in other parts of the world. The FBI has worked with immigrants rights groups to break up slavery operations in agriculture in southern Florida, where workers are held under armed guard and forced to work, supposedly to pay off the debt to their smugglers. Latin American women, along with women from other countries, are trafficked into the US and kept in an endless cycle of debt bondage doing domestic work or sex work. US authorities have uncovered brothels where immigrant women are held against their will in unassuming suburban homes working as prostitutes. Latin American women are also trafficked for sex work from poorer to better off countries. In some cases they are tricked into sex work after being told they will be maids, waitresses or dancers. In other cases they do the work willingly, because of a lack of other options.

Women involved in sex work, out of economic necessity or

against their will, face a high risk of violence and exposure to HIV and other infections. Latin American children, boys and girls, also regularly turn to risky prostitution for lack of other alternatives while living on the streets in US and Latin American cities. For example Balboa Park in downtown San Diego was long known as a spot where young Central American boys, often high on sniffing inhalants, could be picked up for sex.

As difficult as conditions may be for Latin American women and children in today's global economy, women are in many ways leading the resistance to neo-colonialism, unwanted free trade agreements, exploitation by multinational companies, political repression and sexism in their own communities. They are leading the struggle through their everyday efforts to make a living, often as single mothers. And through specific political and community struggles, for example as part of the Zapatista movement in Chiapas, through women's health and education co-operatives in Venezuela, through centres for former prostitutes in El Salvador, or women's squatter communities in Honduras. Wherever women migrate they become the force behind countless community initiatives and groups – organizing, for example, for better working conditions in maquilas in Mexico and better schools in immigrant neighbourhoods in the US.

In Reynosa, Aneth Delgadillo and other women who have seen family members die of strange cancers and maladies have formed a maquila workers rights group called DODS (Derechos Obreros Democracia Sindical) that has won concrete victories, such as fighting age discrimination and the pregnancy checks. In her yard planted carefully with pink flowers above a ravine filled with trash, an older woman from Veracruz in southern

Mexico describes how DODS helped her get back her job in a maquila cafeteria after she was fired because of her age. Her shy, dark eyes in her lined leathery face light up as she describes working with the committee.

In Chicago, Mexican immigrant mothers whose children were warehoused into overcrowded schools in the La Villita neighbourhood staged a hunger strike to force the city to build a new high school, huddling for weeks without food in damp blankets and makeshift shacks at the proposed site. The school opened in 2005, directed by the community with a social justice focus.

In the Atlantida department of Honduras, for several years hundreds of women, mostly single mothers, have been occupying land which they've developed into a functioning community. They continue to petition for legal recognition from the government under land reform laws, facing daily threats of violence from security guards and police.

And in small autonomous communities in Chiapas, women in a weavers' collective brave military checkpoints, and even their husbands' jealousy and anger, to take their goods to market and carve out financial independence for themselves. 'Our husbands don't want us to go to the city alone, they think we're having affairs,' one weaver told a group of visitors, laughing stoically at the everyday sexism they face, along with so many other obstacles.

These are just a few of the countless examples of Latin American women's bravery and leadership in the face of adversity and oppression. So what more can be done to support Latin American women and children's struggles? For one thing, more light must be shed on the specific injustices

287

and problems that they face. It took the mothers and sisters of murdered women in Juarez years of speaking out to finally gain international attention and grudging movement from the Mexican state and federal government. But even as people around the globe have become aware of the femicide in Juarez, their sisters who are being similarly attacked in Guatemala City and the like die in silence. Activists, non-governmental organizations and government institutions around the world need to take note of human rights travesties like this going on in Latin America – and make them a priority.

Another crucial piece of the puzzle involves strengthening women's control over their own bodies: increasing and protecting women's rights to sexual and reproductive health care, awareness and services including access to contraception and abortion. A woman's ability to determine when and with whom she has children and to protect herself from sexually transmitted infections including HIV is crucial to her well-being on physical, financial, emotional and social levels, and of course these factors affect her children's well-being too. United Nations figures show that more than half of new HIV infections are in youth aged 15–24, the vast majority of those in young women. A major cause of the new infections is sex trafficking and marriages or relationships where women don't feel empowered to demand safe sex from their partners.

Yet the US government specifically is attempting to cut gains in these areas, in part by blocking US aid to organizations that provide access to and counselling about abortion. Since these are usually the same organizations that provide access to condoms and information about safe sex, limitations on funding abortion services also directly harm disease prevention efforts. International delegates were angered at a June 2005 United Nations meeting on women's rights when US officials continued to insist that abortion was not classified as a human right under the platform of the historic 1995 Beijing women's conference.

Meanwhile the US and other governments have made strides in reaching out to victims of trafficking, offering services and asylum instead of deportation. This trend must continue and coalesce with broader policy decisions that are empathetic toward and supportive of all immigrant women, not just trafficked ones.

Ultimately, to really fight all these injustices and hurts to Latin American women and children, a systematic problem must be addressed at its root. That is, the problem of economic globalization as it is currently being played out, impoverishing and displacing people throughout Latin America and fostering political repression and internal conflict in numerous regions.

Of course women and children (and men) have always suffered human rights abuses during dictatorships, civil wars and regional conflicts in Latin America, as in most parts of the world. And there is a long history of grinding poverty, even though ironically the region is so rich in natural resources. But the specific problems and violations described here are very clearly tied to the new global economy, and therefore the harmful effects could be greatly reduced by rethinking some global economic paradigms. Women in Latin America have come up with plenty of alternative ways to stimulate local economies and provide for their families. They just need to be given more freedom – from domestic and sexual violence, political repression, economic strangulation – to make their dreams and plans a reality.

Further Reading

Bacon, D., *The Children of NAFTA: Labor Wars on the US/Mexico Border* (Berkeley: University of California Press, 2004).

Guillermoprieto, A., *The Heart that Bleeds: Latin America Now* (London: Vintage, 1995).

International Human Rights Law Institute, *In Modern Bondage: Sex Trafficking in the Americas* (Chicago: DePaul University, College of Law, 2002).

Lydersen, K., *Out of the Sea and Into the Fire: Latin American-US Immigration in the Global Age* (Monroe, Maine: Common Courage Press, 2005).

Randall, M., *Sandino's Daughters: Testimonies of Nicaraguan Women in Struggle* (Rutgers, New Jersey: Rutgers University Press, 1995).

Washington Valdez, D., *Harvest of Women/Cosecha de Mujeres* (Mexico: Oceano, 2005).

Websites

Coalition for Justice in the Maquiladoras: www.coalitionforjustice.net

Global Fund for Women: www.globalfundforwomen.org

Kari Lydersen: www.karilydersen.com

Mexico Solidarity Network: www.mexicosolidarity.org

Pious Aspiration or a Tool for Change? The Significance of the UN Convention on the Rights of the Child

GERISON LANSDOWN

The late twentieth century bore witness to countless gatherings of heads of state, under the auspices of the United Nations, to adopt blueprints for building a better world. And in 2002, for the first time in history, the UN General Assembly held a Special Session on Children at which world leaders signed up to 'A World Fit for Children', a powerful vision of progress for improving the lives of children. Undoubtedly, when these high-flown commitments were made, the intentions were honourable. Most governments would argue that in their country, children are highly valued, they are given priority and that their best interests are a primary influence on policy. Every government in the world, except the US and Somalia, has committed to the UN Convention on the Rights of the Child, a detailed set of principles and standards setting out the entitlements of every child to respect for, and fulfilment and protection of their rights. But the reality on the ground for nearly half the world's 2 billion children remains starkly and brutally at odds with the rhetoric, with poverty, armed conflict and HIV/AIDS, in particular, posing huge threats to childhood. And even in the world's richest nations, the rights of many children are being violated or neglected. So what needs to change in order to create a world in which the commitments to children become more than pious aspirations gathering dust on the bookshelves of politicians and civil servants?

Real change can only be achieved through commitments to profound political and economic reform at the global and national levels. But it also requires a radically new approach to looking at children – a willingness to view their lives through the lens of human rights in order to re-assess the scope of changes needed, the goals for change themselves, and indeed, the process by which those changes are introduced. As the most widely endorsed human rights treaty in history, effectively achieving a global consensus on the terms of childhood, the Convention on the Rights of the Child, if rigorously and consistently implemented, has significant potential for contributing to transformation in the lives of all children, including the most marginalized children on earth.

The scope of the Convention obligations to children
The Convention on the Rights of the Child is a comprehensive treaty incorporating civil and political, as well as social, cultural and economic rights. This places a range of different obligations on governments. They must provide the necessary environments to ensure children's optimum development, and protect them from abuse and exploitation. However, less well understood, and more radically, it acknowledges children as subjects with civil and political rights. All these rights have to be understood

as indivisible and interdependent. In other words, there is no hierarchy – all rights have equal status. And the violation of any individual right can impact on others. Any strategy to improve the situation of children needs to adopt a holistic approach. For example, efforts to promote girls' right to education can only be achieved by tackling other rights violations – including discrimination within families, the classroom and the curriculum, sexual abuse and violence by teachers and male pupils, disproportionate domestic workloads, early marriage, and lack of appropriate hygiene and sanitation facilities in schools.

However, the scope of the Convention needs to be understood not only in terms of the range of rights it embodies, but also in its inclusion of all children. It defines a child as every human being under the age of 18 years. This has significance at two levels.

Firstly, it demands that everyone under that age be recognized as having additional rights to care and protection by virtue of their youth and relative vulnerability, irrespective of culture, religion or local values. Furthermore, it places clear obligations on governments to take appropriate measures to provide that care and protection. The forms that those measures take, and the part that the children themselves play in their own protection, will obviously differ according to age and capacity. Nevertheless, obligations do exist to all children until they reach 18. In practice, however, too little emphasis is afforded to the needs and interests of children as they get older, despite the fact that teenagers, grappling with a world that differs so dramatically from the one in which their parents grew up, can be extremely vulnerable. Too often, inadequate recognition is given to addressing their rights to protection from sexual abuse, early marriage, illegal drugs, harmful media, trafficking, engagement in armed conflict, harsh criminal justice systems, and exploitative or harmful employment. Too little is invested in the development of services designed in response to the expressed needs and wishes of young people. Too little attention is given to providing young people with the information, resources and services to build the capacities to protect themselves – through education, knowledge of their rights, health care, including reproductive health services, and access to the media and the courts to challenge abuses of their rights. Real respect for the rights of children must involve empowering them to make increasing claims for those rights themselves.

In many societies, teenagers are viewed not as young citizens entitled to protection, opportunities and support, but rather as a problem to be tackled, a threat from whom society needs protecting. In the UK, for example, young people are pathologized, rather than valued or respected. Analysis of the media reveals an almost uninterrupted construction of a drug-addicted, sexually excessive, shallow, violent, drunken and morbidly anti-social youth population. Their talents, experience, contributions, fears and aspirations largely fail to penetrate the national consciousness. And this deficit model of youth leads inexorably to a policy focus on containment and control, rather than dialogue on how to promote their rights and offer opportunities to exercise responsibility.

Secondly, the Convention requires of governments that they protect the rights of all children, without discrimination, living within their jurisdiction. This poses a huge challenge to the status quo in many countries, where some groups of children are systematically afforded lower priority and less respect for their rights. The widespread and severe discrimination against girls in many parts of the world is now increasingly understood, and although far from resolved, is the focus of considerable efforts to achieve change. However, the Committee on the Rights of the Child, the international body charged with responsibility for monitoring governments' implementation of the Convention, has identified at least thirty different grounds on which children are discriminated against, many of which are poorly understood and little recognized.

Just to take one such group, millions of children with disabilities experience profound and unrelenting discrimination in their daily lives. Education for All has completely failed to respond to the rights of these children. Indeed, it is estimated that only 2 per cent of disabled children in developing countries have access to primary school. And without access to education, they are condemned to a lifetime of desperate poverty and dependency. They are disproportionately vulnerable to both physical and sexual abuse. And in many countries in the world, they are socially isolated, spurned within their communities, denied access to friendship or contained in loveless institutions. Even more shocking is the widespread lack of respect for the life of children with disabilities, and the relative impunity afforded to parents and the medical profession who either kill or allow such children to die. The Convention provides a clear obligation to take action to address these and many other forms of discrimination perpetrated on this vulnerable group of children.

The Convention, therefore, requires significant action on
the part of governments, in terms of the scope of rights to be
implemented, the age range of children entitled to fulfilment
of those rights, and the recognition of all children to
entitlement to equal protection without discrimination on
any grounds.

The goals for childhood

The Convention offers a vision for childhood in which children
are enabled to fulfil their potential, free from exploitation and
abuse and through increasing degrees of active citizenship.
Although people develop throughout their lives – learning
and growth do not cease at the age of 18 years – childhood
represents a unique period of both opportunity and
vulnerability. Of course, childhood is defined and perceived
differently across cultures, and different cultures vary in their
goals for childhood. In so far as it is possible to generalize,
countries in the North, for example, tend to prioritize the
attainment of personal, social and political autonomy,
independence and self-sufficiency, and aspire to rational
thinking as an ultimate goal in development. However, these
goals are far from universal. In most cultures in the world,
interdependence and integration tend to be more valued as
the outcome of development. These different goals influence
how families structure their children's environment, and the
way in which they consequently develop. For example, research
indicates that whereas parents in the US emphasize goals of
becoming a good person, being self-reliant and independent,
parents in Turkey, Indonesia and the Philippines place greater
stress on deference to elders and obedience.

However, across all these different environments, and regardless of the aspirations parents have for their children, children have universal needs that have been codified and recognized as entitlements in the Convention on the Rights of the Child. By setting out a comprehensive framework of rights, it provides both a set of standards and a tool for promoting children's development, competence and emerging personal autonomy throughout a defined period of childhood. And although the approach to the realization of those rights will vary according to the economic, social and cultural context, the principles they embody are universal and provide a benchmark for every child. What, then, does the Convention require of governments in fulfilling these goals for childhood?

It demands recognition that children have the right to survival, food and nutrition, health and shelter. They have the right to be encouraged and educated, both formally and informally from birth. They have the right to a family environment where their best interests are given primary consideration. They have the right to guidance appropriate to their evolving capacities, to prepare them for life in a spirit of peace, dignity, tolerance, freedom, equality and solidarity. They have the right to play and to take part in sport and cultural activities. And they have a right to respect for their dignity, and to be free from violence and exploitation. Conversely it places obligations on governments to acknowledge the importance of the family as central to children's development, and to provide them with necessary support to meet their children's needs. It requires governments to ensure that the best interests of children are a primary consideration when any action is taken which might affect them, and that all possible efforts

297

are made to implement the rights in the Convention.

In other words, the Convention aspires to goals for children that necessitate that they be given a greater priority. In practice, children rarely do have priority in the political arena. In too many countries, spending on education and health is dwarfed into insignificance by defence expenditure. It has been argued that no economic policy is child neutral: all policies will impact either positively or negatively on their lives. Yet how often do finance ministers subject their budgets to scrutiny in order to assess implications for children? In how many countries does the apportionment of public expenditure on children reflect their needs and their representation within the population as a whole? How many cities are designed to accommodate the needs of children – offering child-friendly communities and spaces? How many children get heard above the voices of the multinational corporations clamouring for concessions, exemptions, legal protections, freedom from taxation, regulation and accountability?

Yet if the goal of optimum development for all children is to be fulfilled, children must be rendered more visible. Children lack the vote and access to the key decision-makers. They lack influential advocates to lobby and influence government agendas. This relative powerlessness renders it too easy for governments to disregard their rights. The Convention introduces a clear set of obligations, voluntarily made to children, by almost every government in the world. Those governments must now be held to account on their commitments by civil society, non-governmental organizations, international agencies and by children themselves, in order to ensure that children are placed far higher up the political agenda.

298

The process of realizing rights

Finally, the Convention poses a fundamental challenge to the way in which change for children must be introduced. Its underlying philosophy of respect for children embodies a clear acknowledgement that children are entitled to be participants in their own lives, agents in the realization of their own rights. It does not merely construct children as passive recipients, entitled to adult protective care. Rather, it recognizes them as subjects of rights entitled to be involved, in accordance with their evolving capacities, in decisions that affect them, and to take growing responsibility for those decisions they are competent to take for themselves. Governments must not, and indeed cannot, fulfil, protect and respect those rights without engaging children themselves as partners in the process. This approach turns prevailing attitudes towards children upside down. It questions the assumption that adults alone know best and have the expertise, wisdom, and understanding necessary both to create the best possible environments for children and to address the rights violations they experience. In its place, it posits children as citizens entitled and, with differing degrees of capacity according to their environment, age and circumstances, able to contribute towards decisions that affect them.

The past 15 years, since the Convention was adopted by the UN, have shown that children have unique perspectives and experience with which to shed light on the challenges they face and the strategies for resolving them. During that period, as the concept of involving children as participants in their own lives began to be explored, an extraordinary proliferation of initiatives has emerged to create a space for children to be heard. They have been engaged in advocacy, social and economic analysis, campaigning, research, peer education, community development, political dialogue, programme and project design and development, and democratic participation in schools. And repeatedly, even the most hardened sceptics, who feel that such engagement represents little more than tokenism or gesture politics, become convinced of the added value when they are brought face-to-face with children making claims for their rights.

Children's participation leads to better outcomes. It ensures that legislation, policies, services and resource allocation targeted at children are directly informed by the beneficiaries. The benefits are comparable to the changes that ensue when women are empowered to inform the political agenda to reflect their life experiences, aspirations and priorities. It leads to better protection. Children who are silenced and passive can be abused by adults in authority with relative impunity. As countless public enquiries across the UK have revealed, where children live in institutions that offer them no voice, abuse can continue unchallenged for years. Furthermore, it is striking to note that as children from all over the world have been given the opportunity to speak out, one of their most passionate and consistent demands is an end to the violence they experience – at home and in schools. Physical punishment has not, in the past, been taken seriously by adults as a fundamental breach of the human rights of children. But for children it represents a profound violation. It is only now, as their repeated evidence revealing the scale and severity of the problem has emerged, that it is beginning to be addressed as a serious child protection issue, worthy of adult attention. Participation

300

enables children to understand and learn the value of democratic processes. Genuine learning about democracy can only take place by experiencing it. If a child learns that he or she has the right to express views, then it is axiomatic that the same applies to other people. So, it is possible to build a culture of respect in which decision-making is undertaken through negotiation, rather than conflict. Children also learn that human rights are reciprocal and mutual and not a route to selfish individualism. The sustained benefits from children's participation are evidenced in Colombia where a system of democratic schools was widely introduced some thirty years ago. In the villages where such a school was established, there is a continuing positive impact, not only on academic outcomes, but also on the strength of civil society, the commitment to non-violent conflict resolution and, in a culture renowned for machismo, high self-esteem amongst girls.

Conclusion

Children in the world of 2005 experience the widest possible of extremes. Globalization may have made the world smaller, but it has certainly not reduced, and indeed many would argue it has exacerbated, the injustices and inequalities. Despite the glaring and unconscionable gap between the lives of the wealthiest and poorest children, there remains widespread complacency or indifference about the status quo between nations and their populations. And amongst those who are neither complacent nor indifferent, there is, too often, a belief that nothing can be done to overcome the problems. Of course, there are no magic wands; there is no instant solution to the devastating poverty, insecurity and abuse that dominate the

301

lives of so many children. But the Convention on the Rights of the Child provides us with a clear set of principles and standards both to aspire to and against which to measure what needs to be done.

As governments continue to meet to frame future policy for tackling the world's ills, it is imperative that they use these standards, and in doing so ensure that they take account of the Convention's scope and the goals it seeks to achieve, while also constructing a process in which children are both visible and actively engaged. The case for greater respect for the rights of children is clearly a legal and moral imperative but, as Kofi Annan has argued, 'Only as we move closer to realising the rights of all children will countries move closer to their goals of development and peace'. In other words, there are also political, economic and social imperatives. Societies that respect and value children's rights are better places for all people to live in. Everyone who cares about children, and about dignity, justice, humanity and freedom from discrimination should be pressing home this message to governments now.

The Politics of Sexuality: Faith – the Final Frontier?

STEPHEN BATES

Just about all religions have difficulty with homosexuality.
A certain degree of disapproval is written into their cultural
and theological codes and sometimes into their sacred texts,
though why this should be is not always entirely obvious.
Certainly the antagonism towards homosexuality as an
inclination and particularly as a practice seems not to have
dispassionate intellectual as opposed to sociological roots
and although it is clear that God – or at least the scriptural
authorities – forbids it, it is much less certain why He should
do so. Jesus never mentioned it in his recorded remarks.

Is it because the practice is medically harmful? Or
undignified? Or debilitating to the individual and his tribe?
Or is it just viscerally distasteful?

If it is a matter of taste, then surely we have mechanisms
now for coping with this. Indeed there are clear indications
that in western societies in recent decades, the secular world
has been doing so, without too much distress. There have been
openly gay cabinet ministers in Britain, much loved and
appreciated gay artists, even the daughter of the Vice
President of the United States, in the most overtly religiose
administration in that country's history, is an acknowledged
lesbian – all phenomena that would not have been publicly

303

admitted even thirty years ago, but which are now greeted with a shrug of indifference in polite society.

This may not be true throughout these societies as a whole, but the fact that there is now revulsion and condemnation when gay people are attacked and that no one would stand up in public and say as Lord Montgomery, the hero of El Alamein, did in the House of Lords during the passage of the Sexual Offences Act in the late 1960s that 'homosexuality in any form [was] the most abominable bestiality that any human being could take part in' – this from a man fully aware of the real bestialities of the Nazi concentration camps – does seem to indicate a certain sea-change in attitudes. But this change in secular mores is causing more increasing disquiet among religious bodies than in any other section of society. It is a part of modern life that they find difficulty dealing with. They feel threatened by it. And, almost for the first time, they find themselves seriously out of step with secular morality. It is causing them a convulsion particularly in Christian and post-Christian societies. In the Vatican, they rail against the objective disorder of homosexuality as part of a would-be crusade against wider social immorality, while one authority – former principal of a large seminary – calculates that half the priests in training in the US are now homosexually inclined. And in worldwide Anglicanism, the faithful are tearing themselves apart over the election of an openly gay bishop in the diocese of New Hampshire in the US, with bishops from the developing world making common cause with conservative evangelicals to overturn long-standing traditions of tolerance in church government and theological autonomy.

In the battle which is being waged for control of the soul of these churches, the Bible plays a central role, partly because of the long-running and still unresolved debate over precisely what authority to give to a text written over several centuries 2,000 years ago by a succession of men living in and addressing societies vastly different to our own, also because the defence that 'it is in the Bible' is about the only acceptable means of avoiding accusations of blind prejudice and homophobia.

Not that the sacred texts of any religion are particularly absorbed by homosexuality, at least not in the way that some religious followers, particularly in some of the Christian denominations, now are. The Indic religious texts appear generally relaxed about the practice, the Koran, it is generally accepted, contains just four references to the issue and even the Bible only about eight of any significance.

These certainly give their adherents some textual justification for their condemnation, but scarcely for the sometimes savage punishments that they have meted out and in some societies continue to exact. Although in Britain the last execution for homosexual behaviour took place in 1835, in the Middle East the death penalty is still sometimes carried out, even though the Koran states: 'if two men among you commit indecency, punish them both. If they repent and mend their ways, let them be. God is forgiving and merciful' (4.13).

The biblical references are scattered and sufficiently problematical to have spawned a small modern exegetical industry among theologians with differing views. The most famous single reference, the account of Sodom and its destruction in Genesis 19, now appears not to be referring to homosexuality at all, but to a breach in traditional customs of hospitality, while the most unequivocal, that in Leviticus, which in the Authorized Version condemns homosexuality as an 'abomination' may have been rather less sweeping than has customarily been assumed. The original meaning of the relevant word '*to'ebah*' now appears to have been a reference to a ritual impurity or ethnic contamination.

Even St Paul, the only New Testament author to raise the subject, seems as much concerned with the purity of the tribe and its avoidance of contamination by alien or foreign practices as with the activity itself. Indeed there are scholars, of whom one is Dr Jeffrey John, the canon theologian forced to stand down from his appointment as suffragan bishop of Reading in 2003 following evangelical protests that he was gay, who argue ingeniously if not entirely convincingly that the Pauline reference in Romans 1 to men 'leaving the natural use of the woman' can scarcely be a condemnation since, as we now know, for homosexuals their nature is to go with men, not women.

What the references have in common in their apparent warnings against homosexual practice (lesbianism is not mentioned specifically) is a fear of dilution of the tribe and a wasting of its reproductive and survival potential. These may well have been legitimate societal and cultural fears in Roman and pre-Roman Palestine, but they can scarcely be said to be so today and can hardly merit the weight of condemnation that they are still required to bear.

Nevertheless, such concerns about homosexuality have arisen across cultures and throughout history. It is an example of otherness, an affliction of foreigners that may yet dog, dilute and threaten the purity and virility of society.

There are numerous examples of this, as is evident from the

THE POLITICS OF SEXUALITY

names by which the threat has been known: 'the Italian vice'
to the English, *l'amour allemand* to the French, and 'the Turkish
disease' to the Spanish. And it is a fear that has commonly been
exploited in times of crisis, at least from the time, in 541 AD,
when the emperor Justinian blamed a plague which wiped out a
third of the population of Constantinople on God's wrath at the
city's sins 'especially ... the defilement of males which some men
sacrilegiously and impiously dare to attempt'. This is not an isolated
example, but has recurred well into the twentieth century.

From the Middle Ages onwards the biblical injunctions were
expanded and amplified by a succession of Christian writers who
proclaimed that all sexual activity was unclean, unwelcome
and to be avoided except where absolutely necessary. Gradually,
too, homosexual activity, which had hitherto been regarded as
an offence like any other and no more serious than most, took
on an especially repugnant quality. It was St Thomas Aquinas
in the thirteenth century who pronounced it unnatural in the
eyes of God and therefore disordered and who maintained (as
some evangelicals including the current bishop of Carlisle do
to this day) that it was a violation of the Creator's design of
the genitalia.

But there was always a heavy pragmatism behind state
persecution of such an unnatural practice. In England the
'detestable and abomynable vice' of homosexuality only
became a civil crime in 1533, coincidentally just as Henry VIII
was embarking on the dissolution of the monasteries which,
among other crimes, he declared to be hotbeds of the activity:
a convenient example of combining moral retribution with
financial expediency.

It is clear though that, however savage the punishments in

307

the statutes, across Europe laws against homosexuality were
usually applied only periodically and not invariably savagely.
Not only did they not have the effect of suppressing the
activity – modern research in court records indicates that its
incidence has remained remarkably stable across societies
and throughout generations – but there was also a frequent
degree of toleration and even protection of practitioners.
There was often indeed a reluctance to prosecute (as in the
case of the most famous gay victim of all, Oscar Wilde). Thus
too, Napoleon who, when told of a gay community in Chartres
in 1805, remarked: 'Nature has seen to it that [these offences]
are not frequent. The scandal of legal proceedings would only
tend to multiply them.'

And, of course, it was perfectly possible for homosexuals in
the higher ranks of society to avoid prosecution altogether, or
even to be robust in their denial of charges against them.
James I, charged before the Privy Council in 1617 with acts
of sodomy with his favourite 'sweet child and wife' George
Villiers, defended himself by referring to the mention in St John's
Gospel of the evangelist leaning on Christ's bosom during the
Last Supper. The king told the council: 'Jesus Christ did the
same and therefore I cannot be blamed. Christ has his son
John and I have my George.'

The historian Alan Bray has pointed to a number of funerary
monuments which clearly celebrate close male friendships
across the centuries. Even Cardinal Newman was buried with
his closest friend at the end of the nineteenth century without
scandal or comment. Of course it is impossible to know whether
these were sexual partnerships or not at this distance, but it is
possible to know what would be the reaction of some modern

clergy, particularly of an evangelical persuasion, should such a burial request – or monumental commemoration – be made today. They would not be happy about it. Such research by historians like Bray and William Naphy has produced a much more complex and variegated picture of historical attitudes to homosexuality than some Christian groups, with their sweeping references to a uniformity of condemnation across 'two thousand years of history' would like to pretend. But the question remains: Why now should this definition have become so important to them?

The answer lies of course in both the decline in religious adherence in recent decades and the fear of marginalization in a society that no longer shares their morality or at any rate no longer gives it unquestioning deference. Partly this must be due to changing social patterns, Sunday no longer being a day of rest and religious observance – some suggest that the decline in church attendance may be dated back to the 1950s when mothers ceased to see it as their duty to take the children to church – but partly also to the churches' own loss of authority. In a number of societies which were previously theocratic in outlook, such as Ireland and Spain, the Catholic Church has been undermined by ill-addressed sexual abuse scandals. In others, such as England, society has just moved on and traditions of church-going have died, though not necessarily among some communities such as those originating from the Caribbean.

Additionally and crucially, society's understanding of the condition of homosexuality has moved on, whereas the understanding of the churches has stood still. It is now widely appreciated that being gay is not a frivolous lifestyle choice (who would choose it if they were interested in religion, given the condemnations it receives?) or a perversion for those who are inherently psychologically inclined to it, but a naturally occurring condition that occurs in a number of species and one that cannot be sublimated without difficulty and often damage. Many in the churches still do not appreciate this.

The churches have had limited success in combating their decline and the prescription of the Vatican on the one hand and conservative evangelicals on the other that the drop in observance has been caused by an excess of liberalism or an equivocation in the churches' message seems subjectively not to work: people like certainty but not necessarily censoriousness. There is a reservoir of potential believers: two-thirds of those questioned in regular surveys claim to want to find some form of spirituality in their lives but fewer than 10 per cent can be bothered to try to find it in a church on any given week.

Homosexuality plays into this problematically for the churches in modern society, precisely because they find themselves (or fear they will find themselves) increasingly out of step with the secular world in which they wish to proselytize. This is especially the case not only because, anecdotally, some in the gay community appear to be disproportionately drawn to religious observance and even ordination (figures here could only be speculative), but also because it is clear that there is a whiff of hypocrisy in the Catholic and Anglican Churches' current obsession with the practice. Conservative evangelicals in England who campaigned against Dr John's appointment as a bishop in 2003, even though he fulfilled the Church of England's criteria for promotion, were surprised and perturbed to discover how little sympathy their arguments received in the media.

But as one of my tabloid colleagues said: 'Everyone knows the church has always had gay bishops. Why the fuss now?'

In the United States where a similar campaign against Gene Robinson, the Bishop of New Hampshire, who is indeed in an active sexual partnership, has also been waged, other issues are involved, especially a battle for political control of the Episcopal Church. But even in a much more religiously observant society, where the debate on culture wars has been highly politicized, there is a sense of disjunction. Gays and their practices may be condemned from pulpits but are a highly visible strand within mainstream society. President George Bush during his re-election campaign in 2004 promised a constitutional amendment formally to define marriage as being between partners of the opposite sex only – but the promise was quietly shelved once he returned to the White House.

In England, however, there is an additional problem because the Church of England is the established church, a cornerstone of the constitutional settlement, and paranoid about losing its authority because of its declining support. If it is not available to all sections of the community and able to speak to them in a direct and positive fashion, can it any longer be considered the national church? It is being pulled in several directions, dragged into a debate it would really rather not have, pummelled both by events across the Atlantic and by the injunctions of bishops from the developing world who may overlook the problems in their own backyards – little matters such as AIDS, corruption, genocide, even ritual child sacrifice – but find the West's acceptance of homosexuality morally and biblically repugnant. And it finds a resurgent and rancorous

311

conservative evangelical faction determined to insist that its own version of orthodoxy and vision of the church should prevail as a means of countering secular drift.

The result has been a series of sticking plaster solutions and compromises to reassert a societal control that has, in truth, already largely been lost. It needs new solutions and new thoughts to cope with a pluralist society and a new boldness of vision, leadership and authority which it conspicuously lacks. 'We have a special relationship with the cultural life of our country and we must not fall out of step with this if we are not to become absurd and incredible,' said one Rowan Williams. Unfortunately it was before he became Archbishop of Canterbury.

Two hundred and thirty years ago Jeremy Bentham argued of homosexuality: 'This crime, if crime it is to be called, produces no misery in society.' Given the paucity of divine revelations these days, it may be time for the Church of England at least to revisit that utilitarian consideration. And lighten up.

Further Reading
Bray, A., *The Friend* (Chicago: Chicago University Press, 2003).

Furlong, M., *C of E: The State it's In* (London: Hodder, 2000).

Heskins, J., *Unheard Voices* (London: Darton, Longman and Todd, 2001).

Naphy, W., *Sex Crimes from Renaissance to Enlightenment* (Stroud: Tempus, 2002).

Robb, G., *Strangers: Homosexual Love in the 19th Century* (London: Picador, 2003).

Church House Publishing, *Some Issues in Human Sexuality: A Guide to the Debate* (London: Church House Publishing, 2003).

Tannahill, R., *Sex in History* (London: Abacus, 1980).

Vasey, M., *Strangers and Friends: A New Exploration of Homosexuality and the Bible* (London: Hodder, 1995).

Surviving Ourselves: Environment, Society and the Future of Our Civilization

RICARDO NAVARRO

Social conditions

Our generation has witnessed a lot of advances in every field of science and technology, particularly in the second part of the twentieth century, when new inventions and discoveries brought a considerable improvement in the quality of life of millions of people. Yet the benefits of so-called development have certainly not been uniform for all. If we take a look at social conditions across the planet, we still find that 20 per cent of people do not have access to clean water, 40 per cent do not have proper sanitation facilities and 5 million people die every year from diseases related to lack of water and water pollution. In a world saturated with weapons, we can certainly say that poverty has proven to be a very effective weapon of mass destruction.

Poverty is not just the consequence of bad management or lack of resources in a given country, but rather the result of a process of impoverishment that began with colonialism and continues under free market capitalism. If we compare consumption levels throughout the world, we realize that 20 per cent of the global population – living mostly in industrialized countries – consume 80 per cent of the resources in the world, and therefore generate 80 per cent of the waste. A corresponding 20 per cent of people living in the southern hemisphere consume less than 5 per cent of these resources. Likewise, if we compare the income of the 20 per cent population sector with the highest consumption with that of the 20 per cent with the lowest level of consumption, we see that the ratio increased from 30 in 1960 to 80 at the end of the century. This means that the world's social and economic disparities are dramatically increasing over time. Another vivid picture emerges when we realize that half of humanity lives on less than US $2 a day, while at the same time Exxon Mobil makes US $100 million profit every day and the world spends US $3,000 million on weapons and war-related activities, also every day.

A conclusion that becomes glaringly obvious when we look at the conditions and history of the social and economic disparities in the world is that the process of impoverishment of most of humanity can only be explained by looking at the process of enrichment of the other part of humanity. Or, to put it in other words: poverty and wealth are two sides of the same coin.

It is extremely important to bear this conclusion in mind when planning so-called poverty reduction strategies, for often these strategies simply attempt to reduce poverty by well-meaning technical and social projects, without addressing the interconnectedness of poverty and wealth. To eradicate poverty entails stopping the process of impoverishment of a sector of the population, which in turn implies stopping the process of enrichment of another population sector – at least in the way that has been taking place up until now. Poverty reduction strategies will not be effective without seriously considering corresponding wealth reduction strategies.

Ecological conditions

Looking at the ecological conditions of the planet, we can see that the underground aquifers are releasing on average twice as much water as is being replenished, so eventually these aquifers are going to run out of clean drinking water. A superficial assessment of this problem might suggest that this water depletion is a consequence of overpopulation and that it is, therefore, caused by countries in the South, in which populations grow more rapidly. The facts prove otherwise. Whilst an average person in Somalia uses 0.9 litres of water per day, the average US citizen consumes 350 litres per day. While human population must eventually stabilize, since this is an evolutionary requirement on a planet of finite size, the main cause of environmental deterioration is not overpopulation per se, but rather the excessive consumption on the part of a small percentage of the world's population in the northern hemisphere and amongst the upper and middle classes in the southern hemisphere.

Continuing with ecological indicators, more than half the trees that once covered the face of the Earth are gone, generating a serious erosion of soils, a permanent destruction of water catchment areas and an irreversible loss of habitat for thousands of animals and plant species, undermining the biodiversity of the planet. This deforestation, together with the emission of greenhouse gases from the combustion of fossil fuels, have increased the temperature of the atmosphere by close to 0.7°C, generating an increasingly dangerous climate

317

change affecting the lives of millions of people every year, including the loss of thousands of lives and billions of dollars in property damage.

Scientists estimate that, if present trends continue, the temperature of the atmosphere at the end of the century might increase by up to 6°C, generating climatic conditions unknown to the human race. Again, a situation of climate injustice arises. Climate change is the result of the accumulation of greenhouse gases in the atmosphere, a result of having world emission levels that exceed the capacity of the planet to process them. High emission levels are the result of an excessive consumption of fossil fuels by the people who have the resources to consume. The impact of climate change is of course larger upon the population sectors that are most socially or ecologically vulnerable. Those who live in poverty-stricken areas suffer more from the devastation caused by hurricanes or droughts. So we have a situation in which those who generate climate change are from the population sectors that have the resources to consume and those who suffer the consequences are mainly those who do not have resources to consume. This climate injustice can be conceived as a situation in which an ecological debt has emerged: those who consume owe those who do not consume. If we interpret this in political and geographical terms we can say that environmental deterioration has occasioned an ecological debt, owed by the northern countries to the southern countries. In socio-economic terms, it can be said that the ecological debt is something that the rich owe to the poor of the world.

If we look at the historical context for the processes of impoverishment and enrichment arising out of colonialism and

318

other forms of exploitation, together with the environmental deterioration of our planet, we cannot deny that an overwhelming social and ecological debt has developed: a debt that the rich owe to the poor, that white people owe to black and indigenous peoples, a debt that modern cities owe to rural areas, a debt that men owe to women, a debt that our generation owes to future generations and a debt that our species owes to the other species on the planet.

The future of humanity

Looking at the future, there are no signs that this irrational process of environmental and social injustice is going to change. For example, with climate change scientists are telling us that we should reduce our carbon emissions by up to 60 per cent immediately, but the Kyoto Protocol demands a total reduction of only 5.2 per cent by the year 2012, taking 1990 as the base year. However, some nations, notably the US, do not even wish to ratify this. Meanwhile, over-consumption of resource, propelled by market forces, continues as if nothing is happening.

The planet is being bombarded by about 50 per cent more waste than it is capable of processing, and this figure is increasing. Despite the fact that this consumption system is the fundamental cause of climate change, the trans-national corporations are pushing for greater consumption, removing all barriers to national and international trade in a 'free market'. We have seen in the past few years how corporations are pushing governments to sign all kinds of treaties, such as free trade agreements, the Free Trade Area of the Americas and the Panama Puebla Plan in Central America, all designed to remove every barrier to investment and exploitation of resources, so that trade and consumption can increase. What is ironic is that some of the governments that are pushing for these agreements claim that one of the modern dangers to the world is fundamentalism – without acknowledging that they are firm believers in the fundamentalism of the market.

In Latin America, for example, the US government is pushing for the Free Trade Area of the Americas, so that the corporations can have access within South America to the largest reservoirs of water and biodiversity in the planet. Biodiversity is going to be one of the main resources that corporations will require to develop new genetic engineering technologies. In 2004 the US President, George Bush, claimed that the terrorists of Al Qaeda were regrouping in the triple frontier of Brazil, Argentina and Paraguay, which came as a surprise to their inhabitants since nothing unusual had been noticed. However, that region is known for having one of the largest underground aquifers on the planet: the 'Guarani Aquifer'. As water is a resource that is becoming more and more strategic with time, it is difficult not to conclude that the main concern of the US government in this respect is not terrorism but water. If this demand for resource is not managed in the proper way, we will soon see Latin America becoming a new global hot spot, like the Middle East.

One thing that can be concluded from this analysis is that the world as we now know it is certainly not sustainable, which in turn means that we are heading further and further into crisis. Governments and agencies are fond of talking about sustainable development, but the only things that have managed to be sustainable up to now are poverty, violence and environmental deterioration. Besides, what should be of concern to us is not the sustainability of development but, rather, the sustainability of the world. To compare development and the world is like comparing an engine and a boat: what really matters is the sustainability of the boat, not that of the engine. It is true that the boat needs the engine to move forward, just as the world needs development to solve many problems, but what happens when a boat like the *Titanic* is faced with an iceberg? What happens when the world has to face up to the iceberg of climate change, or other icebergs such as poverty and violence? The engine must be stopped or, better still, put into reverse.

Non-sustainability of the world

Assuming that we humans wish to continue sharing the planet with all other living organisms, it is of utmost importance to identify what makes our world non-sustainable. The primary cause of non-sustainability is our economic system, for the simple reason that it contradicts the logic of nature. While our economic system is based on unlimited growth, nature follows a logistic growth, which is basically an initial rapid and increasing growth, followed by a reduced rate of growth (the inflection point) until, finally, growth ceases. In addition, our production system is founded on an unfair principle, because it privatizes the benefits of production, such as economic profits, but it socializes the costs, such as pollution. With such performance, our economic system generates huge disparities that in turn generate unacceptable levels of violence, sometimes in the direct form of wars, other times in structural ways such as poverty and environmental deterioration.

321

Following this line of reasoning, another important cause of
non-sustainability is the existence of the military-industrial
complex. With an expenditure of US $3,000 million per day
in this sphere, there is no way that the world can ever be
sustainable, not only because of the huge amount of resources
being used but, more importantly, because of the damage that
the products of this industry generate, including the motivation
underlying the use of military means to solve social, economic
and political problems. What has been seen in Iraq in the last
few years is that two wars have been motivated by the economic
imperative of petroleum. As Von Clausewitz would probably
say if he were alive, war is just the extension of business by
other means.

Another key cause of non-sustainability is the existence and
influence of large, powerful entities such as the United States
of America. The world cannot be sustainable as long as the US
continues to fill its current role. In the past few years we have
witnessed the tremendous capacity for destruction vested in
the US. In the first US war in Iraq, promoted by George Bush
Senior, there were more than half a million people killed in direct
and indirect ways. In the second US war in Iraq, promoted by
George Bush Junior, more than one hundred thousand people
have already been killed. The war continues, and there are no
international bodies capable of stopping the bloodshed. In the
context of the second of these wars, George Bush Junior said
that if the United Nations did not accept the decision of the
US to invade, the UN would become irrelevant – and it did.

All of these problems would not exist if the US government
were directed, as a matter of course, by decent and well
meaning people, but at present the problem appears insoluble

322

because the leadership of the US government is not economically accessible to capable and decent individuals, but rather to a conglomerate of large trans-national corporations whose objectives are to increase their wealth at any cost. To run a presidential campaign in the US at least US $1,000 million are required – every four years. These sums cannot, of course, be found by ordinary US citizens. This problem could be solved if the US were to divide into fifty or so different nations, as the former Soviet Union did. Many countries presently feel threatened by the US, but perhaps no one would feel threatened by the Republics of Idaho or Oregon. Then, and only then, might peace stand a chance.

Opportunities for sustainability

To make our world sustainable, or at least to push it in that direction, many radical measures have to be taken. But remember – the word radical comes from the Latin 'radix' which means 'root'. To do something radical means going to the root or being profound. Radical is not synonymous with violent. Doctors often have to be very radical to save lives.

The main radical measure to be taken is a complete change in our system of values. At present our values are primarily based upon money and power: the more of these that a person has, the better he or she is. This obnoxious equation is based upon human weaknesses, such as prepotency and ambition, but if we wish to continue sharing the planet with all other creatures these values have to be exchanged for others more in harmony with nature and humanity. Wisdom begins when we acknowledge our limitations; therefore, we need to be humble and realize that we live in a finite world

323

alongside many other living species, and to ensure that both they and us have a satisfactory life. It is interesting to note that, among the 30 million or so species living on the planet, only humans take from nature far more than we need to survive, and that in that process many millions of our fellow human beings are left without the basic means of survival, generating a non-sustainable social, economic and political world. At the same time, this irrational behaviour endangers our own living conditions because it threatens the ecological base on which we all depend. In other words, we are producing a non-ecologically sustainable world.

At the forefront of a new set of values we should place equity, justice and solidarity. We have to put into practice many concepts already enshrined in many important written documents, including constitutions, such as 'All men are equal' – but we should not forget women in so doing. Minority rights, and sometimes even majority rights, have to be observed in practice. Poverty should shame each of us and one of our many challenges should be its eradication, which, as already stated, requires an analysis of the processes of impoverishment and enrichment. We may need to get our heads around new ideas – such as limiting wealth and consumption.

A proper environmental philosophy can be summarized by the phrase 'We are all one and the same life', therefore any damage to the environment or to my fellow human beings should also be considered as direct damage to me. This should be one of the main principles of development. At a practical level, we need to develop and implement many new ideas advanced by many talented people, such as promoting the use of renewable energy sources – wind, solar or small hydro.

Bicycles should be the main mode of everyday transportation.

All these may seem Utopian or impossible to achieve, but that is precisely the challenge that humanity is facing nowadays. If we do not find a way to live in peace and harmony with our fellow creatures, what will happen to us is what happened to the dinosaurs 65 million years ago. We will be left with no representatives on the planet. And that will be unfortunate.

Members of the Kayapo tribe, carers for the eastern Amazon rainforest (photo: Simon Counsell)

Greenbacks in the Garden of Eden: an Essay on How Not to Save the Rainforests

SIMON COUNSELL

In 2005 a unique assemblage of some 1,600 scientists and specialists (of which I was one) produced a report on the state of the planet that has unsettling implications for all of humanity. The 'Millennium Ecosystem Assessment' concluded that humankind's activities are putting intolerable and unsustainable pressure on Earth's natural systems, including fresh water, atmosphere, fisheries and terrestrial ecosystems such as forests. By doing so, we are possibly undermining the very basis of our survival as a species. These findings confirmed what environmentalists and conservationists had been predicting for many years. They indicate in the starkest terms the need for concerted government action. But they also force us to ask questions about 'conservation'. Specifically, why is it that, despite some four decades of large-scale, organized, international conservation efforts, the planet remains in such a parlous state?

In this essay I suggest that, along with the quickening pace of technological and economic development, this failure has resulted from fundamentally flawed approaches to conservation. In particular, we have ignored the strikingly obvious fact that

327

many traditional or 'pre-industrial' societies have, for millennia, sustainably managed and even enhanced the environment that they inhabit. Instead of looking to such societies for solutions to a crisis that is largely not of their making, we have sought to impose *technocratic* conservation measures over vast swathes of the Earth. These measures may, in fact, serve to alienate, dispossess and undermine the very societies that could hold some of the keys to global ecological recovery.

Nowhere is this better illustrated than in current efforts to save the world's remaining rainforests. As I will describe later, international conservation organizations have effectively 'muscled in' on indigenous forest lands, in some cases deliberately undermining traditional authorities and cultures and replacing them with modern technocratic management – often with dire consequences.

Adam and Eve, hunter and gatherer

In modern Judaeo-Christian societies, notions of 'nature' and wilderness flow from, and are inextricably linked with, the myth of Eden. It seems to be a common feature of many societies through the stages of their evolution that they tend to displace the 'ideal' relationship between themselves and their physical surroundings to some notional time in the past. Curiously though, despite the Bible's original, mythical, location of humankind *within* Eden, modern conceptions and metaphors for Eden often define it as a space unsullied by humans, as a wilderness to be 'protected' against plundering by humanity.

According to the *Oxford English Dictionary*, a wilderness is 'Land which is wild, uncultivated, and inhabited only by wild animals'. But where exactly are these untouched areas inhabited only by animals? Some places on Earth – Antarctica, the bottom of some of the deepest seas and the tops of some of the highest mountain ranges – could genuinely qualify as 'wilderness'. But the use of the term wilderness, and other similar expressions, as applied to most other parts of the world, requires much closer scrutiny. Conservationists use a plethora of such terms when talking about the world's forests, including 'virgin forest', 'primary forest', 'pristine forest', and 'old growth forest'. But even in some of the supposedly remotest, 'wildest' forests, such as Amazonia and the Congo Basin, there is growing evidence of the importance of human agency.

One view of the Eden myth is that it is a transcription of a dimly recorded oral history – a story passed down from generation to generation over possibly thousands of years – recounting the transition of *Homo sapiens* from hunter-gatherer to primitive agriculturalist. Whatever our interpretation of the Bible's Genesis chapters 2 and 3, modern scientific studies – whether from an anthropological, a structural, a sociological, or an energetic perspective – have tended to support the basic view of hunter-gatherer societies 'freely eating from the fruits of the orchard', which 'swarms with creatures' (many of which, it transpires, taste good and fill the belly). This is to be compared with life in early agricultural societies, with its endless and desperate struggle against 'thorns and thistles', and which was often nasty, brutish, violent and very short.

Despite a precipitous decline in the last 5,000 years (and, especially, in the last 500), many hunter-gatherer societies – and other indigenous peoples variously engaged in subsistence farming and herding of animals – persist to this day. Such people occupy many of the remotest places considered to be the most worth 'conserving' – from the Inuit people of the northern Polar regions, to the Yanomami of northern Brazil, the San of southern Africa and the Dayaks of Borneo, to name but a few. In fact, more than 80 per cent of the world's remaining 'biodiversity' is believed to exist within indigenous peoples' lands and territories. This is clearly not a coincidence. Despite this, our knowledge of the ecology of such societies remains desperately scant.

Engineering the wilderness

The anthropologist Dr Darrell Posey, in his studies of the Kayapo tribe of the eastern Amazon rainforest, was one of the few scientists to have investigated closely the ecological relationship between an indigenous forest people and the environment in which they live.

The Kayapo inhabit the rainforest–savannah border. Within the forest, small patches are cleared of large vegetation, and planted with species useful for food, medicines and building and ritual purposes. The plot may be intensely cultivated for several years – using a complex pattern of fertilization, 'sympathetic planting' and irrigation – before 'natural' regeneration is allowed to take over. The Kayapo do not abandon their forest 'gardens' but return to them over many years, as they continue producing fruits and medicines and form habitat for wild game. Trails up to 4 metres wide, criss-crossing the forest, are constantly enriched by the Kayapo with preferred species. Significantly, the Kayapo do not distinguish between cultivation and 'natural environment'. They do not even have a word for 'forest'; what we perceive as 'rainforest' is considered by the Kayapo as 'old fields'.

But the Kayapo's 'ecological engineering', as Dr Posey termed it, in the savannah is perhaps even more significant. Often starting at the site of an old ants' nest, the Kayapo introduce plants from parts of the forest with similar ecological conditions into a 1–2 metre diameter area. Working out from this in concentric rings, more than a hundred species might be planted, eventually forming a 'forest island', which is rich in foods, medicinal plants, shade, wildlife-attracting species and plants that can provide fresh water. Staggeringly, 'forest islands' of around 10 hectares have been found to contain plant varieties collected and transposed from a geographical area the size of Western Europe.

We have no reason to believe that the Kayapo are unique; this anthropogenic selection of species – a cultivation of Eden on a continental scale – has had profound impacts on parts of what is usually considered to be the 'unspoilt wilderness' of Amazonia. Some evidence from the Congo Basin indicates that what is now perceived as Africa's 'primeval jungle' may also have been the product of hundreds or thousands of years of (totally unrecorded) human modification. Charcoal layers found deep in soils across large areas of the Congo suggest that fire – possibly of human origination – has created the conditions in which the abundance of the present rainforest is possible. For many Bantu agriculturalists in the Congo Basin, their present pattern of rotational 'slash and burn' farming has probably changed very little since their ancestors started migrating into the region 3,000–5,000 years ago (when they may have found that 'Pygmy' hunter-gatherers were already present in the forest). Though colonial regimes and the independent states that succeeded them deliberately depopulated large areas of the forest, much of the Congo Basin is still claimed as traditional territory by one tribe or another.

Perhaps we owe it to the Kayapo in the Amazon Basin, the Ba'aka 'Pygmies' and various Bantu people in the Congo Basin, and countless other forest peoples – for their selective gathering, hunting, planting, fertilizing and rotational forest agriculture – that we now have forest 'wildernesses' worth 'conserving'. Yet, in most current conceptions of 'conservation', this human agency is anathematized as 'destructive'.

Creating, and killing, the forest that gives life

If the 'eco-historical' relationship between indigenous forest people and their environment is profound, then it should be of no surprise that the forest continues to play a key role in providing them with crucial resources. Again, our detailed knowledge is rather scant, but we are at least beginning to understand how some indigenous 'forest economies' work.

One of the great trees in the Congo Basin rainforest is the moabi (*Baillonella toxisperma*), which can grow to 60 metres tall and 5 metres in diameter. For Bantu forest farmers and Ba'aka 'Pygmies' (particularly for women), moabi is important in economic, cultural and medicinal terms. Moabi fruits are highly sought after. As well as being a nutritious food source, the seeds yield oil used for cooking and lighting. Extracts from the bark of the tree provide medications for a range of conditions, including dental and back problems, and a footbath to ease sore feet after a long day walking in the forest.

Another tree important to the people of the Congo Basin rainforest is sapele (*Entandrophragma cylindricum*). Like moabi, parts of sapele trees provide various medicines, including treatments for headaches, bacterial infections and eye complaints. But large sapele trees are also the unique host of the *Imbrasia* caterpillar, a highly regarded local delicacy. These 3-inch-long caterpillars are so important in local diets that the time each year when they fall from sapele trees is known as 'caterpillar season'. Sapele caterpillars are a highly valued trade item in local commerce, being easy to dry and preserve. Collecting caterpillars is a communal task, providing an important source of income for women and older people.

Examples of indigenous forest economies are numerous and varied; extracts of the seeds of the greenheart tree are used as a reliable contraceptive by Amerindian women in Guyana; illipe nuts from various Southeast Asian *Shorea*-species trees are used in cooking, for oils and fats, and also medicine; wild honey is also used for medicinal and culinary purposes, collected with astounding skill and bravery from high in the forest canopy, by Ba'aka 'Pygmies' in the Congo.

These examples are deliberately chosen: as well as being important to local people, moabi, sapele, greenheart and *Shorea* (usually known as meranti) are all also felled for their timber and traded internationally. The removal of these trees can have devastating impacts on local people. Production of moabi oil is one of the few sustainable sources of cash income currently available to Pygmy people in many areas. But the moabi tree only starts to flower when it is 50 to 70 years old, and then only blooms every three years or so. It is thus very vulnerable to extinction from indiscriminate logging. Yet estimates suggest that the revenues gained from the sustainable production of moabi oil are greater over a ten-year period than from the one-off sale of the tree's timber. Moabi timber is mostly exported to Britain and Europe.

Sapele wood is frequently used as a veneer on low-quality internal doors, which are likely to last only a few years before being thrown away or burned. This wilful waste can mean life or death to the forest inhabitants: the sapele caterpillar season occurs during the rainy periods, when game is difficult to hunt, fishing is unsuccessful and next season's crops are not yet ripe; studies have shown that 75 per cent of the protein eaten by Pygmies at this time is from caterpillars.

The reliance of some indigenous people on forest resources is almost complete, but it is not unique. In the Democratic Republic of Congo, some 35 million people (out of a total population of 55 million) are dependent on the forests for their livelihoods and well-being. Globally, it is estimated, some 80 per centy of the poorest of the poor – those living on less than US $1 per day – rely to some extent on forest resources for their survival.

Greenbacks in Eden, and the disappearing tribes
So we are now beginning to understand that much of what we perceive as 'virgin rainforest' may well have actually undergone significant modification by indigenous people, or indeed even be the product of their cultures. Where these cultures still exist, they often have a profound understanding of the forests' functions and ecology. To many, the forests still play a crucial role in their livelihoods and survival. Western scientists, conservationists and, perhaps, all of us, still have much to learn from them.

It seems obvious then that, when we consider how we should conserve the forests for the future – be it for research, for leisure, for biodiversity or for production of valuable resources – indigenous forest people should be an important and integral part of our plans. Sadly, this is rarely the case; in many cases, efforts to 'protect' rainforests are actually speeding the demise of the forests' original inhabitants.

In order to understand this, it is necessary to look briefly at how the conservation movement has evolved. Broadly, in the forty or so years since, say, the World Wide Fund for Nature (WWF) was established, there has been a shift from conservation focus on single wildlife species, through to 'ecosystems', to 'biodiversity'. This has reflected advances in ecological understanding, as well as early failures to protect single, so-called charismatic species, such as the giant panda, the white rhino and the Sumatran tiger. Many organizations now talk about conserving 'landscapes' and whole 'eco-regions'.

Given that, as we have seen above, indigenous people have been protecting and, in some cases, enriching, the landscapes in which they live, it has been inevitable that many of the areas conservationists have identified as being the most valuable are, in fact, indigenous territories. Many early efforts at large-scale conservation of rainforests adopted a western, specifically a US, model of 'wilderness National Parks' – conveniently forgetting that, as with many areas of tropical rainforest, some of the great North American 'wildernesses' are very much the product of thousands of years of indigenous land management. In many parts of the tropics, some of the best-protected areas have been those where indigenous people have fiercely resisted the incursions of loggers, cattle-ranchers, mining companies and invading colonists. These areas have been very attractive as 'ready-made' conservation areas.

As conservation groups have sought to protect whole 'landscapes' and 'eco-regions', the challenges and the costs

335

have grown exponentially. In fact, the funding requirements have escalated to such a scale that it is often only the larger international agencies – such as the World Bank, the US Agency for International Development, and the European Commission – that can afford them.

However, many conservation projects face a profound problem when dealing with these agencies. Understandably, aid donor institutions have become more demanding in terms of the expected outcomes of their spending of scarce public resources. They wish to see specific indicators of projects' achievements, and tangible means of verifying these achievements. But, ultimately, the very basis of many conservation projects is, of course, that something *doesn't* happen rather than that something *does*; species X or Y do *not* disappear from the face of the planet; so many trees are *not* cut down. This can be very hard to demonstrate in a rigorous or convincing way.

Often, the temptation has been for conservation organizations to find what can be called 'proxy indicators' of project success, especially for areas of land set aside for protection. Usually, these relate to the suppression of supposed threats to the wildlife – the number of 'eco-guards' trained, the number of animal traps collected, guns confiscated, poachers arrested, slash and burn farmers evicted, and so on. Where the real numbers for these kinds of outcomes might not be terribly impressive for donors, so conservation managers might be inclined to intensify 'command and control' measures in order to increase the demonstrable outcomes of their project.

These are, of course, precisely the activities that impinge most directly on indigenous peoples, especially where they are

336

still dependent on traditional hunting-gathering lifestyles. In other words, the very logic of large-scale protected areas, and the associated reliance on large-scale donor agency funding, may have tended to drive conservation organizations into direct conflict with indigenous people. Such conflicts are now endemic within global programmes to establish protected wildlife areas; in some parts of the world, especially Africa, they are ubiquitous. In the worst cases, indigenous forest people have seen their traditional land management practices condemned, their farms destroyed, their subsistence foodstuffs confiscated, and their settlements destroyed or relocated outside National Park boundaries. Indigenous people say that the activities of conservation organizations are now the single largest threat to the integrity of their territories.

During the 1990s, in the face of growing disquiet about the impacts of their activities on indigenous people, most of the big conservation groups – such as WWF and Conservation International – adopted people-friendly policies. But these have been, at best, patchily applied; often, little appears to have changed on the ground. For example, a recent survey carried out by Michael Cernea, Professor of Anthropology at George Washington University, found in a sample of twelve protected areas in the Congo Basin rainforests that a total of some 54,000 people, including Bantu farmers and various hunter-gatherer Pygmy groups, had been evicted or had their lands expropriated by conservation organizations.

To the many millions of 'internally displaced people' suffering from the conflicts that have raged across the Congo region are now being added 'conservation refugees'. In practice, many such people end up living in urban shanty-towns, begging at

337

the side of the road, or seeking poorly paid jobs in unhealthy and violent timber-felling camps in the forest. There is evidently still a long way to go in reconciling conservation with indigenous peoples' rights.

Get rid of the people, and the wildlife will soon follow ...
In addition to abuses of international human rights standards, such an exclusionary approach to conservation may be counter-productive even in terms of protecting wildlife. As Professor Cernea has pointed out:

> The customary tenure of certain resident forest groups acts as an in built protective shield over flora and fauna resources against other local and outside groups. The presence of those resident groups has been often quite an effective deterrent. Eviction of resident people eliminates the customary protector, and it is doubtful whether 'the state' can be as effective against other users, local or remote ...

This is exactly consistent with my own observations in Africa and more widely. In the West-Central Africa country of Cameroon, donor funding has recently ended for what were once two 'flagship' protected areas projects (which between them have consumed more than US $20 million in international aid funding over the past fifteen years or so). In both cases, the reserves were quickly re-invaded by displaced and alienated local communities, along with outsiders, and their natural resources plundered. In short, remove people as an ecological factor in many rainforests and you may end up, at best, with a 'fossil forest' – preserved temporarily, but doomed inevitably

338

to slow degradation. At worst, we may be removing the very people who could protect wildlife in the long term. We disregard the role of people in Eden at our own peril.

We are now at the end of the first big phase of international efforts to protect tropical rainforests, which kicked off in the late 1980s and early 1990s. My prediction is that, as donor support for protected areas inevitably falls away, we will see many repetitions of what has happened in Cameroon. The exclusionary model of protected wildlife areas is, in all but a very few cases, indefensible in terms of human rights. In many cases, it could be totally counter-productive as a means of conserving biodiversity. The task of finding different approaches to global conservation is increasingly urgent.

From scarcity to abundance
If the 'technocratic' approach to conservation is failing, perhaps we can learn lessons by returning to the source of much of the ecological and cultural diversity we still benefit from – the world's remaining indigenous and traditional people. This could require a profound change in the way we think about, and describe, the relationships between humankind, the environment and the land upon which we all, ultimately, depend.

We need to rethink the very language of conservation – language that, through words such as 'wilderness', can 'disappear' from the landscape the very people who created it. In many areas, we could do worse than thinking not in terms of 'conservation' or 'exploitation', but in terms of indigenous 'stewardship'. Dr Jerome Lewis, an anthropologist at the London School of Economics and one of the few people in western society who has a deep understanding of Pygmy hunter-gatherers in the rainforests of the Congo Basin, has described the difference in the Pygmy view of the world from that of Western 'technocratic' society as this: the loggers' and conservationists' mutually reinforcing view of the forest is as a place of scarcity, in which resources are selectively locked away, or priced according to level of demand in the international market, extracted and sold. This contrasts with the Pygmy view, which is one of abundance, where the forest, if managed according to age-old traditions, will always provide, and is thus treated with the respect with which one's own body is treated.

We need to find ways that help to strengthen and support cultures that bind such peoples to their land and environment – rather than contributing to the destruction of those cultures. As with many other 'wild' parts of the Earth, the conception of the rainforest as an uninhabited Eden is not only erroneous, but also dangerous. It is a construct of the recent international conservation movement, with no precedent in historical or cultural reality. A recent press release from a major international conservation organization exclaimed how a piece of land was to be added to a protected area in Congo. It unwittingly proclaimed 'Africa's Last Eden to become a National Park'. For the people who had formerly lived in the National Park – which is now totally depopulated of its indigenous inhabitants – the arrival of the conservationists may, indeed, have brought with it the end of their life in the 'Garden of Eden'. It may also, ultimately, bring with it the end of Eden itself.

Website

For more information on the work of the Rainforest Foundation: www.rainforestfoundationuk.org

Ourselves and Other Animals: the Ethics of Farming

JOYCE D'SILVA

Down on the farm. Chickens scavenging and strutting in the yard, gentle cows wandering in from lush pastures for milking, pigs snuffling for titbits in the orchard, sheep and gambolling lambs in the more distant fields. The rural idyll. Now, more likely, the rural myth.

The easiest way for us urban-society folk to see some chickens is likely to be in the freezer at our local supermarket. Dead, of course. 'They'd rather be . . .', I think, wearing my animal welfare hat. 'But isn't any life better than no life?' asks my rural-idyll-conditioned self.

So, why would a chicken prefer to be dead, if he or she could make the choice (I prefer not to refer to gendered living beings as 'it', if you don't mind)? And, let's be honest, I could be completely wrong in my presumption. Why don't you be the judge? Not that any real judges have done much for chickens in the courts – as yet.

Chickens – and laying hens – are all descended from south-east Asian jungle fowl – chirpy birds, still in existence, who lay two or three clutches of eggs a year, live in fairly small groups and, sensibly, avoid predators by perching in the trees at night.

Our own human ancestors, like us, preferred to obtain food

easily. We do the supermarket one-stop shop; they found chickens easy to keep, tasty to eat and spare eggs added variety to evolving diets. Better than a scary boar-hunt any day. They discovered other uses for chickens too, like making cockerels fight each other – which was a bit of a tendency of theirs anyway. And sometimes you could breed chickens whose plumage was so beautiful – the deep blue-greens and burnished coppers catching the sunlight – you would just want to look at it and admire it – even paint it for the record. Old or injured chickens made a tasty meal.

All these 'developments' in chicken keeping took place over thousands of years and in different places at different times. Some continue to this day. But they have little to do with the supermarket chicken any more. He is not only very different from his egg-laying cousins, but is a different breed of creature altogether. Well, almost – but, it's useful to keep in mind that both egg-layers and meat chickens – 'broilers' – share this common, jungle ancestor.

Globally, we eat about 45 billion chickens every year. The vast majority of these are now descended from breeding birds owned by just three major international companies and a couple of second leaguers. These chickens are not bred for egg laying, for beauty of plumage or additional aggression in fighting cocks – they're bred to grow BIG – and to grow big FAST.

Over the past 40 years or so, the actual numbers of days it takes a chicken to grow to an average slaughter weight (just over 2 kg/4 lbs) has been halved – in fact, it's still being reduced by about one day a year. So a chicken that used to take 80 days to get to the desired weight now does it in 40.

You may well have spotted a hitch here – presumably there

will have to be a future cut-off point. You couldn't, in 40 years' time, go from day-old newly hatched chick to 2 kg in just one day – I presume ...

So far this sounds like a good capitalist success story. Turnover time for end product has been halved. Costs are down, profits are up. Modern distribution methods have made a former luxury product widely accessible to all. Much of the industry is now vertically integrated, so one company and its subsidiaries can supply the chicks and their feed, control their pharmaceutical intake and vaccination programme, collect the end product, slaughter the chickens, freeze them and market them.

Farmers are now 'growers' and one batch of chickens is referred to as a 'crop'. (No 'who's' there then!) Very few farmers can now raise chickens profitably unless they are tied in to supply contracts. Freedom of choice as to breed of bird and method of rearing is mostly a pipe-dream. The self-respect and dignity of the traditional farmer – the qualities that made those of us who would never muck out a pig-sty still respect the people who did – have gone. If your animals are reduced from names to numbers to 'crops', any possibility of individual care is ruled out.

The farmers/growers have lost their self-esteem; the chickens have lost so much more. Selected for larger breast development – as that's the most valuable part of the carcass – the birds grow up front-heavy, slightly off-balance. Their skeletal structure has difficulty in supporting the huge muscle mass that develops long before its time. Overweight and ungainly, the chickens strut ever more awkwardly as they near their slaughter weight. They sink down on the litter floor for longer and longer, resting those painful legs. But the litter (usually wood shavings) becomes dirtier and smellier as the weeks go by and the droppings accumulate. Ammonia builds up. Automatic ventilation keeps the air just about breathable, but the chickens' legs and feet are often burned. Sores may develop on the foot-pad. Hock burns – which have been compared to the bed sores suffered by the infirm in poorly managed hospitals and homes – develop around the 'knee' joint, where the birds' weight presses down during their prolonged resting periods.

You can go detective yourself in the supermarket. Check out the number of chickens who have dark pinkish brown marks around the knee. As recently as 2004, an informal Compassion in World Farming survey found an average of 28 per cent of chickens with hock burns in a range of British supermarkets.

Scientists from Bristol University have developed a 'gait scoring' method (from 0 – normal, to 5 – unable to walk at all) to analyse the walking ability of these chickens as they near slaughter weight. Many score in the range 3 to 5 (Kestin *et al.*, 1992). In the worst cases, the birds become unable even to struggle painfully to the feed and water points and they lie where they are, dying of hunger and thirst. If lucky, the person in charge will put them out of their misery when he or she makes their daily round.

But does all this matter? And can chickens really experience any great degree of pain anyway?

Experiments by the Bristol scientists give a decisive 'yes' answer to that question. Given two feed options – identical except that one has been laced with a painkilling analgesic – the lame birds soon learn to choose the latter (Danbury *et al.*, 2000). Having eaten the painkilling feed, their walking gait also improves when they traverse an obstacle course (McGeown et al., 1999).

There's another hidden scandal in the modern chicken story. The chickens we've been describing only just make it to slaughter weight in sufficient numbers for everyone to make a profit. Keep them for another 40 days – or even 80 more – and many would die from severe lameness and inability to access nourishment. Substantially more would die from another scourge of the chicken house – Sudden Death Syndrome (heart failure). More would die from ascites, brought on by a particular type of heart failure and change in liver function leading to accumulation of fluid in the abdominal cavity. Their metabolism is in overdrive. If you didn't know that chickens could pant frantically, visit a modern chicken farm towards the end of the rearing period and observe.

Chickens don't reach puberty until 18–20 weeks of age. So, how can the breeding flock – the parents of all those chickens – be kept alive long enough and healthy enough to breed at all? The breeding companies have devised a neat and inhumane way of achieving this – counteracting the chickens' in-bred growth spurt by severely restricting their feed. Instead of being encouraged to eat to maximum capacity to enhance their inbuilt growth rate, like their offspring, these breeding birds are kept for many weeks in a state of chronic hunger, being fed only once a day. 'You should see the mad rush when the food comes through,' a flock manager told me. 'And it's all gone in 10 minutes.' As it's sometimes as little as 25 per cent of what the birds would eat, if allowed to eat freely, this means that for 23 hours, 50 minutes of each 24 hour period, the birds are feeling hungry and wanting to eat, but have nothing to feast on.

345

I've chosen to write about chicken farming because it's the most challenging aspect of intensive animal production.

We probably can all agree that keeping a handful of hens in a tiny barren battery cage is wrong. Hens look so much better off in a well-run free-range farm. Believe me, they are – here they are able to nest, perch, forage in the outdoors, spread their wings, dust bathe – all the things that hens like to do.

We have little difficulty in condemning the narrow wooden crates in which calves are raised for veal, unable to turn round and fed an unnatural liquid-only diet for their few months of miserable existence. These social creatures are deprived of mothering and peer group, play, exercise and good health – just for the production of 'white veal'.

If we know about it, it's likely that we also abhor the keeping of pregnant sows in equally restrictive sow stalls – or gestation crates as they are called in North America, where their use is still widespread and ferociously defended by the agribusiness giants. Never mind that the sow's natural behaviour, like that of all pigs, is to spend most of her waking hours in seeking food with her highly sensitive snout, or generally exploring her environment. Pigs can operate computer challenges with more ability than dogs – but that's only proving to us that some pig intelligence is not unlike our own. Pigs are, of course, uniquely intelligent at being pigs. The concrete and slats floor of the sow's narrow stall, lacking straw bedding and comfort, with metal bars surrounding and immobilizing her, reduce her pig intelligence to desperate despondency or frantic stereotypic, repetitive behaviours, such as bar chewing.

The good news is that, thanks to well-supported campaigning and lobbying by organizations like Compassion in World

346

Farming and its European partner groups, these notorious systems either are already banned in the UK (veal crates, sow stalls) or are all in the process of being phased out in the European Union over the next decade. Worryingly, the ban on conventional battery cages is under huge threat from a fight-back by the egg industry and the possible threat to the ban posed by the World Trade Organization, which may forbid the EU to ban imports of battery eggs even when it becomes illegal to produce them within EU borders.

But let's go back to those meat chickens – the broilers. At a casual glance they've escaped some of these worst aspects of the factory farm. They're not caged, they're not confined, they're not individually isolated.

Yet they are the ultimate example of the most insidious and unethical aspect of the whole infamous agribusiness arsenal: the breeding of animals whose own bodies are their worst enemy – animals whose genes predispose them to ill-health and pain and whose death would likely follow before they even reached their own puberty (let alone old age!) if they were either not killed or – as with the breeding flock – semi-starved. Can it be ethical to intentionally breed such creatures?

Here I must add that the slippery science of selective breeding not only has played its role in producing mutant chickens, but it has affected cattle, sheep and pig farming too. Modern dairy cows – such as the ubiquitous black and white Holstein breed – have been selected for productivity. Now the high-yielding Holstein cow produces more than ten times the amount of milk her calf would have suckled from her, had he been allowed to do so. (In the interests of productivity, the calf is removed permanently from the cow within 48 hours of

birth – a procedure that appears to cause anguish to both.)
The Holstein cow is massively prone to mastitis (painful udder
infection) and to scandalous rates of lameness, not helped by
her long physique, huge, leg-buffeting udder nor by the highly
infective and constantly re-soiled floor of the average cow
shed. Worse still, because the Holstein is a 'milk machine'
in industry terms, neither she nor her offspring make for
good quality beef. Her daughters may be reared as herd
'replacements', her sons are generally unwanted. Thousands
are shot soon after birth, some are reared for veal (which is
why veal comes almost exclusively from the male calves)
with a small minority reared for low quality burger beef.

Even beef breed cattle haven't escaped the breeders'
control. A natural genetic mutation in a muscle gene has now
been intentionally bred for, so we have special double-muscled
breeds like the Belgian Blue, whose mighty hind-quarters
make for a great yield of beef, but entail Caesarean births for
over-stretched mothers who are unable to deliver their giant
progeny by normal means.

Pigs too have been bred for faster growth and heavier,
meatier bodies, with the unsurprising result that lameness is a
problem with the breeding herd.

Merino sheep have been bred for such huge curly fleeces
that Australian farmers routinely cut off the skin (not just the
wool) from around the tails of the lambs to prevent fly-strike.

I believe that our selective breeding for 'genetic improvement'
has gone too far. Surely animals have a right to some kind of
bodily integrity? A 1998 EU Directive even goes so far as to
say 'No animal shall be kept for farming purposes unless it
can reasonably be expected, on the basis of its genotype or

phenotype, that it can be kept without detrimental effect on its health or welfare'. This implies that farm animals do have a purpose – to grow and be killed and provide us with food, but it recognizes limits on what we can do to the animals during that process – and it surely implies that creatures such as the fast growing broiler chicken should never have been bred in the first place.

Of course, if we stand back a little (why not be the extra-terrestrial newcomer, fathoming out what kinds of beings exist on Earth) we could question whether it is right for one species to enforce a purpose on another species. From where do *we* get that right?

You might believe it is a God-given right. There are biblical and Koranic texts amongst others that support this view. Far be it from me to attempt to undermine anyone's religious belief. If you favour a scientific cosmology, you may have ideas about humans being top of the intellectual order, top of the food chain (who *invents* these guides to easy conscience I wonder ...). So, our intellectual superiority ordains that we are entitled to premier position and to control over the lives and deaths of the animals we eat.

Sadly, this is just the kind of argument used by fascists and slave-owning societies throughout history. Although they applied this 'because I'm a superior being I can do this to you' justification for the foul deeds they perpetrated on other humans, I find it hard to see why applying this kind of logic to animals is in any way morally distinct.

You may or may not believe that animals have rights. You may reflect that they are sentient beings, capable of joy, pain, a state of well-being or a state of suffering. You may take account of their apparent intelligence, of their emotional well-being and their capacity to feel deprived of mothering or play, of activity or comfort or to be frustrated in their attempts to co-operate with their environment – finding perhaps metal bars, wire mesh or concrete where there should be grasses, earth and trees. The more radical choice then is to forsake chicken and all other meats.

Even if farm animals don't have rights, you might yet agree that they have a right to a reasonable quality of life before they are slaughtered. Even on these terms, modern chicken farming fails the litmus test of acceptability.

You may ask, is there not a middle way of obtaining the chicken without the suffering?

You're right, you can, of course, breed slower-growing chickens whose metabolism and bone structure are not under assault. They will take maybe twice as long to reach slaughter weight. They will need to be cared for and fed for longer. They can be given access to the outdoors – extra pickings for their dietary health and more exercise for their legs and hearts.

The net result is that they will definitely cost more to produce and will no longer be cheap meat.

I would argue that this – the purchase of free-range or organic chicken – is the only morally valid response we can make if we want to eat chicken. The greater cost to us is balanced by the reduction in cost (of suffering) to the chicken.

An increasing number of consumers are now making this chicken-friendly choice and the supermarkets are starting to take note. Availability of organic and free-range chickens is improving. The use of slower-growing breeds is encouraged by organic bodies, such as the Soil Association.

Farming of the traditional peasant type was not without its cruelties – many perhaps perpetuated in ignorance. The logo of factory farming should perhaps include the intentional cruelties of the cage, chain and crate, but also the scandal of the outrageous selective breeding that has come to dominate the industry.

Sadly, the future may lie with the genetic engineers and cloners who are the obvious heirs of the breeding industry's methodology and philosophy to date.

A more compassionate future, where animals are bred with sustainable bodies, are kept in social groups suitable for their species and in environments that stimulate their intelligence and provide creature comforts is possible – but only if our collective human voice speaks loud and clear.

References

Danbury, T. C., Weeks, C. A., Chambers, J. P., Waterman-Pearson A. E., and Kestin, S. C., 'Self selection of the analgesic drug carprofen by lame broiler chickens', *Veterinary Record* 146 (2000), 307–11.

Kestin, S. C., Knowles, T. G., Tinch, A. E., and Gregory, N. G., 'Prevalence of leg weakness in broiler chickens and its relationship with genotype', *Veterinary Record* 131 (1992), 190–4.

McGeown, D., Danbury, T. C., Waterman-Pearson A. E., and Kestin, S. C., 'Effect of carprofen on lameness in broiler chickens', *Veterinary Record* 144 (1999), 668–71.

Website

Compassion in World Farming: www.ciwf.org

The Human Race – a Marathon, not a Sprint: the Millennium Development Goals and their Ethos

EDMUND NEWELL AND SABINA ALKIRE

When Band Aid 20 was recorded in 2004, the teenage singing star Joss Stone famously referred to Sir Bob Geldof as Bob Gandalf. This may reflect on Ms Stone's knowledge of current affairs as well as of her profession, but it's also a telling reminder about the importance of the study of history.

Joss Stone, like a large proportion of the world's population, was not born when plain Mr Bob Geldof launched Band Aid and Live Aid in 1984 and 1985 and rapidly became one of the most recognizable people on the planet. Her ignorance reminds us that learning the lessons of history involves looking back to the recent past as much as to the dim and distant. We cannot assume that people will know about what happened even a generation ago; and if they do not know, how can they interpret or build upon this knowledge? The process of reviewing and learning from what has gone before is important, which is why the study of history – ancient, modern, and contemporary – is so valuable. History is an underrated and under-utilized tool for decision- and policy-making.

353

Sir Bob Geldof is clearly someone who understands the importance of studying history. In his 2004 Bar Council Human Rights Committee lecture at St Paul's Cathedral, 'Why Africa?', he looked back and candidly assessed the limitations of Band Aid and Live Aid. Band Aid was an apt name, because the money it and other initiatives raised for aid in famine-hit Ethiopia was merely a sticking-plaster, a temporary and partial solution that helped relieve some immediate suffering but did little to address its underlying causes. Much of his lecture detailed the lessons he had learnt from past experiences, and would draw upon as a member of the recently formed Africa Commission. Modesty may have prevented him from highlighting the success of his past endeavours; the distribution of £60 million in emergency relief and an unprecedented raising of public awareness of poverty are not insignificant achievements.

In the years that have followed, much has been done to build on the foundation laid by Band Aid and Live Aid. Twenty years on, both projects had reprises in the form of Band Aid 20 and Live 8, but these have taken place in a completely different political and economic climate. Not only have campaigns such as Jubilee 2000 and Make Poverty History enjoyed broad-based public support, but the process of globalization has made the world a smaller and more interconnected place. The ability to establish and mobilize global networks has the potential to make things happen that would have seemed impossible in the days when 'Do They Know It's Christmas?' first topped the charts.

It is for this reason that the fine words of the Millennium Declaration, delivered by the Secretary General of the United Nations, Kofi Annan, at the Millennium Summit in New York

354

in September 2000, give grounds for optimism. What could be seen as lofty rhetoric does contain an important commitment, made by the heads of all 189 member states of the United Nations, to achieve the eight Millennium Development Goals (MDGs) by 2015. The central aim of these goals is to reduce by half the number of people living in extreme poverty throughout the world by 2015.

While the MDGs have been criticized for being overly complicated and bureaucratic (the goals contain 187 targets and are monitored using 48 indicators), they nevertheless provide the most comprehensive strategy to address extreme poverty so far devised, with a set of goals that are realistic and achievable. Yet, as the world is aware, progress towards the MDGs is already significantly behind schedule. As Gordon Brown warned, 'If we let things slip, the millennium goals will become just another dream we once had, and we will indeed be sitting back on our sofas and switching on our TVs and, I am afraid, watching people die on our screens for the rest of our lives. We will be the generation that betrayed its own heart' (from a speech delivered on 16 February 2004).

This is why 2005 has been such a crucial year, both in terms of political action through the G8 Summit, the Africa Commission's report and the follow-up to the Millennium Summit, and through popular awareness-raising activities such as Make Poverty History and its international counterparts. Five years after the announcement of the MDGs there is a real need to reinvigorate the MDG campaign, and it will require constant vigilance to keep up the momentum for another decade if the goals are to be met.

355

So what are the Millennium Development Goals? The eight goals are as follows:

1. Eradicate extreme poverty and hunger.
2. Achieve universal primary education.
3. Promote gender equality and empower women.
4. Reduce child mortality.
5. Improve maternal health.
6. Combat HIV/AIDS, malaria and other diseases.
7. Ensure environmental sustainability.
8. Develop a global partnership for development.

The goals, together with their eighteen associated targets, are described in more detail in the Appendix to this volume.

One reason why the MDGs inspire optimism is that they acknowledge the interconnectedness of the many factors that impoverish the lives of billions of people. Often in the past poverty reduction strategies have been narrowly focused. The MDGs are not only a set of discrete objectives; they interrelate to provide a comprehensive and integrated approach to poverty reduction that takes into account causal linkages. For example, low incomes restrict diet. Poor nutrition causes suffering through hunger, but it also impairs the ability to concentrate and learn. Poor education not only restricts opportunities for employment and income generation, but also limits knowledge about health care, family planning and childcare – including the preparation of nutritious meals. The MDGs recognize these connections and circular relationships, and seek to address them.

As well as taking a holistic approach to poverty reduction,

the MDGs take account of the need for significant structural changes to take place in the global economic system to ensure resources are channelled into developing countries and that these countries are given the opportunity to utilize global markets. They also acknowledge that many of the solutions to overcoming poverty require simple, inexpensive measures, particularly in the areas of education and health care. Furthermore, the MDGs are based on lessons learnt by professionals in development in previous decades, that it is often the small-scale, local solutions, worked out within communities in developing countries, that are the most effective and fulfilling. While some poverty reduction measures have to be thrashed out at political summits by the leaders of the wealthiest nations, many others have to be determined by those who are impoverished themselves, within the context of their local situation.

Underlying the MDGs is a fundamental shift in thinking from poverty reduction strategies of the past. The lessons of history show that creating the conditions for those in developing countries to lift themselves out of poverty is more effective than imposed 'solutions' from outside. This insight is changing the shape not only of development policies, but of relations between the so-called developed and developing worlds. This can be seen in a variety of contexts, including business and religion. For example, western Christian mission agencies have largely shed the paternalistic approach to work overseas that characterized their activities in the past. This is partly due to the somewhat embarrassing situation that faith communities are thriving in the 'mission field' but in decline in the West. But it is also due to an increasing sense of equality and an ending of a colonial mentality. Today, overseas mission is increasingly about partnership: of agencies providing resources for uses determined by local churches and their leaders.

From the perspective of a highly secular Western European culture, it is tempting to play down the role and importance of religion in society. Certainly the churches in Western Europe not only are in numerical decline, but they have long ceased to play a key role in the provision of a range of welfare and other services – perhaps with the exception of education. Yet in other parts of the world, religious activity is increasing. The Christian churches and other faith communities are expanding numerically in many places, and they are also proactive in providing a range of community services. This helps explain an unlikely but important alliance that was forged in 1998 by the then President of the World Bank, James Wolfensohn, and the then Archbishop of Canterbury, George Carey, in establishing the World Faiths Development Dialogue (WFDD). The WFDD brought together faith leaders from around the world and development experts to find ways of working together for poverty reduction. Why should the President of the World Bank be so interested in engaging in the notoriously difficult area of inter-faith dialogue? The reason was made clear in a speech delivered at the 1998 Lambeth Conference, the ten-yearly international gathering of Anglican bishops. Addressing the conference, and with the world's media attention on him, Wolfensohn said, 'Together we can do a lot. We have expertise. You [religious leaders and faith communities] have expertise. We know a lot about development . . . You have the best distribution system of any NGO in the world. You are out there in the fields with your flocks, you and other religions.'

358

(*The Official Report of the Lambeth Conference of 1998*, Harrisburg: Morehouse, 1999, p. 352.)

These were not merely fine words designed to flatter; they were based on solid evidence. The head of the World Bank had identified a key partner in development that had a track record of good delivery at the grass roots level. In a World Bank study across twenty countries, religious organizations ranked as the second most important in their ability to deliver help to the poor. The poor themselves regarded the best to be community organizations in which they themselves participated. Yet religious organizations were found to be more important and effective than kin and family, local leaders, non-governmental organizations, shops and moneylenders, private enterprise and traders, banks, politicians, police, health services, schools, or various government agencies. The identified strengths of religious organizations were their responsiveness to and respect of the poor, their trustworthiness, their honesty and fairness, and their attitudes of caring, loving, and listening. Religious organizations scored less well on the extent to which they empowered poor people to participate in decision-making and help themselves, and on their accountability to local communities, and they were often seen as a source of conflict rather than unity (Deepa Narayan, Robert Chambers, Meera K. Shah and Patti Petesch, *Voices of the Poor: Crying out for Change*, p.184). Overall, however, the findings were very positive, and demonstrate the potential that faith groups have as deliverers of development.

This potential has been recognized elsewhere. In 2005 the Department for International Development (DFID) awarded a grant for a major research project, led by Birmingham

University, into the role faith communities can play in the field of development. DFID has also targeted faith communities in the UK as being particularly effective in raising awareness of poverty issues. Recipients of grants for this purpose include the Micah Challenge, an international evangelical Christian network that is promoting the MDGs, and St Paul's Institute at St Paul's Cathedral, which is running an educational programme on the MDGs called What Can One Person Do? Working in partnership with Muslim, Hindu, Sikh, Jewish and Christian communities, DFID has also produced a series of joint publications under the title Target 2015 focused at how different faith groups can engage more deeply with the MDGs (these can be downloaded from www.dfid.gov.uk).

An important reason why partnerships with faith groups are being developed in this way is that churches and other faith communities have been seen to take a lead on poverty issues in recent years. Jubilee 2000 was mentioned earlier. This campaign provided considerable leverage in bringing about the cancellation of debts owed by developing countries at the turn of the millennium. By doing so, there is little doubt that the campaign also helped pave the way for further cancellations announced by G7 finance ministers in advance of the 2005 G8 Summit. Jubilee 2000 did much to bring the issue of international debt into the public consciousness and on to the political agenda.

Jubilee 2000 started out when a small group of Christians, inspired by the ancient biblical principle of debt remission – Jubilee – found in Leviticus and Deuteronomy – sought to apply it to the context of international loans given to developing countries that had spiralled out of control. This small campaign, which began in the mid-1990s, spread throughout the churches and then beyond the churches. Like so many campaigns and initiatives before it, an issue inspired by a principle of faith captured the hearts and minds of those of other faiths and none. History may rank it alongside other social justice campaigns such as the abolition of slavery and the ending of apartheid – although it would be eclipsed were the MDGs to be achieved.

Jubilee 2000 cannot be seen outside its proper context, which is that it sprang from a religion that has a long and deep history of concern for, and engagement with, human impoverishment. The principle of Jubilee, found in the Hebrew Scriptures, goes back thousands of years, predating Christ. When it comes to drawing upon history for knowledge and inspiration, it is done to great effect within Christianity and other faiths. Because the past seems so present in the way that churches operate – through their buildings, vestments, liturgies, and so on – it is easy to regard them as backward looking, out of touch, or irrelevant. But this is to misunderstand the role of tradition and the use the churches make of history. Ultimately, the churches seek to discover and speak for eternal truths. They do so by seeing the present through the lens of the past, bringing the past into dialogue with the present, as the example of Jubilee illustrates.

It is precisely because the MDGs are concerned with impoverishment in its widest sense that they are receiving widespread support from amongst churches and other faith groups. For as well as being a matter of social justice, which resonates strongly with the principles of many faiths, the MDGs recognize that human flourishing is multidimensional. Although the MDGs do not go as far as considering the

361

spiritual dimension of impoverishment, they nevertheless go beyond regarding the release from poverty as a matter of raising income levels. The wisdom drawn from centuries of reflection across the faiths also provides a vision of what living a good and fulfilled life might be, and this has synergy with the MDGs' all-encompassing approach.

Within Christianity, over the centuries churches have established schools, colleges, universities, hospitals, and developed specialized ministries in similar institutions, and in prisons, refugee detention centres, and so on. The churches have also created relief and development agencies, such as World Vision, Christian Aid, CAFOD, and Tearfund. Similar examples can be found in other faiths. Within Muslim communities, the fact that almsgiving is one of the five pillars of Islam provides a strong rationale for engaging in relief and development work through organizations such as Islamic Relief and Muslim Aid (which is part of the Make Poverty History Coalition).

Will the MDGs be achieved? Their success or failure rests largely on political will in the present and the immediate future. It will be historians of the next generation who will consider whether ours has learnt from the example of Live Aid and other initiatives and built on them to make poverty history. What is certain is that whatever the outcome, people of faith will be at the forefront of seeking to achieve these goals. What is less certain is whether others will share their determination. That is why 2005 is such a crucial year.

We are extremely grateful to Susan Newell for her comments on drafts of this chapter, and to Michelle Brown, our colleague at St Paul's Cathedral, for the invitation to contribute to this book.

Further Reading

The line of argument taken here is based on S. Alkire, E. Newell *et al.*, *What Can One Person Do? Faith to Heal a Broken World* (New York: Church Publishing Inc., 2005).

For the MDG goals and objectives see the Appendix, where they are printed.

Narayan, D., Robert Chambers, Meera K. Shah and Patti Petesch, *Voices of the Poor: Crying out for Change* (New York: Oxford University Press for the World Bank, 2000).

Websites

Department for International Development: www.dfid.gov.uk

For the speech by Gordon Brown, 16 February 2004, see full text on www.hm-treasury.gov.uk/newsroom_and_speeches/press/2004/press_12_04.cfm

Appendices
'So you think you know about ... ?'

THE MILLENNIUM DEVELOPMENT GOALS

'The Millennium Development Goals are still achievable
if we break with business as usual and massively accelerate
and scale up action now.'

Kofi Annan, UN Secretary General

In 2000, the largest gathering of world leaders ever assembled
met in New York and agreed to the Millennium Development
Goals (MDGs). They are the world's time-bound and quantified
targets for addressing extreme poverty in its many dimensions
— hunger, disease, lack of adequate shelter and exclusion —
while promoting gender equality, education and environmental
sustainability. They also recognize basic human rights — the
rights of each person on the planet to health, education,
shelter and security.

The MDGs offer an unprecedented opportunity to cut world
poverty by half in the coming decade. Billions more people
could enjoy the fruits of the global economy. Tens of millions
of lives can be saved. The practical solutions exist. The political
framework is established. And for the first time, the cost is
affordable.

365

The Millennium Development Goals and Associated Targets

Goal 1: Eradicate extreme poverty and hunger

Target 1: To halve, between 1990 and 2015, the proportion of people whose income is less than $1 a day.

Target 2: To halve, between 1990 and 2015, the proportion of people who suffer from hunger.

Goal 2: Achieve universal primary education

Target 3: To ensure that, by 2015, children everywhere, boys and girls alike, will be able to complete a full course of primary schooling.

Goal 3: Promote gender equality and empower women

Target 4: To eliminate gender disparity in primary and secondary education, preferably by 2005 and in all levels of education no later than 2015.

Goal 4: Reduce child mortality

Target 5: To reduce by two-thirds, between 1990 and 2015, the under-five mortality rate.

Goal 5: Improve maternal health

Target 6: To reduce by three-quarters, between 1990 and 2015, the maternal mortality ratio.

Goal 6: Combat HIV/AIDS, malaria and other diseases

Target 7: To have halted by 2015 and begun to reverse the spread of HIV/AIDS.

Target 8: To have halted by 2015 and begun to reverse the incidence of malaria and other major diseases.

From S. Alkire, E. Newell *et al.*, *What Can One Person Do? Faith to Heal a Broken World* (Darton, Longman and Todd, 2005)

366

Goal 7: Ensure environmental sustainability

Target 9: To integrate the principles of sustainable development into country policies and programmes and reverse the loss of environmental resources.

Target 10: To halve by 2015 the proportion of people without sustainable access to safe drinking water.

Target 11: To have achieved by 2020 a significant improvement in the lives of at least 100 million slum dwellers.

Goal 8: Develop a global partnership for development

Target 12: To develop further an open, rule-based, predictable, nondiscriminatory trading and financial system (includes a commitment to good governance, development, and poverty reduction — both nationally and internationally).

Target 13: To address the special needs of the least developed countries (includes tariff- and quota-free access for exports, enhanced programme of debt relief for and cancellation of official bilateral debt, and more generous official development assistance for countries committed to poverty reduction).

Target 14: To address the special needs of landlocked countries and small island developing states (through the Program of Action for the Sustainable Development of Small Island Developing States and 22nd General Assembly provisions).

Target 15: To deal comprehensively with the debt problems of developing countries through national and international measures in order to make debt sustainable in the long term.

Target 16: To develop and implement, in co-operation with developing countries, strategies for decent and productive work for youth.

Target 17: To provide, in co-operation with pharmaceutical companies, access to affordable essential drugs in developing countries.

Target 18: To make available, in co-operation with the private sector, the benefits of new technologies, especially information and communications technologies.

What you can do
There are many ways to support the Millennium Development Goals; some suggestions are:

1. Write to your political representatives
Tell them that you support the Millennium Development Goals and the Millennium Project's recommendations for achieving them.

2. Organize letter-writing campaigns
More is always better – you can amplify your voice by enlisting other people in the campaign to achieve the MDGs. Reach out through personal networks and community groups.

3. Write letters to local newspapers
Send a letter to the editor to help you reach a larger audience of people. Take a look at the www.results.org website for useful tools that can be adapted to help you target both politicians and media outlets in your own country.

4. Sponsor a 'house party' or awareness event
Inform your friends and neighbours about world poverty and the Millennium Development Goals and then write letters together.

5. Adopt a 'Quick Win'
The UN Millennium Project has created 'Quick Win' campaigns
(www. http://mirror.undp.org/unmillenniumproject/press/
press3.htm) which range from supplying anti-malarial bednets
to eliminating school fees in low income countries, which are
important, concrete actions that can be taken to support the
Millennium Development Goals. You and your community
group can organize activities around a particular Quick Win
that is meaningful to you.

6. Join existing networks
Many large organizations are already working on poverty
issues, and supporting them is one way to build support for
the Goals.
    The Global Call to Action against Poverty is a world-wide
alliance committed to forcing world leaders to live up to their
promises, and to make a breakthrough on poverty in 2005.
Campaigns are running in 10 countries:
Australia: 'Fair Share Campaign'
Canada: 'Make Poverty History – Canada'
France: '2005: Plus d'excuses!'
Germany: 'Weltweite Aktion Gegen Armut'
Great Britain: 'Make Poverty History'
Ireland: 'Make Poverty History – Ireland'
Japan: 'Hottokenai, Sekai no Mazushisa'
Netherlands: 'Maak het waar'
Spain: 'Sin Excusas 2015'
United States of America: 'One Campaign'

APPENDICES

Bad news:
The timescale has already slipped.

Good news:
The world has made significant progress in achieving many of the Millennium Development Goals.
Between 1990 and 2002:

- average overall incomes increased by approximately 21 percent.
- The number of people in extreme poverty declined by an estimated 130 million. Child mortality rates fell from 103 deaths per 1,000 live births a year to 88.
- Life expectancy rose from 63 years to nearly 65 years.
- An additional 8 percent of the developing world's people received access to water.
- And an additional 15 percent acquired access to improved sanitation services.

Source: UN Millennium Project

THE FACES OF POVERTY

'A world where some live in comfort and plenty, while half of the human race lives on less than $2 a day is neither just, nor stable.'

President George W. Bush

'In this new century, millions of people in the world's poorest countries remain imprisoned, enslaved and in chains. They are trapped in the prison of poverty. It is time to set them free.'

Nelson Mandela

More than one billion people in the world live on less than one dollar a day. Another 2.7 billion struggle to survive on less than two dollars per day. Poverty in the developing world, however, goes far beyond income poverty. It means having to walk more than one mile everyday simply to collect water and firewood; it means suffering diseases that were eradicated from rich countries decades ago.

Following are some basic facts outlining the roots and manifestations of the poverty affecting more than one third of our world.

Health
- Every year 6 million children die from malnutrition before their fifth birthday.
- More than 50 per cent of Africans suffer from water-related diseases such as cholera and infant diarrhoea.
- Every day HIV/AIDS kills 6,000 people and another 8,200 people are infected with this deadly virus.

371

- Every 30 seconds an African child dies of malaria - more than one million child deaths a year.
- Each year, between 300 and 500 million people are infected with malaria. Approximately three million people die as a result.
- TB is the leading AIDS-related killer and in some parts of Africa, 7 per cent of people with HIV also have TB.

Hunger

- More than 800 million people go to bed hungry every night.
- Every 3.6 seconds another person dies of starvation – and the large majority are children under the age of 5.

Water

- More than 2.6 billion people – over 40 per cent of the world's population – do not have basic sanitation, and more than one billion people still use unsafe sources of drinking water.
- Four out of every ten people in the world don't have access even to a simple latrine.
- Five million people, mostly children, die each year from water-borne diseases.

Agriculture

- In 1960, Africa was a net exporter of food; today the continent imports one-third of its grain.
- More than 40 per cent of Africans do not even have the ability to obtain sufficient food on a day-to-day basis.
- Declining soil fertility, land degradation, and the AIDS pandemic have led to a 23 per cent decrease in food

production per capita in Africa in the last 25 years, even
though the population has increased dramatically.
- For the African farmer, conventional fertilizers cost two to
six times more than the world market price.

The devastating effect of poverty on women
- Over 80 per cent of farmers in Africa are women.
- More than 40 per cent of women in Africa do not have
access to basic education.
- The children of a woman with just five years of primary
school education have a survival rate 40 per cent higher
than that of children of women with no education.
- A woman living in sub-Saharan Africa has a 1 in 16 chance
of dying in pregnancy. This compares with a 1 in 3,700 risk
for a woman in North America.
- Every minute, a woman somewhere dies in pregnancy or
childbirth. This adds up to 1,400 women dying each day –
an estimated 529,000 each year – from pregnancy-related
causes.
- Almost half of the births in developing countries take place
without the help of a skilled birth attendant.

Source: The Millennium Project

MODERN-DAY SLAVERY

'Trafficking in human beings is nothing less than a modern form of slavery. As President Bush has said, nearly two centuries after the abolition of the trans-Atlantic slave trade and more than a century after slavery was officially ended in its last strongholds, the trade in human beings for any purpose must not be allowed to thrive in our times. We must all work to end this terrible tragedy.'

US Secretary of State Condoleezza Rice

Slavery is something that we relegate to the past rather than the present. **Yet slavery today is the worst it's ever been in human history.** There are 27 million slaves in the world today – more than twice the number of people brought over from Africa during the entire trans-Atlantic slave trade, according to conservative UN figures.

The new global economic development during the last half of the century has fuelled a resurgence of slavery. Today millions of economically and socially vulnerable people around the world are potential slaves. This 'supply' makes slaves today cheaper than they have ever been. Because they are so cheap, they are dispensable and if they get sick, are injured, outlive their usefulness or become troublesome to a slaveholder, they are dumped or killed.

Today's slaves are victims of forced labour, servile marriages, debt bondage, child labour, serfdom and forced prostitution. Modern slaves can be concubines, camel jockeys or cane cutters; they might weave carpets, build roads or clear forests.

What is different today is that slavery, in all of its forms, has been outlawed in four major international human rights treaties, in international labour rights agreements and in almost every country worldwide. Yet it still exists as a grave human rights abuse on every continent except Antarctica.

While the moral argument against slavery has been won, the practical struggle to end slavery is by no means over. It will take genuine political will and greater awareness to enforce laws and treaties abolishing slavery and ultimately close the chapter on modern slavery.

SCARS OF SLAVERY – case studies
Anna, United States
'Anna is from Ukraine in Eastern Europe. She is in Atlanta, Georgia, but could be in any city in the United States. She doesn't speak the language and doesn't know anyone except the people who keep her enslaved and the other women working as prostitutes in a house in the city centre. She is forced to work as a prostitute but she never gets any of the money she earns. She can only speak to other women in her house. She has no identity or residence papers and is in the country illegally. If she goes to the police, she will probably be deported straight back to her country, where her family will reject her, as she has worked as a prostitute. She lives in hope of being able to escape and get a proper job, but she doesn't know how and she is very scared of her male captors who beat her regularly.' (*Free the Slaves*)

Ashiq, Pakistan
'My name is Ashiq. I am 11 years old and I have been making

bricks at the factory since my father took a loan of 20,000 rupees [$500] for my sister's marriage, six years ago. My father and elder brother also work there.

I work every day except Sunday. My father and brother and myself earn 30 rupees [$0.77] per 1,000 bricks. We can make around 2,500–3,000 bricks a day. Our wage is cut by 50 per cent for loan repayments. We do not understand the loan interest which always seems to be increasing.

I went to school for three months only. The brick factory owner made my father bring me back. We go to work around 2 am when it is still dark and return at 6 pm after sunset. We have a short rest of half an hour between 7.00 and 7.30 am. I am given no time to play. I am not beaten but my father often is. I am called names. My hope is to enjoy freedom, if I am released from slavery, so that I may learn about some other trade in a better way.' (*Free the Slaves*)

In the world today there are:
a) 27 million slaves
b) no slaves
c) 2 million slaves

How many people were taken from Africa during the entire trans–Atlantic slave trade?
a) 13 million
b) 30 million
c) 1 million

Slavery is:
a) Illegal everywhere

b) legal in some countries
c) legal everywhere

Answers: 1) a 2) a 3) a

Sources: Free the Slaves; Anti-Slavery International;
Abolish, The Anti-Slavery Portal

WOMEN'S RIGHTS

'Women power is a formidable force ... Women will not become more empowered merely because we want them to be, but through legislative changes, increased information, and redirection of resources. It would be fatal to overlook this issue.'

> Gro Harlem Bruntland
> first female Director-General of the
> World Health Organisation 1998-2003;
> former Prime Minister of Norway

'The extension of women's rights is the basic principle of social progress.'

> François Marie Charles Fournier
> Théorie de Quatre Mouvements, 1841

Millions of women throughout the world live in terrible conditions that deprive them of their fundamental human rights for no other reason than that they are women. They face exploitation, abuse and discrimination that prevent them from attending school, working for wages and taking part in civic life.

While their status has improved in recent decades, gender inequalities remain pervasive. Today the scenario for women is one of unharnessed potential and unrealised goals.

- 70 per cent of the world's 1.3 billion poor – those living on the equivalent of less than $1 a day – are women.
- At least one out of every three women has been beaten, coerced into sex, or otherwise abused in her lifetime.

378

- Every minute, a woman somewhere dies in pregnancy or childbirth.
- Two thirds of the 880 million adults in poor countries who can't read or write are women.
- Women make up just under half of the total people living with HIV/AIDS.
- Women cultivate, plough and harvest more than half of all the food in the world.
- Women make up over 50 per cent of the world's population, earn 10 per cent of the world's wages and own 1 per cent of the world's property.
- Two thirds of all children worldwide who don't go to school are girls.
- Countries where women are not permitted to own land: Chile, Egypt, Ethiopia, Iraq, Kenya, Nepal and Panama.
- Of the 192 countries in the world, only 12 have a female head of state. Women have only 10 per cent of the world's seats in parliament.
- Women represent over 40 per cent of the global labour force. Approximately 70 per cent of women in developed countries and 60 per cent in developing countries are engaged in paid employment.
- Worldwide, women on average earn two-thirds of what men earn.
- Women hold only 1 to 3 per cent of the top executive jobs in the largest corporations.

Good News:
Educate a woman ... educate a nation.
- If a girl is educated for six years or more, as an adult her

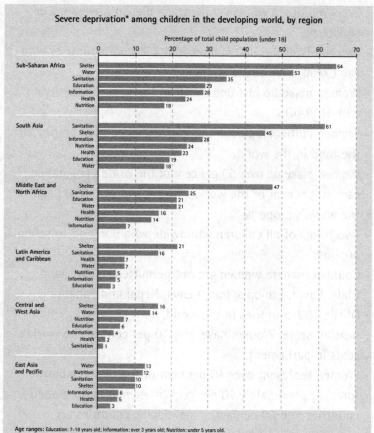

Severe deprivation* among children in the developing world, by region

Percentage of total child population (under 18)

Sub-Saharan Africa
- Shelter: 64
- Water: 53
- Sanitation: 35
- Education: 29
- Information: 28
- Health: 24
- Nutrition: 18

South Asia
- Sanitation: 61
- Shelter: 45
- Information: 28
- Nutrition: 24
- Health: 23
- Education: 19
- Water: 18

Middle East and North Africa
- Shelter: 47
- Sanitation: 25
- Education: 21
- Water: 21
- Health: 16
- Nutrition: 14
- Information: 7

Latin America and Caribbean
- Shelter: 21
- Sanitation: 16
- Health: 7
- Water: 7
- Nutrition: 5
- Information: 5
- Education: 3

Central and West Asia
- Shelter: 16
- Water: 14
- Nutrition: 7
- Education: 6
- Information: 4
- Health: 2
- Sanitation: 1

East Asia and Pacific
- Water: 13
- Nutrition: 12
- Sanitation: 10
- Shelter: 10
- Information: 6
- Health: 5
- Education: 3

Age ranges: Education: 7-18 years old; Information: over 3 years old; Nutrition: under 5 years old.

Sources: Gordon, David, et al., *Child poverty in the developing world*, The Policy Press, Bristol, UK, October 2003. **Note:** The data used in the original study have been updated using Demographic and Health Surveys (DHS) and Multiple Indicator Cluster Surveys (MICS).

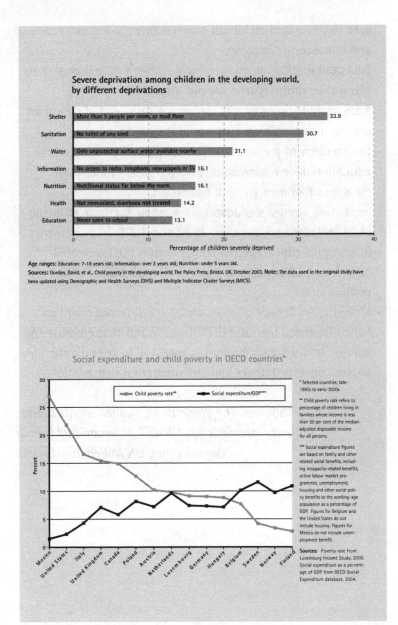

Severe deprivation among children in the developing world, by different deprivations

Shelter	More than 5 people per room, or mud floor	33.9
Sanitation	No toilet of any kind	30.7
Water	Only unprotected surface water available nearby	21.1
Information	No access to radio, telephone, newspapers or TV	16.1
Nutrition	Nutritional status far below the norm	16.1
Health	Not immunized, diarrhoea not treated	14.2
Education	Never been to school	13.1

Percentage of children severely deprived

Age ranges: Education: 7–18 years old; Information: over 3 years old; Nutrition: under 5 years old.
Sources: Gordon, David, et al., *Child poverty in the developing world*, The Policy Press, Bristol, UK, October 2003. **Note:** The data used in the original study have been updated using Demographic and Health Surveys (DHS) and Multiple Indicator Cluster Surveys (MICS).

Social expenditure and child poverty in OECD countries*

Child poverty rate** — Social expenditure/GDP***

Countries: Mexico, United States, Italy, United Kingdom, Canada, Poland, Austria, Netherlands, Luxembourg, Germany, Hungary, Belgium, Sweden, Norway, Finland

* Selected countries; late-1990s to early-2000s

** Child poverty rate refers to percentage of children living in families whose income is less than 50 per cent of the median adjusted disposable income for all persons.

*** Social expenditure figures are based on family and other related social benefits, including incapacity-related benefits, active labour market programmes, unemployment, housing and other social policy benefits to the working-age population as a percentage of GDP. Figures for Belgium and the United States do not include housing. Figures for Mexico do not include unemployment benefit.

Sources: Poverty rate from Luxemburg Income Study, 2000. Social expenditure as a percentage of GDP from OECD Social Expenditure database, 2004.

prenatal care and childbirth survival rates will dramatically
and consistently improve.
- Educated mothers immunize their children 50 per cent more
often than mothers who are not educated.
- AIDS spreads twice as quickly among uneducated girls than
among girls that have even some schooling.
- The children of a woman with five years of primary school
education have a survival rate 40 per cent higher than
children of women with no education.
- Increasing women's education is a major factor in reducing
child malnutrition. Between 1970 and 1995, improvements
in women's education and status within the household
contributed 55 per cent to the overall reduction of child
malnutrition.
- More than a decade of research by the International Food
Policy Research Institute (IFPRI) has found that empowering
women in developing nations is essential in winning the fight
against poverty, hunger and environmental degradation.

Sources: The World Bank, Human Rights Watch,
Amnesty International, UNICEF, International Labour
Organisation, UN Millennium Project

CHILDHOOD UNDER THREAT

'Only as we move closer to realizing the rights of all children will countries move closer to their goals of development and peace.'

Kofi Annan, United Nations Secretary-General

'If we fail to secure childhood, we will fail to reach our larger, global goals for human rights and economic development. As children go, so go nations. It's that simple.'

Carol Bellamy, Executive Director of UNICEF 1995–2005

'A willing world can end child poverty.'

Joseph E. Stiglitz, economist and Nobel Laureate

More than half the world's children suffer extreme deprivations from poverty, war and HIV/AIDS – conditions that effectively deny children a childhood and hinder the development of nations.

Every second child is being denied a healthy and protected upbringing as promised by 1989's UN Convention on the Rights of the Child, the world's most widely adopted human rights treaty. The failure of governments to live up to the Convention's standards causes permanent damage to children and in turn blocks progress toward human rights and economic advancement.

Poverty is not exclusive to developing countries. In 11 of 15 industrialized nations, the proportion of children living in low-income households during the last decade has risen.

383

Enhanced global commitment is needed for the millions of children who continue to die of easily preventable and treatable diseases ... for the many more who go to bed hungry every night, for the millions who do not receive an education, or are at risk of physical or sexual violence.

- 640 million children do not have adequate shelter.
- 500 million children have no access to sanitation.
- 400 million children do not have access to safe water.
- 300 million children lack access to information.
- 270 million children have no access to health care services.
- 140 million children have never been to school.
- 90 million children are severely hungry.

Survival
- 10.6 million children worldwide died in 2003 before they were five. *Equal to the total number of children under five living in France, Germany, Greece and Italy.*
- In developing countries, one child in ten dies before its fifth birthday, compared with one in 1,443 in high-income countries.

Ten countries where children are most likely to die before their fifth birthday (starting with highest mortality rate):
Sierra Leone
Niger
Angola
Afghanistan
Liberia
Somalia

Mali
Burkina Faso
Democratic Republic of Congo
Guinea-Bissau

HIV/AIDS
- 15 million children have been orphaned by HIV/AIDS worldwide – *equal to the total population of children in Germany.*
- Over 2 million children under 15 are infected by HIV.

Conflict
- 1.6 million children have been killed in conflicts since 1990.
- 20 million children have been forced by conflict or human rights violations to leave their homes – *equal to the total population of children under five in the United States.*
- Over the past decade, girls have been kidnapped and forced into wartime service in at least 20 countries.
- Some 300,000 children are serving as soldiers in current armed conflicts.

Child labour and exploitation
- One out of six children in the world today is involved in child labour.
- 22,000 children die in work-related accidents every year.
- Nearly three-quarters of working children are engaged in what the world recognizes as the worst forms of child labour including trafficking, armed conflict, slavery, sexual exploitation and hazardous work.
- 2 million children are trafficked each year – *equal to the number of children living in Australia.*

385

- 2 million children are sexually exploited in the multi-billion-dollar commercial sex industry – *equal to the number of children living in Belgium.*

Good News:
Children's rights are higher on the public agenda than ever before. Never before have children's voices been heard as clearly and distinctly by the international community.

Sources: The State of the World's Children 2005 – UNICEF, International Labour Organisation, Human Rights Watch and the Millennium Project

DISABILITY RIGHTS

'Disability is a natural part of human diversity, and the problems that people with disabilities face in fully enjoying their human rights stem from the failure of society to be inclusive of people with disabilities.'

> *Venus Ilagan, chair of Disabled People's International*
> *and the International Disability Alliance*

'I am amazed that governments create democracies that exclude 10 per cent of their populations. No nation can achieve its full economic potential by excluding some of the brightest members of its population.'

> *Victor Pineda, disability activist and independent film producer*

The global disabled population is increasing and will rise dramatically as the population ages and more people become disabled by HIV/AIDS. The failure to avert preventable diseases and to treat curable diseases is fuelling the increase.

In both developed and developing countries, segregation and marginalization have placed disabled people on the lowest rung of the social and economic ladder. Physical or social barriers limit their lives, often denying them access to essential services. This affects not only disabled people and their families, but also the economic and social development of entire societies, where a significant reservoir of human potential goes untapped.

387

- More than 600 million people in the world are disabled – some 10 per cent of the global population.
- 80 per cent of people with disabilities are in developing countries.
- One in five of the world's poorest people are disabled, meaning that disabled persons are twice as likely to be living in poverty.
- About one family in four includes a disabled person.
- Diseases such as meningitis, also armed conflict and landmines are among the major causes of disability in the world.
- The UN estimates that at least 250,000 people have had to have false limbs fitted because of landmines.
- In Cambodia alone 1.4 million of the population of eight million have been disabled as a result of poverty, war and human rights abuses.

Good news
A UN Convention on the Rights of Persons with Disabilities is on the threshold of being established.

Sources: Rehabilitation International;
International Disability Alliance;
World Health Organisation;
World Bank

THE DEATH PENALTY

'A sign of hope is the increasing recognition that the dignity of human life must never be taken away, even in the case of someone who has done great evil.'

Karol Wojtyla, Pope John Paul II, 2004

'It is always unlawful to put to death a man, whom God willed to be a sacred character.'

Lucius Caecilius Firmianus Lactantius,
Christian apologist, fourth century

The death penalty is the ultimate denial of human rights. It is the premeditated and cold-blooded killing of a human being by the state in the name of justice. It violates the right to life as proclaimed in the Universal Declaration of Human Rights.

Despite the worldwide trend towards abolition, there is an ongoing need for concerted action by the international community to consign the death penalty to history.

More than 3,797 people were executed in 25 countries in 2004 and at least 7,395 were sentenced to death. These were only minimum figures; the true figures were certainly higher. In 2004, 97 per cent of all known executions took place in China, Iran, Viet Nam and the USA.

- China: 2,400
- Iran: 159
- Viet Nam: 64
- USA: 59

APPENDICES

Abolition

- 120 countries have now abolished the death penalty in law or practice.
- 85 countries and territories have abolished the death penalty for all crimes.
- 11 countries have abolished the death penalty for all but exceptional crimes such as wartime crimes.
- 24 countries can be considered abolitionist in practice: they retain the death penalty in law but have not carried out any executions for the past 10 years or more and are believed to have a policy or established practice of not carrying out executions.
- 76 other countries and territories retain and use the death penalty, but the number of countries which actually execute prisoners in any one year is much smaller.

Child executions

Eight countries since 1990 are known to have executed prisoners who were under 18 years old at the time of the crime.

- China
- Democratic Republic of Congo
- Iran
- Nigeria
- Pakistan
- Saudi Arabia
- USA
- Yemen

The USA executed more child offenders than any other country (19 between 1990 and 2003).

Amnesty International recorded four executions of child offenders in 2004 – one in China and three in Iran. Another child offender was executed in Iran in January 2005.

Execution of the innocent

- Since 1973, 117 prisoners have been released in the USA after evidence emerged of their innocence of the crimes for which they were sentenced to death. There were six cases in 2004.

The death penalty in the USA

- 59 prisoners were executed in the USA in 2004, bringing the year-end total to 944 executed since the use of the death penalty was resumed in 1977.
- Over 3,400 prisoners were under sentence of death as of 1 January 2005.
- 38 of the 40 states provided for the death penalty in law. The death penalty is also provided for under US federal, military and civilian law.

Source: Amnesty International

ARMS AND THE ARMS TRADE

'We can't have it both ways. We can't be both the world's leading champion of peace and the world's leading supplier of arms.'
Former US President Jimmy Carter, presidential campaign, 1976

Did you know?
There are more than 500 million small weapons, nearly one for every ten people, worldwide. Every year, roughly half a million people are killed in armed violence. That's one person per minute. By 2020, the number of deaths and injuries from war and violence will overtake the number of deaths caused by killer diseases such as malaria and measles. Global military expenditure and arms trade form the largest spending in the world at over $950 billion in annual expenditure for 2003; the total budget of the UN – committed to preserving peace through international cooperation and collective security – amounts to about a proportional 1.5 per cent of this amount.

The top five countries profiting from the arms trade – USA, UK, France, Russia and China – are the five permanent members of the United Nations Security Council; they account for 88 per cent of reported conventional arms exports. From 1998 to 2001, the USA, the UK and France earned more income from arms sales to developing countries than they gave in aid.

Half the world's governments spend more on the military than on health care. Just 1 per centof global annual military spending could educate every child on earth over the next decade.

392

The third world is often the destination for arms sales: see page 402.

WEAPONS OF MASS DESTRUCTION

Weapons of mass destruction (WMD) are designed to kill people in large numbers, often both civilians and military personnel. Some weapons can have more of a psychological impact than cause physical damage.

These weapons can be categorized into three main types:
1. Nuclear weapons
2. Biological weapons
3. Chemical weapons

1. Nuclear Weapons

Nuclear weapons have only been used twice in war:

Code name 'Little Boy', dropped on Hiroshima, Japan, 6 August, 1945: death toll 100,000+.

Code name 'Fat Man', dropped on Nagasaki, Japan, 9 August, 1945: death toll 70,000 approx.

Destructive power:

The explosive yield of a nuclear weapon is expressed in the equivalent mass of trinitrotolene (TNT), either in kilotons (kt) of TNT or megatons (mt) of TNT.

First used weapon: 'Little Boy', Hiroshima, yield (12–15 kt), USA.

Largest weapons: Tsar Bomba, yield (50 mt), USSR; EC17/Mk-17, EC24/Mk-24, B41, yield (25 mt), USA.

Comparison: the Oklahoma City Bombing, 19 April, 1995, truck-based fertilizer bomb, yield (0.002 kt).

In 1985 there were 65,000 nuclear weapons worldwide; in 2002 there were about 20,000 weapons worldwide. Nuclear

393

weapons have been used 2,000 times since World War II, but for test purposes only.

The Comprehensive Nuclear Test Ban Treaty (CTBT) bans all nuclear explosions in all environments and was opened for signature on 24 September 1996. Notably, two nuclear powers, India and Pakistan, have not signed.

Treaty Status (15 March, 2005):

Member States: 175; Total Ratification: 120; Annex 2 Ratification: 33; Latest State Signatory: Bahamas; Latest Ratifying State: Rwanda.

The CTBT will enter into force 180 days after it has been ratified by the 44 states listed in its Annex 2. These 44 states all formally participated in the 1996 conference session and possess either nuclear power or research reactors.

2. Biological Weapons

Biological warfare (or germ warfare) is the use of any organism or toxin found in nature as a weapon of war. Ideal characteristics of biological weapons are high infectivity, high potency, availability of vaccines and delivery as an aerosol. Main military advantages are the efficacy and cheap cost of manufacture.

An attack, viewed as effective and successful, could result in thousands or even millions of victims especially within urban environments; several biological agents also can target harvest crops.

Diseases commonly considered for weaponization are: anthrax, ebola, pneumonic plague, cholera, tularemia, brucellosis, Q fever, Machupo, VEE, and smallpox. Naturally occurring toxin options are ricin, SEB, botulism and mycotoxins.

The Biological and Toxin Weapons Convention (BTWC) in 1972 banned 'development, production, stockpiling, and use of microbes or their poisonous products except in amounts necessary for protective and peaceful research'; over 100 countries are signatories.

The following 27 countries have not signed the Biological and Toxin Weapons Convention:

Andorra, Angola, Azerbaijan, Cameroon, Chad, Comoros, Cook Islands, Djibouti, Eritrea, Guinea, Israel, Kazakstan, Kiribati, Kyrgyzstan, Marshall Islands, Mauritania, Micronesia (Federal States of), Moldova (Republic of), Mozambique, Namibia, Nauru, Niue, Samoa (Western), Tajikistan, Trinidad and Tobago, Tuvalu, Zambia.

3. Chemical Weapons

Chemical warfare applies the toxic properties of chemical substances to kill, injure or incapacitate the enemy.

Chemical weapons are classified according to persistency; as being *persistent*, i.e., tending to remain in the environment for up to a week, or *non-persistent*, whose effectiveness lasts minutes or hours.

In 1993, Paris, the Chemical Weapons Convention (CWC), banning the production and stockpiling of chemical weapons, was opened for signature which 130 countries signed.

The Chemical Weapons Convention ban went into force on 27 April, 1997.

WARS, MASSACRES AND ATROCITIES

'War is much too serious to be left to the generals.'
Charles-Maurice de Talleyrand (1754–1838).

'The naked, poor, and mangled peace'
Henry V.1 (Shakespeare)

'As long as war is regarded as wicked, it will always have its
fascination. When it is looked upon as vulgar, it will cease to
be popular. The change will, of course, be slow, and people will
not be conscious of it.'
Critic as Artist II (Oscar Wilde)

Wars, Massacres and Atrocities of the 20th Century
By one estimate between 4 per cent and 5 per cent of all
human deaths in the twentieth century were overtly caused
by other people. However, such estimates will always be
subject to controversy. Statistical calculations and methods
of calculation for deaths incurred can vary widely and
dramatically. In many cases not only may actual physical
evidence and eyewitness accounts be lacking or in dispute but
definitions of what constitutes victim and tragedy and even
the actuality of event be in denial. The figures below include
battle deaths, civilian casualties of war, genocide, democide
and famine caused by economic disruption. All graphs and
statistics derive and are adapted from Matthew White's
website, Twentieth Century Atlas – Top-ranked Atrocities.
(http://users.erols.com/mwhite28/atrox.htm).

GLOBAL LANDMINE CRISIS

'Every 27 minutes, somewhere in the world, a landmine claims another victim. There have been many excellent and high-profile campaigns against this hidden killer but the need for a continued, concerted drive to rid the world of landmines is as great now as it ever was.'

Heather Mills McCartney

'The devastation wreaked by landmines is not only horrendous but immoral.'

Desmond Tutu

'I want a world where every child has a chance to wear two shoes ... When I buy shoes, I have to hide one shoe because the empty shoe reminds me of my missing leg and the horror of landmines.'

Song Kosal

Forty people are killed or injured by landmines every day – at least two new casualties per hour.

When triggered, a landmine unleashes unspeakable destruction causing injuries such as blindness, burns, destroyed limbs and shrapnel wounds. Landmines deprive people in some of the poorest countries of land, limbs, livelihoods and infrastructure.

Landmines are still being laid today and minefields dating back decades continue to lie in wait of innocent victims. A global mine crisis remains.

• A landmine costs as little as $3 to produce; clearing one can cost up to $1,000.

- 200–215 million landmines are stockpiled in the arsenals of 78 countries.
- 15,000–20,000 people are killed or injured by landmines every year.
- More than 300,000 people are living with landmine-related injuries worldwide.
- Landmines lie buried in more than 80 countries; casualties are reported in 65 of these. Some of the most contaminated countries are Afghanistan, Angola, Burundi, Bosnia and Herzegovina, Cambodia, Chechnya, Colombia, Iraq, Nepal and Sri Lanka.
- Over 80 per cent of landmine victims are civilians; 25 per cent are children.
- Landmines most often cause limb loss or death, but can also cause vision loss and other injuries
- Less than 10 per cent of landmine victims have access to appropriate medical care and rehabilitation services.

The **Mine Ban Treaty,** prohibiting the use, manufacture, stockpiling or transfer of anti-personnel mines, was opened for signature on 3 December 1997. It entered into force on 1 March 1999 and became binding as international law. A total of 134 countries are States Parties to the Mine Ban Treaty as of 31 July 2003. Another 13 countries have signed, but not ratified the treaty.

Non-signatories to the treaty are (as of 22 December 2004):
- Armenia
- Azerbaijan
- Bahrain

- Bhutan
- Burma (Myanmar) !
- China !
- Cuba !
- Eygpt !
- Finland
- Georgia
- India !
- Iran !
- Iraq !
- Israel
- Kazakhstan
- Korea, Democratic Republic of (North)!
- Korea, Republic of (South) !
- Kuwait
- Kyrgyzstan
- Lao People's Democratic Republic
- Latvia
- Lebanon
- Libya
- Federated States of Micronesia
- Mongolia
- Morocco
- Nepal !
- Oman
- Pakistan !
- Palau
- Russian Federation !
- Saudi Arabia
- Singapore !

- Somalia
- Sri Lanka
- Syria
- Tonga
- Tuvalu
- United Arab Emirates
- United States of America !
- Uzbekistan
- Vietnam !

! *Antipersonnel landmine producers*

It is estimated by Landmine Monitor that the greatest numbers of antipersonnel mines – between 190 million and 205 million – are stockpiled by states not party to the Mine Ban Treaty.

The largest stockpiles are estimated in:
- China (110 million)
- Russia (50 million)
- United States (10.4 million)
- Pakistan (6 million)
- India (4–5 million)
- Belarus (4.5 million)
- South Korea (2 million)
- Serbia and Montenegro (1.3 million).

Other states not party to the treaty believed to have large stockpiles:

- Burma
- Egypt
- Finland
- Iran
- Iraq
- Israel
- North Korea
- Syria
- Turkey
- Vietnam.

Good News

- The number of mine-producing countries has dropped from over 50 in 1992, when the International Campaign to Ban Landmines began its work, to 15 by mid-2003.
- More than 1,400 non-governmental organizations in 90 countries are working for a global ban on landmines.

Sources: International Campaign to Ban Landmines, Landmine Monitor Report 1999 and Landmine Monitor Report 2003; The Landmine Survivors Network

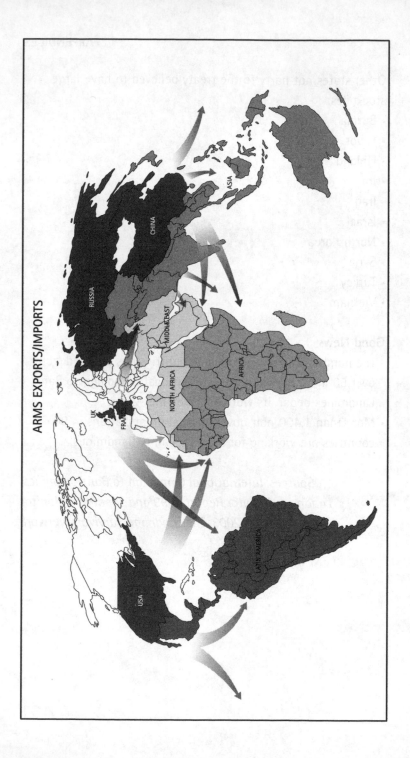

ARMS EXPORTS/IMPORTS

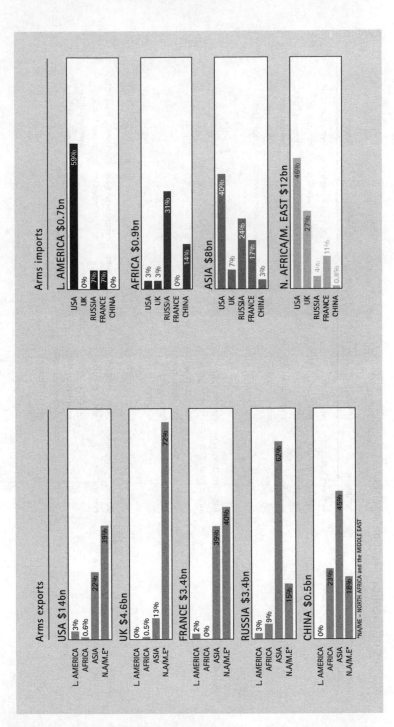

Arms exports

USA $14bn
- L. AMERICA: 3%
- AFRICA: 0.6%
- ASIA: 22%
- N.A/M.E*: 39%

UK $4.6bn
- L. AMERICA: 0%
- AFRICA: 0.5%
- ASIA: 13%
- N.A/M.E*: 72%

FRANCE $3.4bn
- L. AMERICA: 2%
- AFRICA: 0%
- ASIA: 39%
- N.A/M.E*: 40%

RUSSIA $3.4bn
- L. AMERICA: 3%
- AFRICA: 9%
- ASIA: 62%
- N.A/M.E*: 15%

CHINA $0.5bn
- L. AMERICA: 0%
- AFRICA: 23%
- ASIA: 45%
- N.A/M.E*: 18%

*NA/ME – NORTH AFRICA and the MIDDLE EAST

Arms imports

L. AMERICA $0.7bn
- USA: 59%
- UK: 0%
- RUSSIA: 7%
- FRANCE: 7%
- CHINA: 0%

AFRICA $0.9bn
- USA: 3%
- UK: 3%
- RUSSIA: 31%
- FRANCE: 0%
- CHINA: 1.4%

ASIA $8bn
- USA: 40%
- UK: 7%
- RUSSIA: 24%
- FRANCE: 17%
- CHINA: 3%

N. AFRICA/M. EAST $12bn
- USA: 46%
- UK: 27%
- RUSSIA: 4%
- FRANCE: 11%
- CHINA: 0.8%

Classes of chemical weapon agents

Class of agent	Examples	Symptoms	Effects	Rate of action	Persistency	Notes
Nerve agent	Sarin, VX	Difficulty breathing, sweating, drooling, convulsions, dimming of vision	Inhibits the breakdown of the neurotransmitter acetylcholine in the victim's nerves	Vapours: seconds to minutes. Skin: 2 to 18 hours	VX is persistent and a contact hazard; the other agents are non-persistent and present mostly inhalation hazards	Nerve agents are hundreds to thousands times more lethal than blister, pulmonary or blood agents
Blood agent	Hydrogen Cyanide	Rapid breathing, convulsions and coma	Prevents the normal use of oxygen by the body tissues so that vital organs cease to function within minutes	Immediate onset	Non-persistent and an inhalation hazard	All based on cyanide
Vesicant (blister agent)	Mustard gas, Lewisite	Burning or stinging of eyes and skin	Creates extreme burning pain; conjunctivitis; large water blisters on the skin that heal slowly and may become infected	Vapors: 4 to 6 hours, eyes and lungs affected	Persistent and a contact hazard	Used to incapacitate rather than kill, overloading the medical facilities

Classes of chemical weapon agents (continued)

Class of agent	Examples	Symptoms	Effects	Rate of action	Persistency	Notes
Pulmonary agent (choking agent, lung toxicants)	Phosgene	Difficulty breathing, tearing of the eyes	Damages and floods the respiratory system, resulting in suffocation; survivors often suffer chronic breathing problems	Immediate to 3 hours	Non-persistent and an inhalation hazard	These were commonly used in World War 1, but were rendered mostly obsolete by the more effective nerve agents
Lachrymatory agent	Tear gas, pepper spray	Powerful eye irritation	Causes sever stinging of the eyes and temporary blindness	Immediate	Non-persistent and an inhalation hazard	In recent decades these agents are usually used for riot-control purposes, therefore they are often called riot control agents
Incapacitating agent	BZ	Confusion, confabulation, hallucination, and with regression to automatic 'phantom' behaviours such as plucking and disrobing	Decreases effect of acetylcholine in subject. Causes peripheral nervous system effects that are the opposite of those seen in nerve agent poisoning	Inhaled: 30 minutes to 20 hours; Skin: up to 36 hours after skin exposure to BZ. Duration is typically 72 to 96 hours	Extremely persistent in soil and water and on most surfaces; contact hazard	

APPENDICES

THE FULL PICTURE

Nation	CW Possesion	Signed CWC	Ratified CWC
Albania	Known	14 January 1993	11 May 1994
China	Probable	13 January 1993	4 April 1997
Egypt	Probable	No	No
India	Known	14 January 1993	3 September 1996
Iran	Known	13 January 1993	3 November 1997
Iraq	Known	No	No
Israel	Probable	13 January 1993	No
Libya	Known	No	6 January 2004 (acceded)
Myanmar (Burma)	Possible	13 January 1993	No
North Korea	Known	No	No
Pakistan	Probable	13 January 1993	28 October 1997
Russia	Known	13 January 1993	5 November 1997
Serbia and Montenegro	Probable	No	20 April 2000 (acceded)
Sudan	Possible	No	5 May 1999 (acceded)
Syria	Known	No	No
Taiwan	Possible	No	No
United States	Known	13 January 1993	25 April 1997
Vietnam	Probable	13 January 1993	No

The 30 or so worst bloodlettings of the twentieth century have (probably) been …

Rank	Death Toll	Event	Dates
1	55,000,000	Second World War (Some overlap w/Stalin. Includes Sino-Japanese War and Holocaust. Doesn't include post-war German expulsions)	1937/39-1945
2	40,000,000	China: Mao Zedong's regime. (includes famine)	1949-76
3	20,000,000	USSR: Stalin's regime (includes WW2-era atrocities)	1924-53
4	15,000,000	First World War (incl. Armenian massacres)	1914-18
5	8,800,000	Russian Civil War	1918-21
6	4,000,000	China: Warlord & Nationalist Era	1917-37
7	3,000,000	Congo Free State [n.1]	(1900)-08
8	2,800,000	Korean War	1950-53
8	2,800,000	2nd Indochina War (includes Laos & Cambodia)	1960-75
10	2,500,000	Chinese Civil War	1945-49
11	2,100,000	German Expulsions after WW2	1945-47
12	1,900,000	Second Sudanese Civil War	1983-(99)
13	1,700,000	Congolese Civil War [n.1]	1998-(99)
14	1,650,000	Cambodia: Khmer Rouge Regime	1975-79
15	1,500,000	Afghanistan: Soviet War	1980-89
16	1,400,000	Ethiopian Civil Wars	1962-92
17	1,250,000	East Pakistan: Massacres	1971
18	1,000,000	Mexican Revolution	1910-20
18	1,000,000	Iran-Iraq War	1980-88
18	1,000,000	Nigeria: Biafran revolt	1967-70
21	917,000	Rwandan Massacres	1994
21	800,000	Mozambique: Civil War	1976-92
23	675,000	French-Algerian War	1954-62
24	600,000	First Indochina War	1945-54
24	600,000	Angolan Civil War	1975-94
26	500,000	Decline of the Amazonian Indians	(1900-99)
26	500,000	India-Pakistan Partition	1947
26	500,000	First Sudanese Civil War	1955-72
29	450,000	Indonesia: Massacre of Communists	1965-66
30	365,000	Spanish Civil War	1936-39
?	>350,000	Somalia: Chaos	1991-(99)
?	>400,000	North Korea: Communist Regime	1948-(99)

The maps on pp 3XX–3XX display major wars and atrocities of the twentieth century. The magnitude maps display the body count from specific events which are united by cause and engagement but which often spread into different countries. The intensity maps often include several separate events that are united by place and period. 'Per-million' refers to the population of the country at the mid-point of the period, not per million participants in the event.

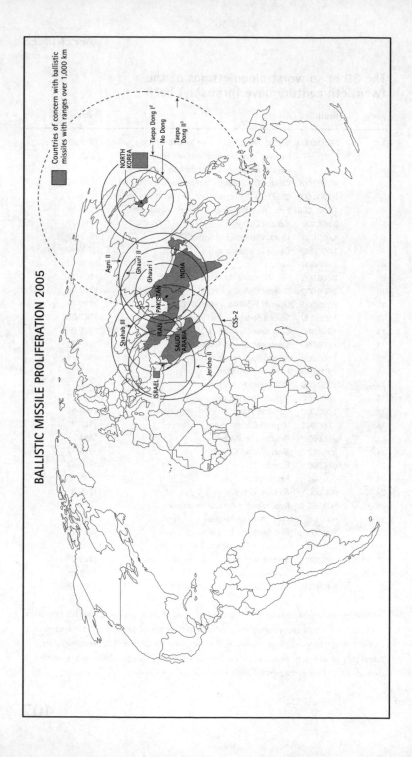

BALLISTIC MISSILE PROLIFERATION 2005

Countries of concern with ballistic missiles with ranges over 1,000 km

NORTH KOREA

Taepo Dong I²
No Dong
Taepo Dong II³

Agni II

Ghauri II
Ghauri I

INDIA

PAKISTAN

Shahab III

IRAN

CSS-2

SAUDI ARABIA

Jericho II

ISRAEL

Strategic Missiles of 5 Declared Nuclear-Weapon States

Country	Missile	Type	Range
China	DF-5A	ICBM	13,000km
France	M45	SLBM	6,000km
Russia	SS-18	ICBM	9,000-11,000km
	SS-19	ICBM	10,000km
	SS-24	ICBM	9,000-11,000km
	SS-25	ICBM	10,500km
	SS-27	ICBM	10,500km
	SS-N-18	SLBM	6,500-8,000km
	SS-N-20	SLBM	8,300km
	SS-N-23	SLBM	8,300km
United Kingdom	Trident II/D-5	SLBM	7,400+km
United States	MX Peacekeeper[1]	ICBM	9,650+km
	Minuteman III	ICBM	9,650+km
	Trident I/C-4	SLBM	7,400km
	Trident II/D-5	SLBM	7,400+km

[1] To be removed from service by October 1st, 2005.

Missiles with ranges exceeding 1,000 km in 6 Countries of Proliferation Concern

Country	Missile Name	Range
India	Agni II	2,000-2,500km
Iran	Shahab III	1,300km
Israel	Jericho II	1,500km
North Korea	No Dong	1,300km
	Taepo Dong I	1,500-2,000km[2]
	Taepo Dong II	5,500km[3]
Pakistan	Ghauri/No Dong	1,300km
	Ghauri II	1,50C-2,000km
Saudi Arabia	CSS-2	2,600km[4]

2. The sole test of the Taepo Dong I flew 1,320km. Some experts speculate that an operational third stage and re-entry vehicle would allow the Taepo Dong I to deliver a light payload over 5,500km.

3. The Taepo Dong II has not been flight-tested. The 2001 National Intelligence Estimate of the Ballistic Missile Threat speculates that, with a lighter payload, it could have a 10,000-km range.

4. Saudi Arabia purchased CSS-2 missiles from China in 1987 and has never tested them.

19 countries only have ballistic missiles with ranges under 1,000 km

Afghanistan	Kazakhastan	Turkmenistan
Armenia	Libya	Ukraine
Bahrain	Slovak Republic	United Arab Emirates
Belarus	South Korea	Vietnam
Egypt	Syria	Yemen
Greece	Taiwan	
Iraq	Turkey	

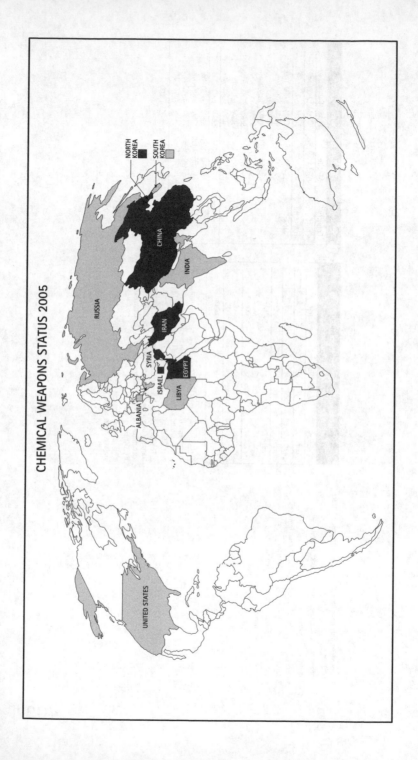

CHEMICAL WEAPONS STATUS 2005

Countries That Have Abandoned Chemical Weapons Programs

Until the Chemical Weapons Convention came into force, many nations had chemical warfare programs. A growing number have since ended their programs and are destroying or have eliminated their weapons, including the United States, the United Kingdom, France, Canada, Germany, India, Italy, Japan, Russia, and other states of the former Soviet Union, South Africa, South Korea, Libya, Albania and the Federal Republic of Yugoslavia.

Possible Chemical Weapons

China, Egypt, Iran, Israel, North Korea, and Syria are believed to have some quantities of undeclared chemical weapons.

Countries with Declared Chemical Stockpiles Slated for Destruction

The United States, Russia, India, South Korea, Libya, and Albania have not yet completed destruction of their chemical weapons. Russia declared 44,000 tons of Soviet era mustard gas, lewisite, sarin, VX, and other chemicals, which it promised to destroy in joining the Chemical Weapons Convention, but many have additional undeclared capabilities.

Significant Countries That Have Not Joined the CWC

North Korea, Syria, Israel, and Egypt.

Other Possible Programs

Some reports indicate that Ethiopia, Myanmar, Pakistan, Saudi Arabia, Sudan, Taiwan, and Vietnam may be interested in developing or may operate chemical warfare programs but the evidence is inconclusive.

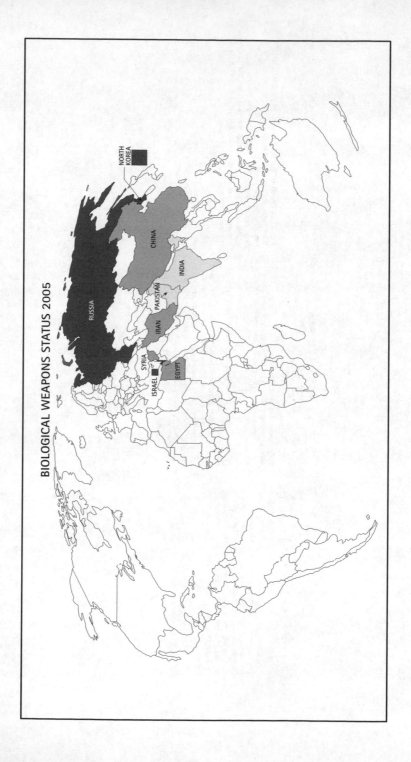

BIOLOGICAL WEAPONS STATUS 2005

Countries That Have Abandoned Biological Weapons Programs

With the Biological Weapons Convention, many nations gave up their biological warfare programs and destroyed their biological weapons stockpiles, including the United States, United Kingdom, France, Canada, Germany, Japan, states of the former Soviet Union, and South Africa.

Possible Biological Weapons

North Korea and Israel may have active offensive biological weapons programs and may be capable of producing biological agents for military purposes. Russia, the successor state to the Soviet Union, may still possess undeclared biological weapons.

Suspected Biological Warfare Research Programs

China, Iran, Egypt, and Syria may have offensive biological warfare research programs. There is no conclusive evidence that Iran or Syria has produced actual agents or weapons.

Countries of Potential Concern

Some are concerned that India and Pakistan possess the industrial infrastructure to support offensive biological weapons programs, but there's no evidence that such programs exist.

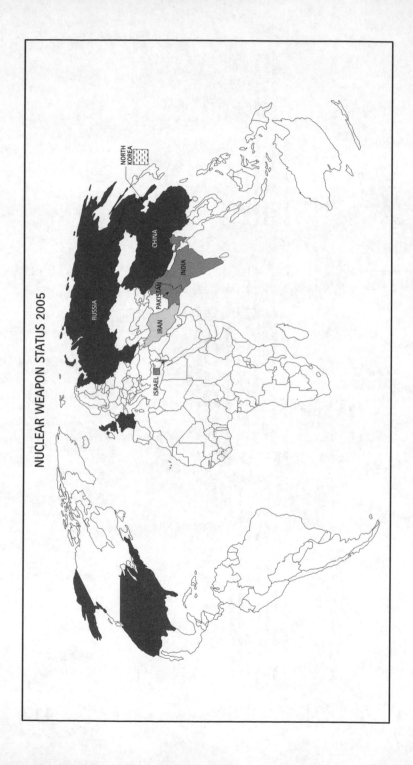

NUCLEAR WEAPON STATUS 2005

RUSSIA

CHINA

INDIA

PAKISTAN

IRAN

ISRAEL

NORTH KOREA

Abstaining Countries

The following countries have the potential ability to develop nuclear weapons, but have chosen not to do so. Some have installations under international inspection that could produce weapons-grade material.

Algeria, Argentina, Australia, Austria, Belgium, Brazil, Bulgaria, Canada, Chile, Egypt, Finland, Germany, Hungary, Indonesia, Italy, Japan, Mexico, Netherlands, Norway, Poland, Romania, Republic of Korea, Slovakia, South Africa, Spain, Sweden, Switzerland, Taiwan, Ukraine.

Recent Renunciations

South Africa produced six complete nuclear bombs during the 1980s but renounced such activities and joined the NPT in 1991. Belarus, Kazakhstan, and Ukraine acceded to the NPT as non-nuclear weapon states and returned all remaining nuclear weapons to Russia to the early 1990s.

Egypt and Sweden both had active nuclear weapon programs but terminated them prior to the founding of the NPT in 1970. After 1970, Argentina, Brazil, Libya, Iraq, Romania, South Korea, Spain, Taiwan, and Yugoslavia all had active programs researching nuclear weapons options. All of these programs were terminated by the early 1990s, except for Libya's, which was renounced in December 2003.

Legend:

- NPT Nuclear Weapon States
- Non-NPT Nuclear Weapon States
- Suspected Nuclear Weapon States
- Suspected Clandestine Programs

Country	Total Nuclear Warheads
China	410
France	350
India	75–110[1]
Israel	100–170[2]
Pakistan	50–110[3]
Russia	~16,000
United Kingdom	200
United States	~10,300
Total	~27,600

1. India is thought to have produced enough weapons-grade plutonium to produce between 75 and 110 nuclear weapons. The number of actual weapons assembled or capable of being assembled is unknown. No weapons are known to be deployed among active military units or on missiles.

2. Israel is thought to possess enough nuclear material for between 100 and 170 nuclear weapons. The number of weapons assembled or capable of being assembled is unknown, but likely to be on the lower end of this range.

3. Pakistan may have produced enough weapons-grade uranium to produce up to 110 nuclear weapons. The number of actual weapons assembled or capable of being assembled is unknown. Pakistan's nuclear weapons are reportedly stored in component form, with the fissile core separated from the non-nuclear explosives.

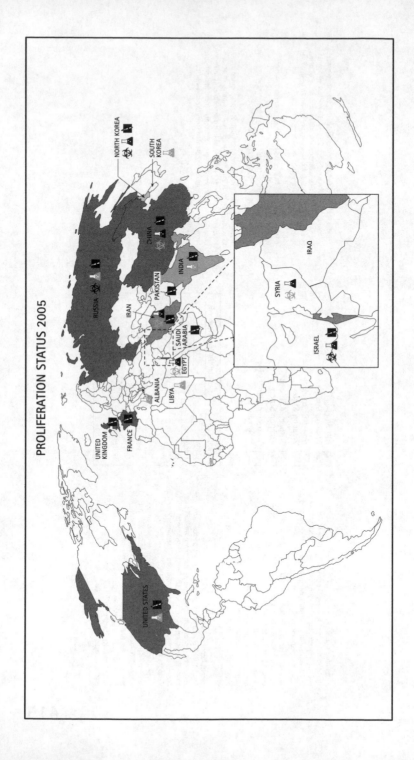

PROLIFERATION STATUS 2005

Chemical, Biological and Missile Proliferation

Suspected Biological Warfare Stockpiles.
(Country may have offensive biological weapons or agents).

Suspected Biological Warfare Research Programs.
(Country may have active interest in aquiring the capability to produce biological warfare agents).

Suspected Chemical Warfare Stockpiles.
(Country may have some undeclared chemical weapons).

Declared Chemical Weapons Slated for Destruction.
(Country has declared its chemical weapons, and committed to destroying them under the Chemical Weapons Convention).

Ballistic Missiles with over 1,000km Range

Nuclear Proliferation

Declared nuclear weapon states

Non-NPT nuclear weapon states

Suspected nuclear weapon states

States with suspected clandestine programs

Worldwide Nuclear Stockpiles

Country	Total Nuclear Warheads
China	410
France	350
India	75-110
Israel	100-170
Pakistan	50-110
Russia	~16,000
United Kingdom	200
United States	~10,300
Total	~27,600

Missiles with ranges exceeding 1,000 km in 6 Countries of Proliferation Concern

Country	Missile Name	Range
India	Agni II	2,000-2,500km
Iran	Shahab III	1,300km
Israel	Jericho II	1,500km
North Korea	No Dong	1,300km
	Taepo Dong I	1,500-2,000km[2]
	Taepo Dong II	5,500km[3]
Pakistan	Ghauri/No Dong Ghauri	1,300km
	Ghauri II	1,500-2,000km
Saudi Arabia	CSS-2	2,600km[4]

2, 3, 4 See notes on Ballistic Missile Proliferation map.

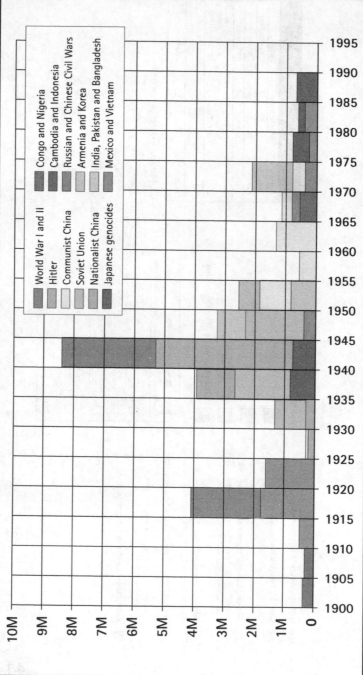

Year-by-Year Death Toll (1900-1995)

Legend:
- World War I and II
- Hitler
- Communist China
- Soviet Union
- Nationalist China
- Japanese genocides
- Congo and Nigeria
- Cambodia and Indonesia
- Russian and Chinese Civil Wars
- Armenia and Korea
- India, Pakistan and Bangladesh
- Mexico and Vietnam

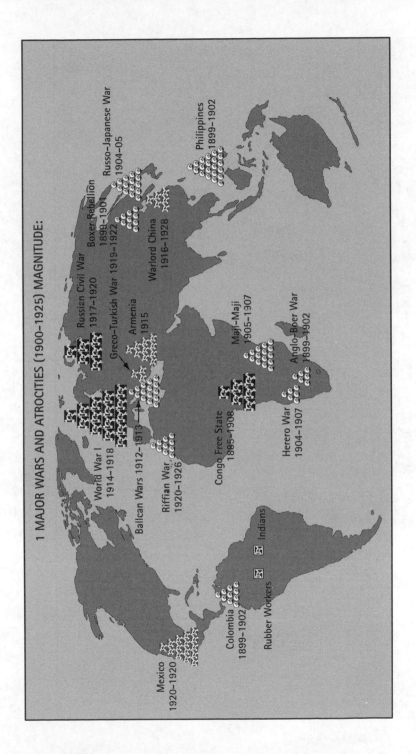

1 MAJOR WARS AND ATROCITIES (1900–1925) MAGNITUDE:

Russo–Japanese War 1904–05

Philippines 1899–1902

Russian Civil War 1917–1920

Boxer Rebellion 1899–1901

Greco–Turkish War 1919–1922

Armenia 1915

Warlord China 1916–1928

Maji–Maji 1905–1907

Anglo–Boer War 1899–1902

Herero War 1904–1907

World War I 1914–1918

Balkan Wars 1912–1913

Riffian War 1920–1926

Congo Free State 1885–1908

Indians

Rubber Workers

Colombia 1899–1902

Mexico 1920–1920

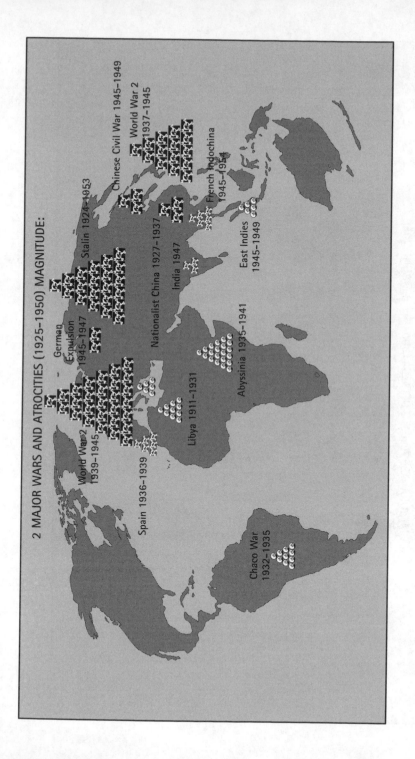

2 MAJOR WARS AND ATROCITIES (1925–1950) MAGNITUDE:

German Expulsion 1945–1947

Stalin 1924–1953

Chinese Civil War 1945–1949

World War 2 1937–1945

French Indochina 1945–1954

India 1947

Nationalist China 1927–1937

East Indies 1945–1949

World War 2 1939–1945

Spain 1936–1939

Libya 1911–1931

Abyssinia 1935–1941

Chaco War 1932–1935

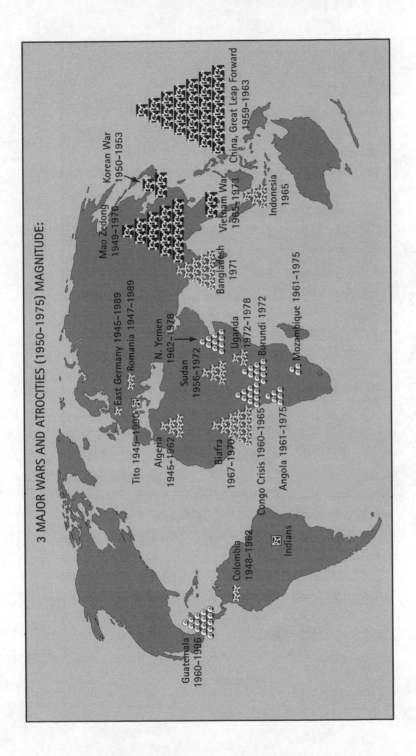

3 MAJOR WARS AND ATROCITIES (1950–1975) MAGNITUDE:

Mao Zedong 1949–1976
Korean War 1950–1953
China, Great Leap Forward 1959–1963
Vietnam War 1965–1973
Indonesia 1965
Bangladesh 1971
East Germany 1945–1989
Romania 1947–1989
Tito 1945–1990
N. Yemen 1962–1978
Sudan 1956–1972
Uganda 1972–1978
Burundi 1972
Mozambique 1961–1975
Algeria 1945–1962
Biafra 1967–1970
Congo Crisis 1960–1965
Angola 1961–1975
Colombia 1948–1962
Indians
Guatemala 1960–1996

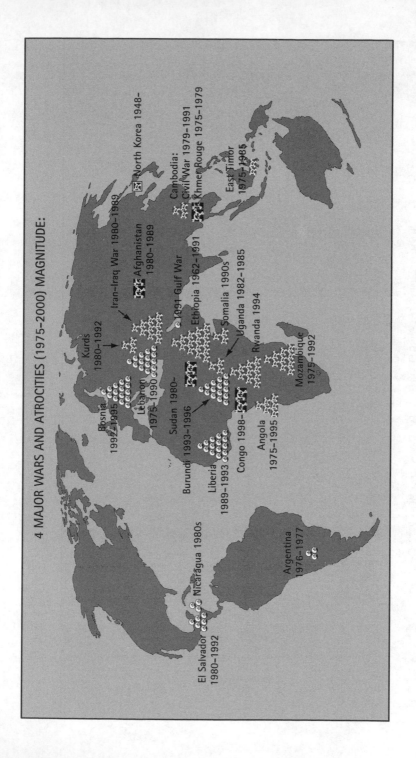

4 MAJOR WARS AND ATROCITIES (1975–2000) MAGNITUDE:

North Korea 1948–

Cambodia:
Civil War 1979–1991
Khmer Rouge 1975–1979

East Timor
1975–1985

Iran–Iraq War 1980–1989

Afghanistan
1980–1989

Kurds
1980–1992

1991 Gulf War

Ethiopia 1962–1991

Somalia 1990s

Uganda 1982–1985

Rwanda 1994

Lebanon
1975–1990

Bosnia
1992–1995

Sudan 1980–

Burundi 1993–1996

Congo 1998–

Angola
1975–1995

Mozambique
1975–1992

Liberia
1989–1993

Nicaragua 1980s

El Salvador
1980–1992

Argentina
1976–1977

Percentage of national populations killed in specific episodes of mass brutality

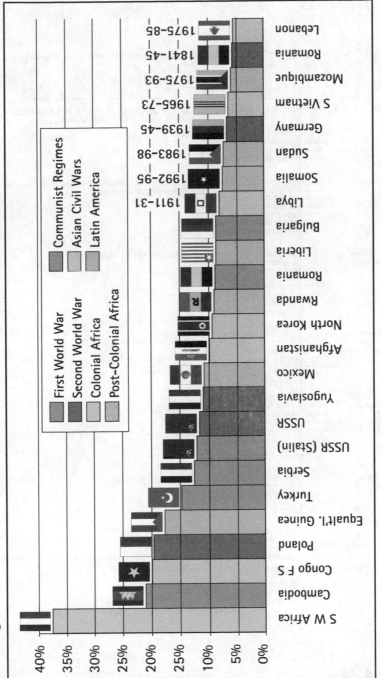

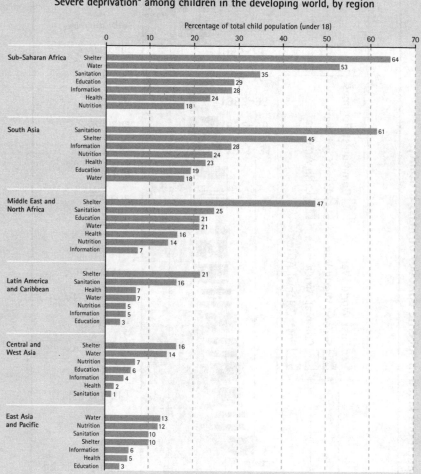

Severe deprivation* among children in the developing world, by region

Percentage of total child population (under 18)

Sub-Saharan Africa
- Shelter — 64
- Water — 53
- Sanitation — 35
- Education — 29
- Information — 28
- Health — 24
- Nutrition — 18

South Asia
- Sanitation — 61
- Shelter — 45
- Information — 28
- Nutrition — 24
- Health — 23
- Education — 19
- Water — 18

Middle East and North Africa
- Shelter — 47
- Sanitation — 25
- Education — 21
- Water — 21
- Health — 16
- Nutrition — 14
- Information — 7

Latin America and Caribbean
- Shelter — 21
- Sanitation — 16
- Health — 7
- Water — 7
- Nutrition — 5
- Information — 5
- Education — 3

Central and West Asia
- Shelter — 16
- Water — 14
- Nutrition — 7
- Education — 6
- Information — 4
- Health — 2
- Sanitation — 1

East Asia and Pacific
- Water — 13
- Nutrition — 12
- Sanitation — 10
- Shelter — 10
- Information — 6
- Health — 5
- Education — 3

Age ranges: Education: 7–18 years old; Information: over 3 years old; Nutrition: under 5 years old.
Sources: Gordon, David, et al., *Child poverty in the developing world*, The Policy Press, Bristol, UK, October 2003. **Note:** The data used in the original study have been updated using Demographic and Health Surveys (DHS) and Multiple Indicator Cluster Surveys (MICS).

Severe deprivation among children in the developing world, by different deprivations

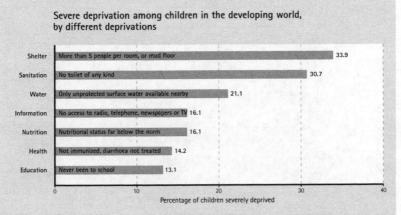

Shelter	More than 5 people per room, or mud floor	33.9
Sanitation	No toilet of any kind	30.7
Water	Only unprotected surface water available nearby	21.1
Information	No access to radio, telephone, newspapers or TV	16.1
Nutrition	Nutritional status far below the norm	16.1
Health	Not immunized, diarrhoea not treated	14.2
Education	Never been to school	13.1

Percentage of children severely deprived

Age ranges: Education: 7–18 years old; Information: over 3 years old; Nutrition: under 5 years old.
Sources: Gordon, David, et al., *Child poverty in the developing world*, The Policy Press, Bristol, UK, October 2003. **Note:** The data used in the original study have been updated using Demographic and Health Surveys (DHS) and Multiple Indicator Cluster Surveys (MICS).

Social expenditure and child poverty in OECD countries*

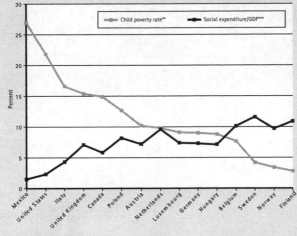

Legend: ● Child poverty rate** ■ Social expenditure/GDP***

Countries (x-axis): Mexico, United States, Italy, United Kingdom, Canada, Poland, Austria, Netherlands, Luxembourg, Germany, Hungary, Belgium, Sweden, Norway, Finland

* Selected countries; late-1990s to early-2000s

** Child poverty rate refers to percentage of children living in families whose income is less than 50 per cent of the median adjusted disposable income for all persons.

*** Social expenditure figures are based on family and other related social benefits, including incapacity-related benefits, active labour market programmes, unemployment, housing and other social policy benefits to the working-age population as a percentage of GDP. Figures for Belgium and the United States do not include housing. Figures for Mexico do not include unemployment benefit.

Sources: Poverty rate from Luxemburg Income Study, 2000. Social expenditure as a percentage of GDP from OECD Social Expenditure database, 2004.

425